Sales Force Automation Using Web Technologies

Navtej (Kay) Khandpur
Jasmine Wevers

WILEY COMPUTER PUBLISHING

John Wiley & Sons, Inc.
New York • Chichester • Weinheim
Brisbane • Singapore • Toronto

Publisher: Robert Ipsen
Editor: Theresa Hudson
Associate Managing Editor: Angela Murphy
Text Design & Composition: Publishers' Design & Production Services, Inc.

This text is printed on acid-free paper.

This publication is designed to provide accurate and authoritative information in regard to the subject matter covered. It is sold with the understanding that the publisher is not engaged in rendering legal, accounting, or other professional service. If legal advice or other expert assistance is required, the services of a competent professional person should be sought.

Netscape Communications Corporation has not authorized, sponsored, or endorsed, or approved this publication and is not responsible for its content. Netscape and the Netscape Communications Corporate Logos are trademarks and trade names of Netscape Communications Corporation. All other product names and/or logos are trademarks of their respective owners.

Library of Congress Cataloging-in-Publication Data

Khandpur, Navtej.
    Sales force automation using Web technologies / Navtej (Kay)
Khandpur, Jasmine Wevers.
        p.   cm.
    Includes index.
    ISBN 0–471–19114–0 (pbk./CD-ROM : alk. paper)
    1. Sales management—Data processing.   2. Selling—Data
processing   3. Marketing—Data processing.   I. Wevers, Jasmine,
1962–   . II. Title.
HF5438.4.K53   1998
658.8′00285′4678—dc21   97–26315

Printed in the United States of America
10 9 8 7 6 5 4 3 2 1

For Dr. Jaswant Singh, a father figure, a role model, and a friend.

Khandpur

For the late Ann Marie Gorowara, my grandmother, who taught me the value of perseverance.

Wevers

Contents

About the Authors

Navtej (Kay) Khandpur is a consultant in Customer Relationship Management. In his 20 years in the field Kay has served in a variety of customer relationship management functions, from managing support operations to business planning for support delivery. Most recently he was with Tandem Computers, where he managed the company's customer satisfaction program for critical accounts. Kay has also taught graduate courses in the business school at the George Washington University in Washington, D.C., and often speaks at industry conferences. His credentials include a BSEE, an MSEE, an MS in Information Systems Technology, and an MBA; he is a member of Beta Gamma Sigma, the honor society for collegiate schools of business.

Kay is currently with Promentis Solutions (www.promentis .com), a management consulting practice located in Santa Clara, California. Many of his clients are technology companies, from startup ventures to Fortune 500 companies, whose goal is to increase profitability through higher customer satisfaction, and manage their customer relationships as cost effectively as possible. Kay's work as a consultant has included process implementation and improvement, strategy development, design and implementation of measurement systems, creation and implementation of customer management programs, and contract program management for technology selection and deployment.

Kay feels strongly that the quality and range of relationships a company has with its customers can materially affect its profitability. He is the co-author of *Delivering World-Class Technical Support*, published by John Wiley & Sons in 1997. He initiated that book in pursuit of his ambition to help develop professional hands-on managers for the vital business function of improving customer satisfaction through superior post-sales service. He wrote this book to help sales organizations improve customer satisfaction and increase profits through superior *pre-sales* service.

In his spare time Kay tries to improve his satisfaction level with his golf game.

Jasmine Wevers is a recreational ski racer and avid mountain and road bike enthusiast. She can be found exploring the mountains of the western United States in summer or winter.

When not exploring the outdoors, Jasmine is president and co-founder of MJM Technologies, Inc. (www.mjmtech.com), a Campbell, California, based consulting and training firm that implements HelpDesk and Customer Service Management systems. MJM's extensive client list represents leading technology companies in the telecommunications, semiconductor, networking communications, and medical equipment industries. MJM has helped implement customer service and help desk solutions for such industry giants as Microsoft, MCI, Hewlett-Packard, Amoco, and Georgia-Pacific, just to name a few.

Jasmine is a veteran of the software support industry with 17 years of technical support, management, IT, and project management positions. Jasmine has held technical support management positions with Golden Bow Systems, Research Information Systems, and Micro-MRP. Jasmine has spent the last ten years implementing MRP, Customer Service, and Help Desk systems, as well as speaking at industry conferences.

Acknowledgments

This book would not have been possible without the help of a great number of people who gave of their time, experience, and wisdom.

First and foremost we would like to acknowledge the assistance we received from Patricia Bruce, a consultant and an expert in Sales Force Automation. Many of the ideas in this book came from her, and the book would not have been possible without her contributions. We owe her a deep debt of gratitude.

Others we would like to thank are:

Dixie Baker and Keith Raffel, of UpShot Corporation

Mark Bonacorso, Judy Hamilton, and Kevin McDonald, of FirstFloor Software

Mitch Bishop and Lyle Ekdahl, of Scopus Technology

Al Campa, of Actuate Software

Keith Carlson and Lara Bliesner, of Andersen Consulting

Kathleen Dempsey and Mike Barnwell, of Netgain

Sherrick Murdoff and Kamlesh Keswani, of NetDynamics

Ed Murphy and Colleen Kelly, of Borealis Technology

Rich Petersen and Steve Farber, of Interwoven

Dave Rome, of Calico Technology

Christina Schuetz, of ONYX Software

Gerard Wevers, of Siemens Components

All our clients and friends, past and present, for giving us the opportunity to try out our ideas

And, of course, we want to thank Terri Hudson and Moriah O'Brien of John Wiley & Sons, for keeping us honest and putting up with our last-minute requests and changes.

There are no doubt others whom we should thank, and we apologize for not mentioning your names here.

Setting the Stage

I am a Bear of Very Little Brain, and long words Bother me.

Alan Alexander Milne in Winnie the Pooh, *1926*

Sales Force Automation

Salespeople have always used some kind of technology to help them manage the knowledge necessary to do their jobs. Centuries ago the technology may have been a stick used to make notations in the sand, later a quill on paper. In the last few decades sales automation technology was in the form of telephone logs, portable recording machines, card files, and three-ring binders. Nowadays the technology encompasses contact management systems, personal organizers, proposal generation tools, and product configurators.

With the rapid increase in computing capability available to companies and individuals, and the equally dramatic decline in the price of this computer technology, more and more sales forces are being equipped with tools that are intended to make them more successful. Companies are investing significant amounts of money in information systems technologies to be used in activities related to the sales and marketing efforts of company personnel. The application of information systems technologies to sales and marketing activities has given rise to the term *Sales Force Automation*.

Some may point out that it is not the sales force that is being automated *per se*, but rather the activities performed in the life cycle of a sale. In fact the Gartner Group, a leading market research company, uses the term *Technology-Enabled Selling* when talking about this topic. While that term is actually more correct, the phrase *Sales Force Automation* has gained widespread acceptance and it is the term used in this book.

Growth has been rapid in this Sales Force Automation (SFA) market segment: some market research companies project a total market size for sales automation software and services of approximately $3 billion in 1998, with a compound annual growth rate of between 40 percent and 50 percent for the next few years. By some estimates there are over 1000 vendors of Sales Force Automation products in the United States at the time of writing; this number is changing almost daily as new companies enter the market. Other companies are unable to compete and drop out, and yet others merge and consolidate. The range of services is also very broad. Some companies sell only products, while others are purely systems integrators; and many provide both products and integration services.

As technology advances, so do the tools available to sales forces. The recent explosion of the Internet, intranets and extranets, and all manner of Web technologies that make use of these networks allows many companies to capitalize on a relatively low-cost approach to Sales Force Automation. This book will show how a company can leverage these new technologies and improve the effectiveness and productivity of its sales force.

WHY AUTOMATE?

Some may question why they should even attempt to automate the activities of their sales force. This is not an unreasonable position. Any attempt at Sales Force Automation is doomed to failure if the management of a company and indeed its sales force are not convinced that automation is a necessary step, and that implementing automation will result in tangible benefits to the company. We believe therefore that it behooves managers to be wary of the promises that SFA holds out, and to apply good business sense before making any radical changes to the company's sales processes and investing significant amounts of money in technology.

There are three reasons that justify investments in Sales Force Automation:

1. Increased sales effectiveness
2. Improved sales efficiency
3. Higher customer satisfaction

Increased Sales Effectiveness

Sales Force Automation promises to increase the effectiveness of the sales organization. *Sales effectiveness* means how well a sales organization performs in the generation of revenues. You can assess the effectiveness of your sales organization by asking the following questions:

- Of all the leads that came in to the company in the last year, how many turned out to be real leads that were appropriate for your products?
- Why were the other leads rejected?
- Of the real leads, how many became valid prospects?
- Why were the rest discarded, and what happened to them?
- Of the real leads, how many reached the proposal stage?
- Why were the rest discarded, and what happened to them?
- With how many proposals did the sales organization make the final cut?
- Why did the sales organization not make the cut?
- How many final cuts actually resulted in a sale?
- Why did you lose the sales you did?

As you answered these questions you probably realized that few leads finally resulted in actual sales and revenues. In other words, the effectiveness of your sales force, as measured by revenues or the ratio of leads to sales, was probably not as high as it could have been. While some of the losses may have been due to factors beyond the control of your sales organization, the primary reasons that your sales force did not close sales probably were:

- Inappropriate leads
- Lack of information
- Missed commitments

Leads are often handed off to the sales force without full qualification; the sales force then spends time qualifying the lead and often finds that the lead is of no value whatsoever. Sales Force Automation can improve the lead generation and qualification processes by imposing strict rules on what enters and leaves the leads system.

Even when the sales force receives good leads, it often does not have the material necessary to keep the leads informed. The sales force may not be aware of new products, configuration, pricing, promotions, and packages that have been made public, and may be surprised by customers who have more detailed and accurate information. Sales Force Automation can ensure that the sales force receives all the material necessary to keep leads, prospects, and customers fully informed.

Most business-to-business sales tend to be complex transactions. Customer requirements often change, products are added and removed from the purchase list, customers demand different pricing and payment terms, new products are released, and so on. In these situations a salesperson must coordinate the activities of many people within the sales organization, and sometimes also the activities of people outside the organization. For example, a salesperson may need some pricing decisions made by a sales manager, and also need to schedule a visit by the Vice President of Research and Development to give the prospect some visibility into product futures. In effect the sales cycle requires a series of discrete actions, all of which must be executed in a timely manner to make the sale. In other words the sales cycle is a project, and the salesperson the project manager responsible for managing an *ad hoc* team working toward the successful completion of the project. And as any project manager can tell you, even in the highest performing teams there is a need to track commitments. Sales Force Automation can provide the commitment tracking functionality required to manage the sales project.

By addressing the preceding issues, you can dramatically improve the effectiveness of your sales force. Your salespeople will receive only qualified leads that have a high likelihood of success, they will have at their fingertips all the information they need to be effective in selling, and they will be able to track and drive to closure all the commitments that are made during the sales cycle.

You should note that increases in sales effectiveness are somewhat independent of Sales Force Automation. Most improvements in effectiveness come from taking a hard look at existing sales process, identifying the issues in those processes that hamper effectiveness, and then addressing those issues. Sales Force Automation is a tool that can implement and enforce good sales processes. Sales Force Automation is also a tool that can implement and enforce bad sales processes. If you have poor sales processes, all automation will do is make the problems all the more pervasive and visible. Sales Force Automation without process improvement will *not* increase sales effectiveness.

Improved Sales Efficiency

Sales Force Automation promises to improve the efficiency of the sales organization. *Sales efficiency* means how much revenue a company can generate for each dollar it spends in the sales organization. You can assess the efficiency of your sales organization by asking the following questions:

- How much time and money did your sales organization spend in pursuing all those leads that resulted in sales?
- How much time and money did your sales organization spend in pursuing all those leads that did not result in sales?
- How many times did individual salespersons have to call on a prospect before closing the sale?
- What is the average time it takes for a salesperson to configure a sale?
- What is the average time it takes for a salesperson to pull together a proposal?
- How many levels of authorization and approval is a salesperson required to get before presenting a proposal to a customer?
- What percentage of a salesperson's average day is spent on following up on commitments, order history, order status, approval status, corporate reporting requirements, or other administrative tasks?

Compare your answers with those of some of the salespersons in your organization. You may be surprised to learn that a significant amount of a salesperson's time (and a higher percentage than what you may have thought) is spent in unproductive ways. There is no reason that a salesperson should have to spend an inordinate amount of time configuring a sale, tracking down order status, or repeatedly visiting a customer to answer questions because a product brochure was never mailed to the customer.

Sales Force Automation can improve the efficiency of your sales organization in two ways: by shortening the time it takes to do something (reducing the *cycle time*); and by managing workflow by tracking commitments, escalating issues, and readily providing the current status of activities related to a sale. For example, a proposal generation system may provide the ability for a salesperson to easily incorporate and customize entire paragraphs and sections from a stock of standard and preapproved paragraphs and sections, as well as from proposals used in other similar proposals. An opportunity management system may keep track of all collateral sent to a customer, as well as a list of all activities associated with a customer, together with the current status of each activity and the next action and its owner.

Realizing efficiencies through Sales Force Automation should be traded off against the costs of using the system. If it takes longer for a salesperson to get into the system and retrieve the information needed than it does to pick up the telephone and ask someone, then there is no efficiency realized because the person at the other end of the telephone will have to get all this information. True efficiencies from Sales Force Automation will be realized only when the tools are an essential and integral part of doing business in your organization, and your sales force thinks no more of using the automation than it would of using a telephone or jotting a note on paper.

Higher Customer Satisfaction

Sales Force Automation promises higher customer satisfaction. Customer satisfaction can be measured in many ways, but relative to the sales organization you can assess the satisfaction of your customer base by asking the following questions:

- Of all the sales you made, how many resulted in customers that are currently referenceable in every way?
- How many customers have you lost to the competition?
- Do you know why you have lost customers?
- How many customers would leave you if a competitive product came into the marketplace?
- How many customers provide you with a continuous revenue stream?
- What percentage of your revenues comes from current customers?
- How does this compare to other companies in your market segment?

Having satisfied customers is absolutely essential to the sales organization. Many studies have shown that satisfied customers are more likely than dissatisfied customers to be loyal to your products. Loyal customers can significantly improve the profitability of your company. An article in the *Harvard Business Review* ("Zero Defections: Quality Comes to Services," by Frederick F. Reichfeld and W. Earl Sasser, Jr., *HBR*, Volume 68, No. 5, September–October 1990) gave an example of a software company that reduced customer defections by 5 percent, and realized a profit improvement of 35 percent. Loyal customers tend to be customers for a longer period of time, thereby increasing your chances of selling to them. Furthermore, the costs of selling to these customers tends to be lower, as they generally require less of a sales effort than new customers. Finally, loyal customers tend to be champions of your products, and provide good references when needed.

Sales Force Automation can increase customer satisfaction because it allows your sales force to more effectively manage the customer account. A good automation tool gives each salesperson complete visibility into all interactions a customer has had with your company, so the salesperson can spot and address issues before they escalate. Effective salespersons will also be quick to notice trends and exceptions in the transactions, and recognize selling opportunities when they come up. For example, a software company salesperson may look at recent customer support interactions and see that the customer has been having problems interfacing your company's products to an internal application; this could result in an opportunity to improve customer satisfaction by helping your customer with the interface. A networking company salesperson may notice that there has been an increase in the number of calls from the customer's network center, requesting assistance in improving the performance of their network; this could be an opportunity to sell the customer more networking equipment.

Higher customer satisfaction through Sales Force Automation can come about in many ways. The automation system must be capable of capturing data that can be analyzed and reported, and the sales organization must be capable of and willing to look at and use the information from the data analysis.

Estimating the Return on Investment

Estimating the return on investment on any large-scale implementation of any kind of enterprise application is a difficult exercise at best, and a nightmare at worst. To accurately estimate returns on investment, you must have good data on your current performance, and realistic assessments of what your investment will do for your performance. In these days of rapid change, your whole environment could change between the time you decide you need Sales Force Automation tools and the time you actually purchase the tools, let alone deploy them. Furthermore, as discussed previously, changes in sales processes are usually required before you can realize gains in sales effectiveness. If these changes are done in conjunction, it becomes almost impossible to determine whether improvements are a result of process changes or automation.

While it may be possible to quantify gains in sales effectiveness and efficiency as a result of Sales Force Automation, it is very difficult to show a causal relationship between this kind of automation and customer satisfaction. Customer satisfaction is influenced by many things, one of which is the sales relationship and another account management. In other words, while Sales Force Automation contributes to overall customer satisfaction and customer loyalty, it is difficult to directly link the implementation of sales automation technologies to increases in

TABLE 1.1   Income Statement Example (All Numbers in $M)

	Company A	Company B	Company C	Company D
Annual Revenues	5.00	10.00	50.00	100.00
Cost of Goods Sold (30%)	1.50	3.00	15.00	30.00
Sales & Marketing (25%)	1.25	2.50	12.50	25.00
Other Costs (25%)	1.25	2.50	12.50	25.00
Income before Tax	1.00	2.00	10.00	20.00

customer satisfaction. Our analysis below is therefore done for only effectiveness and efficiency gains realized from Sales Force Automation.

To illustrate the impact of Sales Force Automation, we consider four companies with similar cost structures but different revenues. The example assumes that companies have a cost of goods of 30 percent, sales and marketing costs of 25 percent, and other costs (such as Research and Development, General, and Administrative) of 25 percent of revenues. A *pro forma* income statement for these companies is shown in Table 1.1.

If we consider only increased sales effectiveness, that is, generating additional revenues for no increase in sales and marketing costs, we could expect an increase in our income. Table 1.2 shows what happens to the income of these four companies if the

TABLE 1.2   Income Statement Example with Increased Sales Effectiveness (All Numbers in $M)

	Company A	Company B	Company C	Company D
Income before SFA	1.00	2.00	10.00	20.00
Income after Sales Effectiveness Increase of:				
1%	1.04	2.07	10.35	20.70
5%	1.18	2.35	11.75	23.50
10%	1.35	2.70	13.50	27.00
15%	1.53	3.05	15.25	30.50

implementation of Sales Force Automation results in increases in sales effectiveness of 1, 5, 10, and 15 percent.

A small company, Company B, increases its income by $700,000 a year with an increase in sales effectiveness of 10 percent. A larger company, Company D, sees its income go up by the same amount with only a 1 percent increase in sales effectiveness. In other words, each of these companies can realize significant returns on the bottom line with investments in automation. The exact return will, of course, depend on the size of the initial investment, the amortization period of the investment, and the ongoing costs associated with the investment.

But what if there is no increase in sales effectiveness, and all the return is in the form of increased efficiency or reduced costs? Table 1.3 shows what happens if there is no change in sales effectiveness, but only improvements in efficiency instead.

Clearly there is a smaller impact on the bottom line: For company B an increase in sales effectiveness of 10 percent resulted in an impact of $700,000; an improvement in sales efficiency of 10 percent resulted in an impact of $250,000. The return on investment, however, may have been higher in the latter case if the initial investment and ongoing costs are lower than those for the increase in sales effectiveness.

As the preceding tables show, the returns on investment in Sales Force Automation can be quite high. Keith Carlson, who manages the Sales Force Effectiveness practice at Andersen Con-

TABLE 1.3 Income Statement Example with Improved Sales Efficiency (All Numbers in $M)

	Company A	Company B	Company C	Company D
Income before SFA	1.00	2.00	10.00	20.00
Income after Sales Efficiency Improvement of:				
1%	1.01	2.03	10.13	20.25
5%	1.06	2.13	10.63	21.25
10%	1.13	2.25	11.25	22.50
15%	1.19	2.38	11.88	23.75

sulting, a leading global management and information technology consulting firm, says that "One of our clients saw a 40 percent reduction in administration time, and a 30 percent increase in revenue per sales representative. Another client in the financial service industry estimates the benefit of implementing a comprehensive sales force effectiveness solution is in the range of \$20M to \$40M a year."

You must be clear in your mind on why you want to implement Sales Force Automation, and then assess the potential return. The leverage of your investment in automation tools will depend on your estimate of the value you expect to realize, be it in the form of increased sales effectiveness, improved sales efficiency, or higher customer satisfaction.

SALES FORCE AUTOMATION TOOLS

There are many applications and functions that fall under the umbrella of Sales Force Automation. Most of these applications are used as tools that enable and assist the sales force to do the job; hence we call them Sales Force Automation *enabling tools* and categorize them as follows:

- Personal Productivity Tools, such as word processors, spreadsheet programs, expense report programs, presentation software, and e-mail.
- Personal Management Tools, such as calendar and schedule programs, contact managers, and account/territory management systems.
- Functional Tools, such as proposal generators, order entry systems, sales configurators, and sales analysis programs.
- Sales Process Tools, such as opportunity management systems, telebusiness systems, and team-selling systems.

If implemented and used properly, personal productivity tools typically improve sales productivity, because the individual salesperson can use these tools to more efficiently do the job. Spreadsheets are more efficient than adding up numbers on a calculator. Writing a letter using a word processor can be much quicker than dictating the content and having someone else type it.

Personal management tools tend to increase sales effectiveness. A salesperson with personal management tools can keep track of all contacts, customers, prospects, and leads; and usually also record notes of past conversations and other interactions. Before making a sales call, the salesperson can improve potential effectiveness by reviewing all contact information.

Functional tools tend to both increase sales effectiveness and improve sales productivity. A sales configurator can dynamically assist a salesperson in the configuration and pricing of a complex order. The salesperson's effectiveness is improved because the proposed configuration will be correct the first time, and the efficiency is improved because the configuration can be resolved in real time, perhaps even as the salesperson is with the customer.

Sales process tools increase sales effectiveness, improve sales productivity, and enhance customer satisfaction. These tools implement *workflow;* that is, they guide the salesperson through the steps required to close the sale, and automate as much as possible of the process and information flow. Using *Computer Telephony Integration* a telebusiness system can guide a call from a customer to the appropriate telesales representative, and present customer information to the representative for review before the call is picked up. This allows the representative to be fully informed before speaking to the customer or prospect.

The four categories of tools described in the preceding may or may not be connected to one another. The extent to which they are connected determines whether they are:

- Stand-alone
- Interconnected
- Integrated

Stand-Alone SFA Tools

As their name may imply, stand-alone Sales Force Automation tools are discrete applications that operate independently of one another. They typically tend to be generic applications in the Personal Productivity tools category, such as time management applications, expense report packages, presentation programs, word processors, and so on (see Figure 1.1).

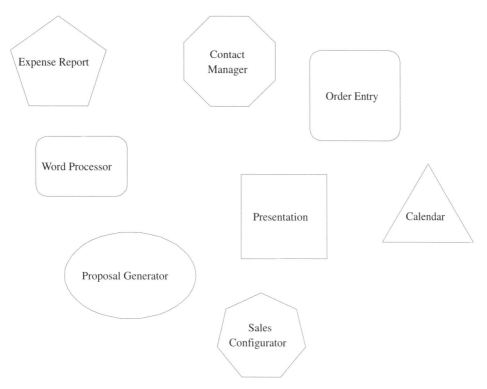

FIGURE 1.1   Stand-alone SFA tools.

The advantages of stand-alone tools are that they are readily available, usually inexpensive, require little training, and are easy to deploy into the sales force. These tools can be found in most computer stores or through mail-order catalogs; in fact many of these tools are already standards in many large corporations. Because of their easy availability, they tend to be inexpensive. Targeted at the mass market they are usually easy to learn, typically requiring a few hours to a day of training before the user is fully functional. Finally, these tools are easy to deploy for the reasons cited earlier.

The disadvantages of stand-alone tools are that they provide minimal and generic functionality, often cannot be customized to any great extent, and do not offer any automatic data sharing. Because of their mass-market nature, these packages tend to provide functions that are generic to the task they are intended to address. For example, word processing programs may be excellent for word processing but may have little built-in support for sales activities. Whatever customization is possible is usually tied to the program itself, not always the application or usage of the program. So an expense report program may allow the user to add some fields, but not be able to provide expense roll-ups by customer account. Finally, many of these applications are designed for stand-alone operation. They generally maintain their data in a proprietary format, and not all the data therein may be available to other programs that wish to use the data. Sharing data with other applications therefore becomes a burden. Tools used in automation are far more valuable if they can share data, for example, a time management system linked to a contact manager.

Interconnected SFA Tools

Interconnected Sales Force Automation tools offer considerably more functionality than stand-alone tools, and provide a greater degree of data sharing. They generally tend to implement whole sales applications in the Personal Management and Sales Functions categories, and provide some ability to automatically share data (see Figure 1.2).

The advantages of interconnected tools are that they support multiple users, provide some facility for reporting, are somewhat customizable, and provide facilities to share data with other applications. Unlike stand-alone tools, interconnected tools tend to be larger applications and so support multiple concurrent users. This means that more than one person in the sales organization may be using the application at the same time, which is useful, for example, in a telesales environment. The data structures used in these tools are usually available for use in report writing; many of these applications provide a set of standard and customizable reports. These tools also tend to be more customizable than stand-alone tools; for example, you can change the content and layout of screens. Finally, these tools usually also provide *Application Programming Interfaces (APIs)* so that other programs can use the data in these applications. For example, a sales configurator may provide an interface to a proposal gener-

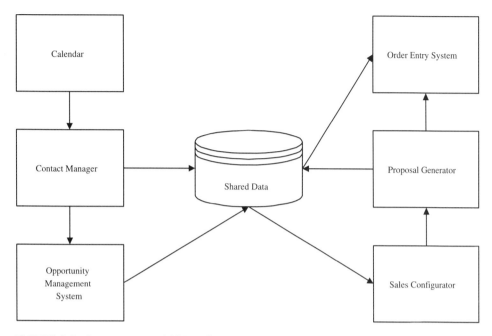

FIGURE 1.2 Interconnected SFA tools.

ation system so that a proposal can automatically and easily incorporate the latest pricing information.

The disadvantages of these tools are that they require a longer implementation time than stand-alone tools, have greater training requirements, generally cost more, and require some level of internal technical support (also known as Help Desk support). Because of the complexity associated with the complete functionality these tools provide, implementation of these tools can be a time-consuming endeavor. Deploying these tools requires planning and coordination of many departments in the sales organization. These tools also tend to change the way work is done, so users of these tools require training not only in the tools themselves, but also in work methods and procedures. As may be expected, this class of tools costs more than the stand-alone solutions to purchase, and also to operate. The size and complexity of these tools, as well as their *mission-critical* nature once they are deployed, dictate the need for an internal technical support staff, such as a Help Desk.

Integrated SFA Tools

Integrated Sales Force Automation Tools differ from interconnected tools in that not only do they provide the functionality necessary for automation, but the applications that make up the tools are also designed to work with one another (see Figure 1.3). For example, a telesales application would be tightly integrated with an opportunity management system (OMS), and leads generated from the telesales application will be available to the OMS for tracking and management. The level of integration in these tools varies: Sometimes just the sales functions are integrated; in others the sales functions and other corporate applications such as customer support, order entry, and supply chain management are able to communicate with the sales applications. These types of tools are available from the larger vendors of Sales Force Automation, as well as from systems integrators that select the appropriate technologies and deliver a seamlessly integrated turnkey solution.

The biggest advantage of integrated tools is that they offer complete functional solutions. They generally utilize sophisticated database and networking technologies, and when they come from one vendor only they generally provide a consistent user interface. Many vendors are moving to provide integrated solutions, and those vendors that do not have the needed functionality are writing interfaces that tightly integrate their products to others with the functionality. A common example is that of sales configurators; many companies that sell integrated tools have aligned with a small number of companies that make sophisticated sales configuration systems, and provide a seamless interface between their application and that of their sales configurator partner.

The disadvantages of integrated tools are that they are very expensive, require a very long implementation time, have a higher ongoing maintenance overhead, and generally present a higher risk. Per-user costs can be very high with these tools, es-

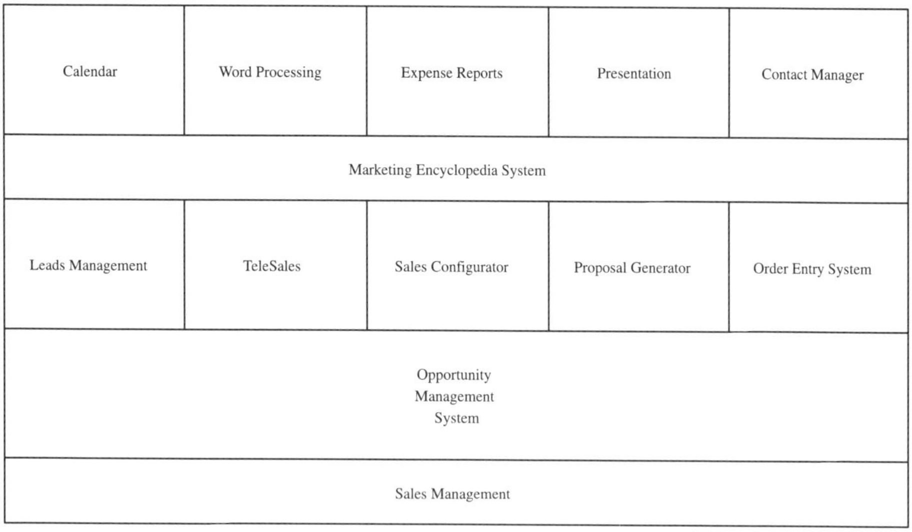

Calendar	Word Processing	Expense Reports	Presentation	Contact Manager
Marketing Encyclopedia System				
Leads Management	TeleSales	Sales Configurator	Proposal Generator	Order Entry System
Opportunity Management System				
Sales Management				

FIGURE 1.3 Integrated SFA tools.

pecially when you factor in the training costs and the costs of the disruptions associated with implementing such a comprehensive set of functionality. This comprehensive functionality also requires a significant amount of time to design, implement, and deploy; a typical rollout may take over a year to complete. Associated with running such a complex environment are the ongoing costs that will be incurred for user training, equipment maintenance, application maintenance, and user technical support. Finally, these tools can be very risky for two main reasons: Your business environment may change before your deployment is complete, thereby putting you in a state of constant change and deployment; or you end up committed to a partner who may not survive the very fragmented and competitive market segment.

Having said all this, the trend nowadays is toward integrated Sales Force Automation tools with rich functionality that can be rapidly prototyped and deployed. The value of Web technologies is that they enable such an environment.

AUDIENCE FOR THIS BOOK

Our target audience is people in companies that want to design, specify, select, and implement Sales Force Automation technologies using the Web. This book will guide the reader through key functions of sales and marketing processes, and demonstrate how these functions may be automated using Web technology. It will provide an enterprisewide sales framework that readers can use when developing their automation strategies, as sales functions (and therefore automation) are often introduced over a period of time. To the maximum extent possible it will provide templates that a reader can use to see how automation can be implemented.

Our audience will be primarily sales and information systems personnel in new, small, or medium-size technology companies. These companies compete in market segments where the typical sales cycle is complex: It lasts more than a few hours and requires more than one interaction with the customer, often by different people in the company. For example, in such a company a marketing assistant may identify and screen a potential customer, and hand off a prospect to a salesperson who will follow up with the customer. The sales cycle itself may involve multiple personnel from both the company and the prospect. Upon closure of the sale, other personnel from the company may need to follow up with the customer to assure product delivery and installation.

It is not our intention to address the specific needs of companies that engage exclusively in *point-of-purchase* sales, in which a sale (usually for a small dollar amount) is initiated by the customer and completed in one transaction (which may in fact be over the Web, also known as electronic commerce or interactive selling). While a company in our target market may sell products in this fashion, such sales will typically make up a small portion of overall sales. Most sales in the companies of our target audience will require the active participation of a sales force and sales teams.

The approach we have taken in writing this book is to provide a comprehensive and rigorous discussion of issues of interest to our target audience. We identify and discuss the issues the reader is likely to encounter. We do this by first developing a framework for discussion, then we identify key issues, discuss the factors surrounding the issue, and finally discuss various approaches to address the issue. Whenever possible we give practical advice and tips that the reader can use. Our goal is to not to direct the reader, but to discuss and guide. We want to give our readers a context in which to view and analyze Sales Force Automation, and by discussing the factors around each issue we expect that the reader will apply the discussions to the context of the reader's own situation.

STRUCTURE AND OVERVIEW

This book is in four main parts. Part I of the book sets the stage, Part II is a discussion of sales processes and models, Part III is about planning and implementing Sales Force Automation technologies, and Part IV is a survey of some commercially available tools used in Sales Force Automation projects.

Part I Setting the Stage

We first set the stage for the rest of the book by defining what we are talking about, and limiting the scope of discussion. This part of the book discusses Sales Force Automation, and the various technologies that are available and being used for Sales Force Automation. The intention is to give the reader an understanding of Sales Force Automation, and the basic technology building blocks that can be used in Sales Force Automation. We include a discussion of the Internet, intranets, and the World Wide Web; and give an overview of the different sales and marketing functions involved in a complex sale.

Part II Sales Processes and Models

The next step is to go over how a complex sale is actually initiated, managed, and completed. This part of the book discusses in detail sales business processes that need to be automated. We cover leads, sales calls, closing the sale, managing customer relationships, and managing the sales cycle. We will show how leads flow through a sales organization, are qualified, passed on to the sales force, and turned into customers. Once a customer relationship is established, we discuss how to manage it. Finally, this part of the book covers the activities involved in managing the sales cycle.

All chapters in this section include examples of how you can automate the different activities and processes using Web technologies. We show screen shots of pages that you can use to develop your own applications, and include all the HTML files we created for the examples on the accompanying CD-ROM.

Part III Planning and Implementation

One of the major reasons for the lack of success of Sales Force Automation projects is the lack of planning prior to implementing the technology. This part of the book will discuss how to plan for implementing Sales Force Automation technologies. We discuss the importance of making a business case for Sales Force Automation before beginning the effort, and then go through all the steps involved in planning for Sales Force Automation.

In all likelihood the implementation of your Sales Force Automation system will require some purchase of technology. We go over how to select the right tools, how to put out a Request for Proposal (RFP), how to evaluate bids, and how to select a vendor and tool. We provide a template RFP on the accompanying CD-ROM that the reader can use to create a custom RFP to send out to prospective vendors.

Part IV Survey of SFA Technologies

The last part of the book covers some commercially available Sales Force Automation technologies and building blocks that you can use to develop your Sales Force Automation solution. In keeping with the emphasis of this book, we have selected as examples vendors that have tools designed for Web usage.

As mentioned earlier in this chapter there are over 1000 vendors of Sales Force Automation products at the time of writing this book. We are very fortunate to be based in an area of the

United States (the San Francisco Bay Area) that is home to a large number of these vendors. The vendors that appear in this book do so for two reasons: They have interesting technology, and it was relatively easy for us to contact them. The purpose of giving examples of commercially available products is to educate and inform using real examples. While we are very grateful to the vendors for all their assistance, we are in no way endorsing any of the products or vendors shown in this book. By the same token, we are in no way rejecting products or vendors that are not mentioned in this book. You, the reader, must make your own assessment of available technologies and their appropriateness to your particular situation.

Work Areas

Many of the chapters of this book include sections called *Work Areas*. These sections contain lists of questions for you to ask yourself and others in your organization when you are considering a Sales Force Automation project. We have also collected all these questions into a file that is available on the accompanying CD-ROM. You can use this file to prepare a functional requirements document.

The questions are intended to initiate discussion and dialog, and not intended to give you a cookie cutter with which to prepare a functional requirements document. For that you must still go through a formal process that works best for your organization.

Accompanying CD-ROM

The CD-ROM that accompanies this book contains all the HTML source code used to create the forms used in this book. If you intend to create your own Web-based Sales Force Automation system, you may modify that source to create many of the forms you need.

We have also included some material supplied to us by some of the vendors whose products are mentioned in this book. This material is intended for your use only, and is not to be reproduced without the permission of the appropriate vendor.

SUMMARY

This chapter has made the case for Sales Force Automation, and described the rest of this book. The next chapter will cover some of the underlying technologies that enable Sales Force Automation.

Overview of Sales
Force Automation
Technologies

2

The plethora of technology options for Sales Force Automation available in the market today boggles the mind. Whether you are implementing an SFA solution for the first time, or are making the transition to the Web, it is essential to understand the technology solutions available today.

The Internet has had a dramatic impact on the way we do business. This impact affects how your organization communicates, delivers service, transacts business, and competes in your marketplace. To take advantage of the latest technological advances that exist today, you will read thorough evaluation of the available tools and technologies, and an understanding of:

- How Web technologies can respond to the ever changing business climate
- How to leverage the automation tools
- How different Web technologies work together or impact each other

This chapter will introduce you to the technology building blocks that will be revisited from chapter to chapter as we set the stage for automating each sales function and process.

OPPORTUNITIES FOR AUTOMATION

So much emphasis has been placed on improving the productivity of the salesperson. No matter how much technology you place in front of your salespeople they will do what they do—sell in the simplest way they know how.

Instead of the focus on improving productivity in and of itself, the effort should be placed on streamlining the information flow by using the Web as an enabling technology. By providing on-demand access to the customer information stream, marketing, telesales, contract administration, and support do not have to waste time in the never-ending paperchase to track down critical information to do their jobs.

A streamlined data flow will remove many of the bottlenecks that exist in organizations today, as well as reduce redundant efforts. The net effect is that processes happen seamlessly, and a by-product of this automation is improved or increased productivity.

Historical Sales Process

In the 1980s, the sales information process followed a somewhat manual sequence of events, with automation typically the last stage of the sales cycle at the time of order entry. Figure 2.1 depicts the old mainframe style model of the primitive corporate database.

The sales process in an organization with a primitive corporate database began when marketing generated print media advertisements, collateral, and white papers. The results of their efforts generated bingo-card leads, letters sent through the U.S. mail, or phone inquiries. Next, literature packs were prepared and sent to customers via U.S. mail. Once prospects were qualified, they were handed off to a salesperson for follow-up.

Salespeople traditionally manage their sales process by keeping all customer information logged into a stand-alone data file on their PC or laptop computer. Thus they created a personal database. The bingo-card leads would be typed into this database, and all subsequent customer contact was logged by the representative. Primitive contact management systems consisted of either 3×5 cards or word processors. Once the contact manager

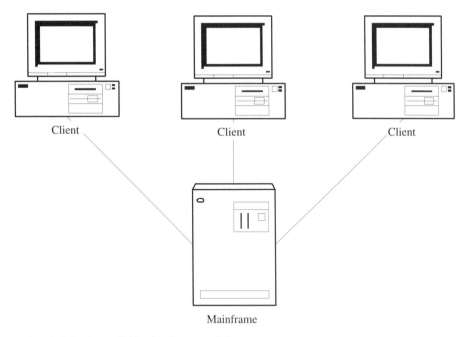

FIGURE 2.1 Monolithic database model.

software packages hit the market (Symantec's ACT!, Telemagic, PackRat), they introduced a new level of complexity requiring more advanced computer skills. Those that could master the necessary skills could run simple reports for marketing, sales, and address labels provided they had tracked the appropriate information in the database. Many of the early systems required customization to track any additional data (like market segment or contact type). At this point, even the most technical salesperson would hit a wall, and the computer departments were too busy to accommodate the custom programming requests.

These personal systems, or contact managers, rarely interfaced with the corporate order entry system. Once the order was placed, the salesperson filled out a paper order form, received the appropriate district manager's signature, and handed off to the sales administrator. The information would then be typed into the corporate order entry system by a sales administrator. At this point the *corporate* information system would know about the customer for the first time. Customer information would be entered into a second customer database.

Now that the customer is in the system, marketing needs to know what geographic region or market segments to which sales is selling. Unfortunately, the early order entry systems did not track geographic regions, market segments, or any other marketing data. Marketing then decided to build its own database (in dBase II or dBase III), with fields to track this important information. Of course, the information was manually typed in by the marketing administrator, who gets his information from check boxes on the order form. If the order was not filled out properly, he would have to track down the salesperson and get this information verbally. This is the third customer database that is created.

The customer service group then needs a mailing list to send out bulletins, technical notes, price catalogs, newsletters, and Christmas cards. Since neither the salesperson nor the corporate order entry system stores contact type, mailings would generally go to all contacts at all companies. To avoid manual generation of labels, customer service would create yet another database of contact names and addresses. This is the fourth customer database. Also in a primitive form, there was no easy way to flag the contacts for deletion when the mail was returned as undeliverable. The proliferation of multiple databases leads to the compartmentalized syndrome illustrated in Figure 2.2, where each database is stand-alone, with no shared information access.

Why This Historical Technology Is Relevant

Believe it or not, there are multimillion dollar companies that operate their sales and marketing organizations like this today. Fortunately, many companies have evolved their information systems to a model that at least has some type of interface between the major legacy systems: Those companies applying a distributed data model have the ability to share data between systems, reducing much of the redundant data entry discussed in the previous section. Figure 2.3 shows the relationships between the separate but linked corporate databases.

By highlighting the opportunities for automation, one can understand, appreciate, and leverage the technology behind the automation process. Imagine the following automated sales process:

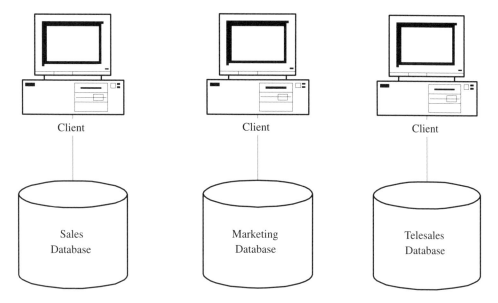

FIGURE 2.2 Departmental (compartmentalized) database model.

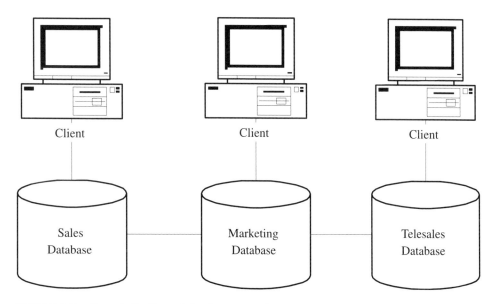

FIGURE 2.3 Shared distributed database model.

Telemarketing Telemarketing is sent an e-mail notification as a new lead enters their system via the corporate Web page. The lead is automatically transferred to the corporate database, and prequalified based on input from the potential customer. The telemarketing representative can pull up the lead information screen within seconds of the lead's entrance into the system. Telemarketing follow-up includes clicking a button to send notification to a fulfillment house to forward glossy marketing materials to the lead. Once this lead is further qualified, the telemarketing representative clicks a button to forward this lead to sales, and the salesperson for the territory is immediately notified.

Sales The salesperson, in a remote office halfway around the world, pulls up the prospect information from the corporate intranet and downloads the latest marketing encyclopedia with up-to-the-minute competitive analysis, market position, and the latest sales figures.

By rating the lead on the corporate opportunity management system via a form provided on the Web page, the district manager can pull together all sales activity instantly, since the lead information has been updated at every step of the way. Since the lead has been classified by market segment and geographic region, the sales management reports can be prepared in a variety of ways by another click of a button (see Chapters 4 and 8 for sample reports).

Order Fulfillment After the sale, the paper trail continues online, because order operations has all customer information on their screen as it was entered by the salesperson. The order fulfillment process happens without incident. All shipment history for that customer can be viewed by anyone in the organization at anytime.

Customer Service When the customer needs to call service or support, the entire customer shipment history is available, with serial numbers and configuration information for each product purchased. In addition, the support representative has the luxury of access to the customer environment information, which was provided by the salesperson at the time the order was placed.

Automation

This automated model may seem like a fantasy. The truth is, the technology to model this process is available today. Through implementing appropriate supporting or enabling technology, you can realize many or all of the benefits of this hypothetical sales organization. Furthermore, the application of Web technologies to your corporate information structure will enable shared information access, as in the Web model in Figure 2.4. The technology building blocks are explored in the next sections.

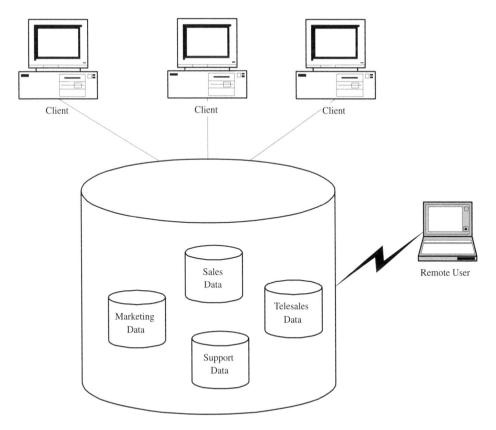

FIGURE 2.4   Web database model.

CORE TECHNOLOGIES

We couldn't begin to list all the core Web technologies in the scope of this book. Included here, however, are the most critical pieces we find as part of common Web infrastructures. You may find that your organization has implemented some of these core technologies already, but hopefully we will introduce you to concepts you never thought possible. Herein lies the value of this book.

Relational Databases

A considerable improvement on the flat file (text file with one data record per line) or proprietary database (used only by the application for which it was generated), relational databases (Ingres, Oracle, Informix, Sybase, ASK, DB2) introduced a more efficient means of data storage and retrieval. Applications that leveraged these common database back ends quickly sprung up for marketing and order entry, as well as financial and manufacturing modules. This gave way to more query and reporting capabilities than ever before. For the first time, corporations were able to integrate the sales and marketing functions with other corporate functions that involve customer contact: technical support and customer service.

Unfortunately this didn't eliminate the salesperson's standalone database on his or her laptop. While on the road, or in a remote regional office, the salesperson had to deal with connectivity issues to the corporate system. Dial-up access was not always available for some of these applications, so remote users were out of the question. The stand-alone contact management systems continued to thrive, and the order-taking process remained somewhat manual. Paper orders where then faxed back to corporate headquarters for entry into the system.

Remote Connectivity

Advances in transport protocols, like TCP/IP, made remote connectivity a reality. The regional office could now dial into the corporate server and enter the prospect information, generate a quote, and even pick up e-mail.

The higher-speed connectivity also became a reality with faster modems and phone or ISDN lines. This made it possible for the salesperson to travel with laptop in hand and still have dial-up access to the corporate office.

Tetherless (Mobile) Connectivity and Data Synchronization

What about times when it is not convenient or possible to work online via a dial-up connection? These mobile professionals face a new challenge.

How about downloading a subset of your corporate database, transferring all data associated with your sales territory to your laptop, editing, then uploading your changes *automagically* into the corporate system? This data process, known as data synchronization, allows for simultaneous changes to be made on the mobile client as well as back at the corporate office, then merges together the two sets of changes.

While the technology for data synchronization has been around for several years, few vendors have been successful in providing a mobile solution. While some software companies are still scrambling to get on the tetherless wave, they may find that by the time they get there, they will be replaced by the mobile Web client, which is discussed in a later section. We are still just breaking the ice on nomadic access to the enterprise.

Wireless Connectivity

Wireless Local Area Networks (WLAN) and Wireless Computing are on the verge of widespread acceptance with the emergence of a new standard known as *IEEE 802.11*. Establishment of this standard will enable different manufacturers of wireless modems to manufacture products that will be able to communicate with one another, removing one of the final barriers that computer manufacturers faced in integrating these products into their laptops and desktop computers on a wide scale. The 2.4 GHz frequency band is allocated on a worldwide basis for license-free radio communications, and the IEEE 802.11 standard calls for 1 and 2 megabit-per-second data transfer rates.

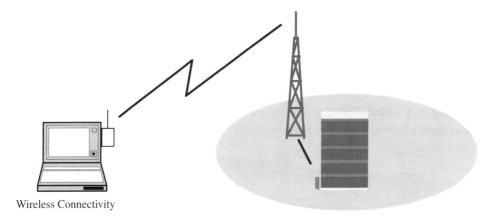

Wireless Connectivity

FIGURE 2.5 Wireless connectivity.

Figure 2.5 shows the radio link between the mobile client and the host base station. While not as fast as hard-wired networks, the enhanced mobility, convenience, and reduced dependence on wired connections make this new technology highly attractive. One can envision a salesperson freely moving from one corporate office to another in a different location, easily establishing a link with which to download electronic mail or other vital information without ever needing to *plug in* to a wired node. In addition, smaller businesses that move frequently will benefit from reduced costs associated with repeatedly laying and moving network cables.

WEB TECHNOLOGIES

The Internet was originated in the 1970s by the U.S. Department of Defense to allow computer systems of different types to communicate with one another. Originally called ARPAnet (Advanced Research Project Agency), this network established communications between military and government locations.

This network idea was adapted by scientists who formulated a network called Bitnet to allow different universities to collaborate on research projects. This network was not originally connected to ARPAnet.

The National Science Foundation (NSF) expanded on this technology in the 1980s, creating the NSFnet to connect college campuses using the Bitnet network with other smaller networks. The term *Internet* was used to represent the interlink between networks.

Although the Internet has had a presence since the early 1970s, the recent emergence of the World Wide Web (WWW) has launched the Internet into a household name.

World Wide Web (WWW)

The Web was formed in 1989 at the European Particle Physics lab as a way for scientists around the world to share information via the Internet. The Web consists of servers that present documents to an end user for viewing. These documents, or pages, can contain links to other servers anywhere in the world.

The fastest growing segment of the Internet today, the Web has grown from less than 50 Web sites in 1990 to over 13,000 in 1995.

The attention of Netscape's IPO in 1995 has thrust this technology into every aspect of media as it exists today. Due to the huge media explosion of the Web, most new computers are equipped with a Web browser preinstalled. The introduction of the Web has enabled an easy marriage between corporate information and an easy-to-use, common graphical user interface.

The Web browser provides the opportunity of a *thin* client. Client/server applications that previously required multiple software pieces to work together are said to be *fat* clients (see Figure 2.6). These fat clients typically required three software programs to be installed and configured to work together before the application would run:

1. Application software
2. Database connectivity software
3. Communications software

While required for the enterprise client/server applications, a fat client presents not only memory and configuration issues, but also presents many support and compatibility issues.

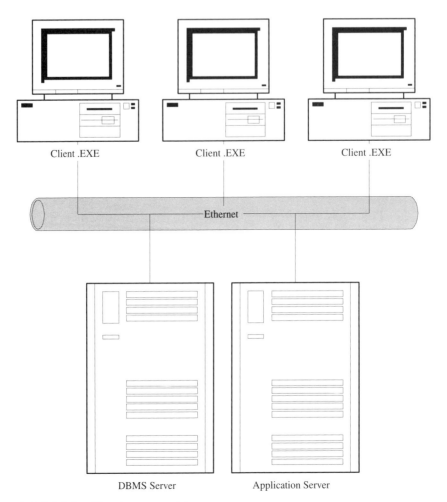

FIGURE 2.6 Client/server model.

In contrast, the thin Web client requires just the one software component to be installed. Moreover, the Web browser is the most universal client component available. Aside from the obvious installation and support advantages, applications designed for a Web client provide additional advantages over applications that have added on a Web interface to an existing product (see Figure 2.7). Applications designed for the Web browser client have the following benefits:

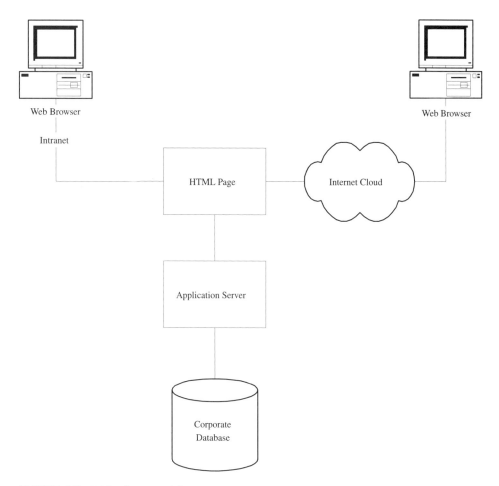

FIGURE 2.7   Web client model.

- Web client functionality is the same whether you are working connected or working offline. Many client/server vendors that have released Web modules do so with very limited functionality. Web access is provided into the application, but often for viewing and minor updating only.
- The Web client enables distribution of upgraded client software without the traditional physical distribution process. A

user simply needs to access the Web page to see any new or updated software.

■ Implementation of a Web client also reduces support overhead normally associated with the traditional client/server model. It is this medium that has driven the popularity of the WWW and the Web browser as the client platform of choice for today's client/server applications.

■ Functionality available with a native Web client encompasses a much more dynamic, interactive, and graphically oriented model. Nonnative Web clients tend toward the static text page with static graphic images.

The additional advantages of the Web have already been realized by millions. The Web:

■ Is inexpensive
■ Provides information on demand
■ Has easy access
■ Has an audience of millions
■ Allows dynamic information flow
■ Is universally accessible

The World Wide Web is a compelling platform for the delivery and dissemination of data-driven, interactive enterprise applications. The Web's ubiquity provides instant and global application availability to both users and companies. Because the Web is architected to be platform independent, it significantly lowers deployment and training costs. Hoping to reap these benefits, organizations are building new applications or retrofitting existing client/server implementations to take full advantage of the World Wide Web.

Until recently, there were few companies building commercial Web/data applications because of the lack of development tools. Applications had to be hand coded from scratch in PERL or C++. As tools that lower the cost of application development and maintenance mature, organizations will increasingly turn to the Web as the platform for commercial applications. Corporations looking to leverage the Web as a strategic platform for implementing innovative business solutions—in effect becoming Web-centric enterprises—need to examine the issues surrounding the development of Web applications.

The next sections explore the technical requirements of the Web/data application environment and discuss the architectural and programming language trade-offs.

Web Page

The basic building block of the Web is the Web page, or in its most basic form, an HTML (Hypertext Markup Language) file. The HTML page displays company information, either in text or graphical form, and can contain links to other pages on the same Web site or another Web site. Since the Web can link together a company with its distributors, channel partners, vendors, and so on, with a universally available client platform, it is the most logical choice for providing an integrated information solution.

The simple, static Web page can be expanded to a dynamic, interactive page by incorporating more sophisticated features, such as user authentication, push technology, tables, interactive maps, frames, forms, graphics, audio, and video. These enhancements transform a standard one-dimensional, read-only Web page into one that can take user input, update databases, submit queries and review query results, record voicemail, provide teleconferencing, and watch video clips.

World Wide Web as an Application Platform

The Web platform can deliver innovative solutions for both inter- and intracompany business issues. As an intranet platform, the Web reduces deployment costs and overcomes performance and scalability limitations of client/server applications. As an Internet platform, the Web enables companies to provide new services and reach new customers through globally accessible applications. Such benefits were not previously available with host-based or traditional client/server applications.

WebData versus Client/Server—Scalable Application Deployment The broad reach and browser-based simplicity of the Web eliminates the time and cost associated with application deployment. In this environment, deployment is instantaneous because the application resides on the server rather than on the client. From the server, the application can be accessed from anywhere in the world. For MIS managers, this server-based implementation eliminates much of the headache involved in maintenance upgrades and administration involved in managing multiple platforms across multiple offices. For business managers, global access of server-side applications provides a compelling new channel for reaching new customers with products and services.

The implementation of a Web-based solution introduces a natural three-tier architecture that provides a foundation for scalability. Current LAN-based client/server applications are typically limited to a small number of simultaneous users. These applications have fat client software that inefficiently processes both screen displays and business logic. Furthermore, traditional client/server users are logged onto the database from the start to the finish of a session. Organizations with these implementations hit the client/server *wall* when the software demands of the application exceed the capability of the client, or when the number of database users has increased to a point where the application can no longer scale. The Web in contrast, due to its thin client architecture, supports a large number of simultaneous clients that access a server-side application. The client browser performs the display of information while all processing intensive business logic is handled on the server. Users on these newly termed *Web/data* applications are also connected to the data source for only the duration of each transaction rather than for the entire session. Optimization in the Web/data application architecture makes database connections readily available to Web application users without incurring the overhead of a persistent and dedicated data source connection.

Lessons from Client/Server Tools—Rapid Application Development In the early phase of the Web, applications were developed from scratch in either C/C++ or PERL due to the lack of mature tools for building commercial applications. This approach is obviously time intensive and costly, and even more so in maintenance of applications once they are built. As Web/data tools evolve, solutions vendors are quickly adopting features seen in client/server tools. This adaptation of current technology for Web/data development thus provides customers with rapid Web application development environments that deliver fast deployment without sacrificing flexibility in development.

In the client/server world, rapid application development (RAD) using a highly visual tool significantly cuts time in application development and subsequent code maintenance. Many successful RAD client/server tools, such as PowerBuilder and Visual Basic, automate the process of client/server application development by providing wizards that generate application objects. These "assistants" eliminate the bulk of programming from commercial applications by determining the application needs and automatically generating code.

Successful client/server tools have also been tightly integrated with underlying languages for business logic and application extensibility. The language integration choice is indispensable if a developer is to reap the benefits of rapid application development without sacrificing flexibility. For example, client/server tools that are based on languages with underlying object-oriented class libraries provide a mechanism for reusing and extending the capabilities of the underlying language. As projects grow in scale and depth, the extensibility and maturity of the language become critical to the project's success. In short, the choice of programming languages dictates the success of the Web/data application.

The Web—New Technical Challenges The Web, while providing significant benefits, introduces new technical challenges with respect to scalability, management of session and state, security, and change.

Scalability. Web applications can face unpredictable and potentially enormous peak loads. Large user loads require a high-performance server architecture that is extremely scalable.

State Maintenance. The Web is a stateless environment in which the client and server are loosely coupled. Applications must keep state information from one page to another if they are to avoid requiring users to reenter information, such as user name and password, from page to page.

Security. Security becomes paramount when companies make internal databases accessible to external browser-based users. User authentication and secure data transmissions are made more challenging in the Web environment because of the large number of potentially anonymous users.

Change. Technology implementations on the Web are changing rapidly and standards are still evolving.

In the past, developers addressed some of these issues through external mechanisms, such as client-side "cookies" for managing state. More recently, development tools have begun to integrate built-in support for solving these issues within a development environment.

Architectural Considerations

Software vendors have taken significantly different approaches in their attempts to integrate Web technology and the application development and deployment architecture. Regardless of the approach, it is clear that in order to reap the full benefits of platform independence, instant global access, and low deployment costs, an application's underlying technology must be optimized for the Web platform. This section explores the different architectural approaches taken by tools for building Web/data applications, and the advantages and disadvantages inherent in these approaches. The approaches examined are:

- Two-tier applications, using:

  Microsoft Windows clients
  Web browser plug-ins
  Java clients
- Three-tier applications, using:

  CGI-based executables
  Web server in conjunction with application server

Two-Tier Applications Two-tier applications connect directly from the client Web browser to the database. They bypass the

Web server and instead use the Internet simply as the communications backbone. The simplicity and uniqueness of the HTML page are not leveraged. Examples of this approach are:

Microsoft Windows Client Applications. These two-tier applications are client/server applications that make use of the Internet rather than the LAN as the communications backbone. The applications maintain the same Windows graphical user interface and are simply downloaded over the Web for execution on the user's machine. The resources required for a traditional client/server application are identical.

Browser Plug-In Applications. Netscape introduced the concept of the Web browser plug-in as a means of allowing existing applications to run within an HTML page. A client-side runtime component is installed on the Web browser. Applications using that runtime are then downloaded each time they are required by the user. The application will require the same amount of resources if it were running as a Windows-based application.

Java Client Applications. Client-side Java applets can be implemented to interface directly with databases using protocols like JDBC. In this approach, the Web server sends the Java applet to the client. The client-side applet then initiates a connection directly to the database, bypassing the Web server.

The first two approaches (Windows clients and browser plug-ins) are typical of most client/server tools vendors who have introduced Web products. However, because these vendors are not significantly changing the client/server architecture, the benefits of operating over the Web are limited.

The advantage of either approach is that, once the application is installed on the client side, users can access data from any remote location that has Internet access. The disadvantage is that the client computer configurations must remain homogeneous. Configuring computers to accept the downloaded software remains a problem. The benefit of instantaneous cross-platform access to applications remains elusive.

Disadvantages of all three approaches, including two-tier Java applets, are that the applications are not efficient in their use of database resources, and the applications do not scale. The client/server architecture, in which a user is exclusively logged into the database for an entire session, limits the number of Web users.

Three-Tier Applications Three-tier applications make use of a Web and/or application server as a middle tier. The middle tier separates the processing tasks, performing the business logic processing while leaving the browser to generate the data displays. Examples of the three-tier application approach are:

- CGI-based applications
- Web server in conjunction with dedicated application server

Three-tier applications, in contrast to two-tier ones, reap the benefits of Web application publishing and distribution. With this architecture, applications reside on the server and can be deployed instantaneously. Through the use of application servers, the three-tier architecture also creates a foundation for scalability.

Early implementations of server-based applications were based on Common Gateway Interface (CGI) executables. Application developers wrote C++ code or PERL scripts and placed them in the CGI directory. When a user requests a page with data, the Web server runs the relevant CGI executable or script. It starts a new CGI process, opens a connection to the data source, passes the request (typically in SQL), receives the data, closes the data connection, and shuts down the CGI process. This cycle occurs each time a new request is received. The overhead involved in starting and stopping the CGI process corresponds directly with the size of the executable. It is also clear to see that with each request substantial overhead is incurred with the opening and closing of a connection to the database. A more optimal solution would require cached application code as well as cached connections.

Application Servers for the Web The application server provides high-speed and scalable three-tier architecture for Web-centric applications. This implementation, whereby the Web server communicates with an *in-memory* application server, eliminates the overhead of starting and stopping CGI processes, and the opening and closing of database connections. The application server negates the burden of restarting CGI processes by providing an optimized CGI interface or a direct interface to Web server APIs (e.g., NSAPI or ISAPI). Applications are cached in memory. There is no need to start and stop individual processes each time a request is to be fulfilled. The application server can also optimize data source connections by caching database connections. Multiple users with identical user privileges can utilize the same cached database connection. A new login or request does not necessitate a new database connection.

Application servers with distributed architectures can also be scaled easily. A distributed server is critical for Web applications with uncertain numbers of users that can increase exponentially overnight. Scalability should be as simple as adding more CPUs to a system. Developers should not need to perform custom coding to handle an increase in the number of Web application users.

Building the Ideal Web/Data Application Implementing a Web-centric solution is not a trivial task. Nor is the implementation process one of shoehorning existing technology to fit a new role. The full benefits of the Web can be obtained only by an architecture that has been optimized for the Web platform. Alternative architectures provide some benefits, but do not provide others. Table 2.1 summarizes the major differences between the approaches discussed in this section.

Enterprise Considerations

The Web-centric enterprise is one that takes full advantage of the Web, and leverages existing core applications at the same time. Corporations today have invested significant time and money to implement fundamental business activities, such as enterprise resources planning, human resources, and supply chain management. Taking the enterprise to the Web does not necessitate the termination of existing application implementations. In fact, Web-centric enterprises should require that their Web/data solutions leverage their existing applications, not dismiss them.

Many businesses have built their human resource administration systems on applications from PeopleSoft. Others have

TABLE 2.1 Web Architecture Options

	Web Native 3-Tier	3-Tier Client/Server	2-Tier Client/Server	Java 2-Tier
Instantaneous, heterogeneous Web application publishing	Yes	No	No	Yes
Scalability	Yes	Yes	No	No

implemented SAP's financial accounting or plant maintenance applications. In their traditional environments, these systems required dedicated client computers. Computers had hefty requirements. Installation and maintenance of these systems on the client computers were significant undertakings. Applications were limited to the existing LAN infrastructure. Transforming these applications for the Web is a natural and obvious step. Web/data development tools must enable this Web-centric transformation, allowing developers to Web-enable these core enterprise applications and at the same time reuse the existing business logic already developed for these systems.

Language Considerations Architectural benefits provided by Web/data tools are also significantly affected by the type of language on which they are based. Like successful client/server tools, successful Web/data development tools must provide the flexibility and extensibility required to build enterprise-scale applications. Languages that have emerged for Web/data applications include Java, Visual Basic (or a licensed variant), C++, and JavaScript. Additionally, client/server vendors have continued to use their proprietary scripting languages as the language underlying their Web application development.

Table 2.2 highlights some of the differences in the various languages used on the Web.

Like the ideal Web/data tool, the ideal Web language should be one that was architected for the Web. It should be portable across the many platforms that support Web browsers. In fact, it should be browser-independent. Furthermore, it must be secure, especially for applications that run over the Internet. And it

TABLE 2.2 Language Considerations

	Java	*Visual Basic*	*C++*	*Java Script*
Secure	Yes	No	No	No
Platform-independent	Yes	No	No	Dependent on browser type
Object-oriented	Yes	No	Yes	Pseudo
Automatic garbage collection	Yes	No	No	No
Built-in threads	Yes	No	No	Yes

must be an object-oriented programming language so that developers can reuse existing code. It must, like its tool, be Web-centric. Java has emerged as the likely winner in the succession of languages on the Web. It builds upon the benefits of existing OOP languages such as C++, removes unnecessary complexity such as pointers and memory allocation, and introduces security and portability features that are important for the Web.

CGI Scripts

To allow for a basic interactive Web page, in which the user can submit information via a form, you must attach code to handle the delivery and processing of the data. Through the use of CGI scripts, you can send and receive information to and from an on-line database.

Multimedia

Multimedia languages provide means of creating dynamic, robust, and visually appealing Web pages, offloading much of the *thinking* to the Web page itself. Consider the standard HTML text type of Web page and its characteristics:

- Static text and graphic images.
- Dynamic data refresh is not handled easily.
- Control of screen content must be managed on the server.

By incorporating ActiveX and Java technologies, the Web page control shifts the paradigm from the server to the client.

ActiveX ActiveX, at a very high level, encompasses both client and server technologies that provide the power of PC computing on a Web platform. The components of ActiveX allow for the creation of interactive applications running on a Web site.

Java For the more robust Web page the effective use of multimedia, graphics, and animation can be created via Java scripts or applets. The Java language was developed by Sun Microsystems in 1991 and was originally intended for consumer electronics applications. It was later adapted as an Internet programming language. Java applets are compiled bits of code that get executed from the Web page. Java scripting, however, must be supported by a Java-enabled browser (such as Sun Microsystems's HotJava).

Some common applications of multimedia technologies you may have seen are:

- Stock market quotes
- Online games
- Pay-per-use software licensing
- Virtual workstations

VRML VRML (Virtual Reality Modeling Language) brings 3D graphics and virtual-reality applications to the Web. As with Java, VRML requires viewing from a VRML browser. Bringing virtual reality to the Web would enable the user to *walk* through a room, open doors, and literally interact with that environment. As with conventional virtual-reality systems, the user would be able to pick up objects, using keys on the keyboard, and turn them around to view all sides.

Security

No Internet discussion would be complete without a discussion on security (see Figure 2.8). Security is typically available in several different methods:

- Application software
- Web server
- Firewall

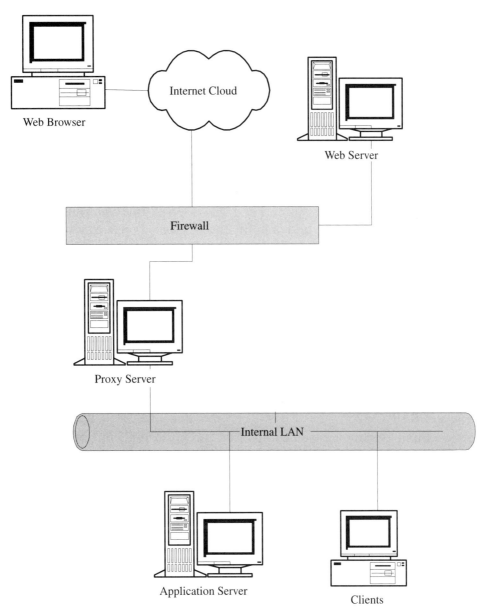

FIGURE 2.8   Web security model.

Your most secure solution would be to incorporate all three levels of controlled access to your corporate database.

Application Security Application-level security is available through a prepackaged Web client solution. By providing user logins and passwords, authentication allows access to only those customers and third-party groups for which you grant access.

Web Server Security The popular Web server software packages available today offer varying degrees of security. Encryption technology is available on many HTTP servers. Proxy servers provide the ability to block inbound connections across the firewall, and restrict outbound connections. Blocking can be based on such parameters as user e-mail address, time of day, port number, application protocol, and domain name. These types of security systems can have an adverse impact on the Web server if the Internet/intranet communications methods are not fully understood. Your system administrator must evaluate all client and server connection types in order to optimize the system security.

Firewall Firewalls further protect internal proprietary data from undesirable outside sources. Available as a third-party software or embedded in some networking products, firewalls reduce the physical access allowed between the outside browser and the corporate database.

Push Technology

Push technology encompasses an information distribution process that sends information and news updates to the user's desktop without requiring the user to visit the Web site. An early example using primitive push technology is e-mail.

The most widely distributed push application in use is PointCast (www.pcn.com). PointCast provides the user with a mechanism with which to configure the types of data being sent, thus filtering out any unwanted information. The PointCast product then acts as a screen saver on the user's desktop, and flashes information in the form of ticker tape of stock quotes, news headlines, weather, sports scores, and so on.

Software vendors are now moving toward a *selective push* technology that builds on the PointCast model by providing information distribution to select user groups within an organization. Information made available on a need-to-know basis, rather than the mass distribution format, has eased the bandwidth issues previously faced with mass distribution. See Chapter 12 for more information on FirstFloor, a leading vendor of selective push applications.

The Web as a Central Repository

Corporate Information is one of your most valuable assets. Access to this information via the Web page ensures the most up-to-date marketing collateral or sales order form that exists at your corporate office. Whether printing the form from the Web page, or entering your order online, you have saved valuable time by not having to track down the latest revision.

While the client/server architecture has produced many benefits, a much more efficient model integrating Internet technologies provides the best of both the departmental and distributed models. Implementing a central repository requires integrating fundamental core technologies into your Web model. The common barriers to productivity that this model addresses are:

Information access is decentralized. As seen earlier in this chapter, information is easily scattered across the corporate network, and the control of this information has become more decentralized. Therefore, it is difficult just to find the correct information you are looking for, not to mention having to scramble to find your way across a network of servers and shared drives.

Data sources are too disparate. Since there are likely many different sources for customer information in your organization, there is not a common, centralized application that supports all data types. For this reason, the management of this data is more complicated and costly.

Data sources are not scalable. As the volume of data and usage grows, the applications that support these data sources are not designed to efficiently support large numbers of users. The result is a network traffic increase, which causes performance degradation. The system administrator ends up trying to address performance tuning on multiple data applications that utilize multiple data sources with multiple data types. The load across the network is therefore difficult to balance.

Global access is too costly. Real-time access to corporate databases worldwide is often accomplished via expensive leased lines. The Web eliminates the leased-line approach by providing a means of connecting offices around the globe via the Internet, a low-cost connection relative to the leased-line charges.

Integrating your corporate and customer data into an online repository is the most cost-efficient form of publishing your data. The Web repository embraces and extends the universal client and Internet technologies. The Web page is the core building block of the information infrastructure required to store, manage, and distribute information across the enterprise. The Web page eliminates the complexity of combining documents and data from disparate sources into one common application, by easily integrating components from such sources as:

- Marketing encyclopedias
- Online color brochures
- Competitive analyses
- Price books
- Interactive catalogs
- Quoting
- Contracts
- Online ordering

The Web as a front end to the central repository adds flexibility to manage the sales and marketing data, as shown in Figure 2.9. The Web client makes it possible for the shared marketing or sales data to exist virtually anywhere on the network. The client application doesn't need to know where a document physically resides. Web administrators can therefore decide the best physical machine on the network to store this critical data. The application has not hard-coded the location of any of these documents.

The corporate information stream is not the only way to leverage your Web investment. Access to your Customer profile enables the entire corporation to see your installed base. This

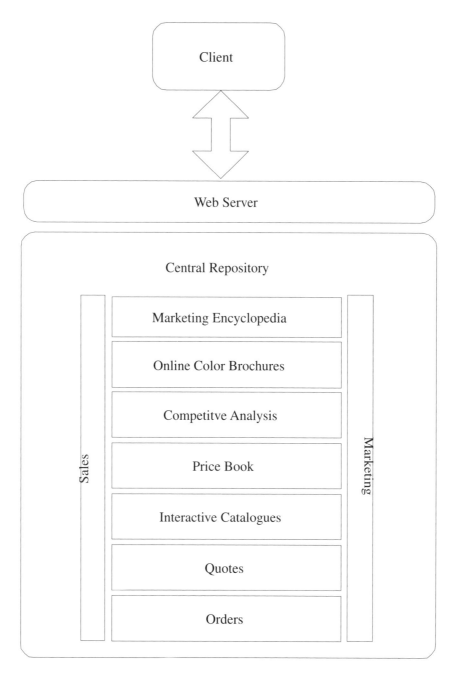

FIGURE 2.9 Shared access to sales and marketing data.

form of Customer Information Asset Management, coupled with the online sales and marketing systems, provides the foundation for a continuous information flow throughout your company—from prospect to sales to support.

The major SFA issues that used to exist (like Account Management, out-of-date price lists, version management) are eliminated by centralizing your sales and marketing operations into one place: the Web site. How many sources of customer data currently exist in your corporation? If the answer is more than one, you should be more than tempted to absorb this book and begin your journey into SFA automation.

IMPORTANCE OF INTEGRATION

Not all companies supply all the tools required to set up and deliver a complete Web solution. It is likely that you will need some combination of a Web server, SFA package, third-party firewall package, and client browser. Anytime you are integrating multiple vendor packages, you must evaluate and test for compatibility, performance, ease of implementation, ease of maintenance, and ease of use. For these reasons, it is important to understand how each component will affect your overall implementation. With careful selection and planning, you can avoid the traps that have historically caused 60 to 70 percent of all SFA projects to fail.

A successful automation project incorporates elements from all four corners of the enterprise: people, process, technology and strategy (see Figure 2.10). In an SFA environment, time to implementation is a critical success factor. It has been widely documented that for an SFA project to be successful, a 1- to 3-month implementation time frame is the only acceptable threshold.

In addition, the ease of customization becomes a factor down the road, since these packages need to be flexible as your business changes. As with any implementation, our experience has shown that minimal, up-front customization reduces time to implement, and allows the user community to experience the *out-of-the-box* system before making unnecessary changes.

All too often, we've seen eager IT professionals trying to closely mimic a legacy system by overcustomizing a new product

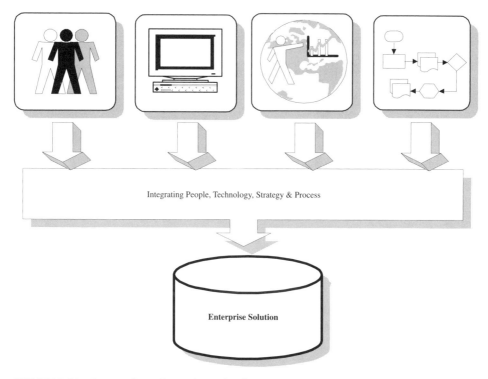

FIGURE 2.10   Integration of people, technology, strategy, and process.

that may have already provided all required functionality. Remember, SFA solutions are designed with the help of industry experts, and have probably incorporated most everything you would want in an out-of-the-box solution.

SUMMARY

This chapter has given a historical perspective of some of the technologies used in Sales Force Automation, and discussed many of the new developments that take advantage of Web and Internet technologies. The pace of technological change is so rapid that much of what we have said will be *historical* information by the time this book is in print. However, we believe that the technologies we have presented will endure the forthcoming changes, and will in all likelihood provide the foundation for the newer technologies.

The next chapter will cover the common sales models used in companies that engage business-to-business selling, discuss some of the functions that are performed while selling, and then review some common Sales Force Automation tools.

The authors would like to acknowledge the assistance of Sherrick Murdoff of NetDynamics in the preparation of this chapter.

3

Sales Models, Functions, and Tools

There is no denying that the most significant contributor to success in a complex sale is the personal selling knowledge and experience of a salesperson. A good salesperson will manage interactions with prospects, and identify the key players in the sales decision-making process. A good salesperson will follow up with each potential influencer in a complex sale, and address the needs and concerns of that influencer. A good salesperson will be available to answer questions as they come up, indeed even before they come up.

With all this emphasis on personal interactions, does this mean that there is no need for Sales Force Automation? Not at all. The purpose of Sales Force Automation is to enable the salesperson to perform precisely those tasks that require personal selling knowledge and experience, and to eliminate or reduce the activities that keep the salesperson from performing those tasks. The previous two chapters have discussed the rationale for Sales Force Automation, and the infrastructure technologies that can be used to implement SFA. But what precisely are we automating?

This chapter will give an overview of the main sales models implemented in most sales organizations, cover the different sales and marketing functions involved in a complex sale, and also cover different sales automation tools and describe their key features.

SALES MODELS

The means by which a company sells products to customers is the *sales model* used by the company. Companies engaged in business-to-business selling may have several different types of sales models to attain their revenue objectives. Although there may be several variations to these, the three most common sales models used in most companies are:

- Field Sales
- Telesales
- Channel Sales

A Field Sales model is the traditional one in which a salesperson works *in the field;* that is, the salesperson spends a lot of time in face-to-face contact with potential customers, usually in the office of the prospect. The salesperson occasionally visits the *home office* to catch up on the latest developments, works on administrative tasks, and meets with sales management. A goal of many sales organizations is to maximize the time a salesperson spends with potential customers, and minimize the time a salesperson spends in the office.

In the Telesales model (sometimes called the *Inside Sales* model), a salesperson works primarily out of an office, usually together with many other telesales representatives. Most of the selling is done through conversations on a telephone, or by other communications methods such as electronic mail and letters and Faxes. Organizations that implement a Telesales model tend to invest heavily in communications and Sales Force Automation technologies.

A company that uses field sales and telesales is said to engage in *direct selling*, because the company sells directly to its customers. Sometimes a company will sell its products to customers through sales channels that it does not own, so-called *in-*

direct sales. In this model the company enters into agreements with selling partners and different types of *resellers*, such as *systems integrators* and *value-added resellers (VARs)*, who sell to the customers that will actually use the products.

The sales cycle for these three sales channels can be similar. In some cases there may be team selling, with more than one individual from a channel involved or multiple channels involved in the same sales opportunity. Using the Web as an enabling tool leverages the value of each of these channels in its own unique way. Given the similarities in these models, our discussion will use generic sales processes whenever possible, and call out the differences in processes when appropriate.

OVERVIEW OF SALES PROCESSES

An overview of the sales and marketing functions involved in a complex sale is shown in Figure 3.1. Each of the elements shown is discussed in a subsequent section.

Capturing the Lead

In a manufacturing process, the quality of the raw materials affects the amount of processing required to convert the raw materials into finished product, and can even affect the quality of the finished product. This is why an efficient manufacturing organization will acquire the best raw materials. A similar situation exists with sales processes. Leads are the raw materials for the sales process, and the quality of leads fed into the sales process affects the amount of time spent on converting the lead to the finished product: a sale to a customer. This section covers acquisition and distribution of leads.

Lead Generation
The beginning of any complex sale, indeed any sale, is the generation of a lead. In a successful business a key goal of the marketing organization is to generate the quality and quantity of prospects your sales organization needs to attain its revenue targets. This is typically done in a number of different ways, such

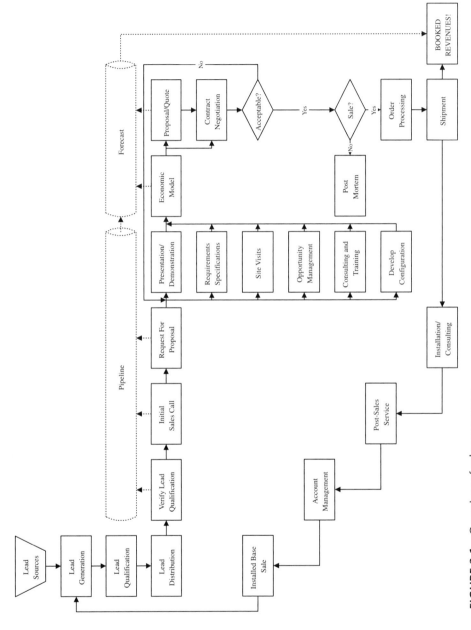

FIGURE 3.1 Overview of sales processes.

as public relations, direct mail, advertising, trade shows, and seminars. Interested parties are identified, and if they show sufficient interest in your products, they may qualify as leads to be pursued for a potential sale.

Two key concerns in generating a lead are the cost per lead and the quality of the lead itself. The cost required to generate a lead includes all the costs associated with creating awareness and the actual acquisition cost itself. The cost per lead should be measured in terms of qualified leads; that is, those leads that meet the quality standards of your lead-generation process. The quality of the lead refers to the suitability of your company's products for the lead's needs, and the intention and wherewithal of the lead to purchase your products. Costs and quality are related: Overall costs of generating leads will be higher when the leads are of poor quality, and lower when the leads are of high quality. In other words, the more leads that result in sales, the lower the overall cost of generating leads.

The advantage of using Web technologies to generate leads is that you can reach a large audience at relatively low cost. For example, the costs of putting up a Web site are low, and the incremental costs of reaching an audience of 1000 or 1,000,000 are marginal. People who make inquiries through the Web site can be asked to complete a questionnaire that collects information that is used to make a qualifying decision. Furthermore, if your Web site has detailed information on your products and services, you can satisfy many questions a casual browser may have.

Lead Qualification

The whole purpose of lead qualification is to separate casual inquiries from genuine prospects. As previously described, leads may come in from a number of different sources. But many of these leads may be from people who have no intention of buying your products. Some of these people may be collecting information for a project (such as writing a book), while others may have filled out a request on a whim. Some inquiries may even come from your competitors. This is a normal part of doing business, and a cost you incur in trying to raise awareness for your products and services. As mentioned earlier, you can lower costs by using the Web to provide enough information to satisfy casual requests. A good automation system should provide a facility for initiating and tracking the information sent to satisfy an inquiry.

Other leads you generate may in fact be viable prospects who have a genuine interest in purchasing your products. Clearly you have to identify these leads, because each one represents a potential customer and a future revenue stream. One way to qualify these leads is to send out a salesperson for each one, and have the salesperson get details on what the person who made the inquiry really wants to do. But this can be a very expensive proposition. Not all of these leads will turn out to be good prospects, and a salesperson could spend a lot of time pursuing leads that have no revenue potential. Every minute a salesperson spends pursuing these useless leads is a minute away from pursuing real leads with revenue potential.

A more common way of qualifying leads then is to minimize the involvement of the salesperson until it is clear the lead appears to be a viable prospect, and to use automation and personnel that focus on qualifying leads. Automation, especially using the Web, typically involves having the person making the inquiry provide as much information as necessary for your organization to make a qualification. This information can be matched against qualifying criteria, and leads that look promising can be quickly passed on to personnel who can get more information and route the lead to the appropriate salesperson. Inquiries that come in without sufficient information, or other inquiries that may not appear to be as promising, can also be routed to in-house personnel for follow-up, perhaps with a lower priority. Leads that clearly are casual requests for information can be handled automatically, without any human intervention. Data collected from these inquiries can be recorded and used to determine the interest levels in the product line.

Lead Distribution

Once the generated leads have been qualified, they must be passed on to the appropriate sales channel. In a direct sales or telesales model, a qualified lead would be distributed to a salesperson or a sales manager. In a reseller model, the qualified lead would be passed on to the appropriate reseller. Although this sounds conceptually simple, leads distribution is often not well executed, because the information that is necessary to route leads is often out of date, not available, not used, or all of those reasons.

The basic requirement for a good leads distribution system is a comprehensive set of rules that specify how a lead should be routed, so-called *routing tables*. These tables define the parameters used in making routing decisions, and the input given by the lead or collected by the person qualifying the lead is matched against values in the table, and the *rules* that are used to resolve routing contentions should they arise. If the tables are well designed, they will give an indication of where the lead should go. Consider a simple example: Your sales territories may be set up by geographic area, but also by industry segment. If a lead comes from California, it may be suitable for your Western Sales Region. However, if the lead's line of business is telecommunications, an industry segment for which you have a separate territory, then perhaps the lead should be routed to a salesperson in the Telecommunications territory. The parameters in the tables would result in a routing contention, but you may have a rule that says that if the lead's company does not have a national presence, then the geographic territory should take precedence over the industry territory.

That was a simple example. In a real business you will have many different channels, territories, salespeople, products, industries, and other criteria for distributing leads; and your rules for distribution may constantly change. Keeping all the routing tables and rules up to date is an essential task and should be given the attention it deserves.

A major advantage of using Web technologies to implement your Sales Force Automation system is that the routing tables can be maintained by many people, spread out all over the world. Senior sales management could decide and maintain the territories and the basic rules for distribution between territories. Sales territory managers could determine distribution within a territory. Individual salespersons could indicate their current availability to accept additional leads.

Managing the Sales Cycle

In a manufacturing process, once the raw materials have been received, sorted, and made ready for further processing, and are delivered to the right place, actual processing of the materials begins. In our sales process, now that the lead has been qualified and presented to the appropriate salesperson, what happens next? This section discusses the activities that are undertaken now that the lead is entering the pipeline (or the *sales funnel,* or the *hopper*). The goal is to move the lead along the pipeline until it results in a sale. This takes a lot of work on the part of the salesperson and other members of the sales team, and all activities must be carefully tracked and managed. For this reason we call this section *Managing the Sales Cycle*.

Verification

After receiving a qualified lead a salesperson will typically have a discussion with the lead. The purpose of the discussion is to get as much information as possible about the opportunity or issue facing the lead so that the salesperson can decide if your products and services can in fact address the needs of the lead. Other factors to consider in decision making include the planned timing of the purchase, whether the size of the potential deal makes it appropriate for the salesperson, and whether initial lead qualification has verified the potential buyer's wherewithal to purchase, both in terms of business stability and budget approval. Other information that is collected by the salesperson at this point can include the names and titles of key decision makers and influencers in the sale, and possibly the names of competitors the lead has contacted. All of this information collected by the salesperson can be logged into a central repository using a Web-based client, and as the lead turns into an opportunity the total information collected can be used to track all the essential details of the sale. If the sale is ultimately lost, this information is vital to the postmortem process discussed in Chapter 6.

Initial Sales Call

If the opportunity is one that will be pursued at this time, the salesperson must schedule an initial sales call with the prospective customer. This often involves a visit to the customer, or sometimes having the customer visit the company's facilities. In addition to scheduling the call in the first place, the salesperson must coordinate the activities of other members of the sales organization that will help with the sales call, and also pull together additional information for the prospect, as well as prepare a presentation to deliver to the prospect.

All of these activities need to be tracked. A Web-based Sales Force Automation System can provide a single interface to the salesperson to accomplish all those tasks. The salesperson can use the system to assign tasks to other individuals or departments, and use the Web to access product and industry information for the prospect. Last, the salesperson can also use the Web to access previously prepared presentations that can be modified and used for the Initial Sales Call, and then use the Web to store the modified presentations.

At (and after) the presentation the salesperson will no doubt meet additional decision makers and other people that may influence the sale, as well as identify new tasks that must be completed to move the opportunity toward a sale. A Web-based system can be used by the salesperson to update the status of the lead (now a prospect); record all completed tasks; add additional contacts, decision makers, and influencers; alert sales management to any special requirements for this prospect; record any commitments made during the sales call; and create, assign, and track new tasks.

Request for Proposal

If the salesperson has shown the prospect that your company's offerings can meet the needs of the prospect, the salesperson will be given a formal Request for Proposal (RFP), and asked to respond to the RFP within a certain time frame. The RFP will typically outline in greater detail exactly what issues the buying organization faces, how they intend to address the issues, the kind of solution they are looking to buy, and often the specific requirements the prospect has for a solution.

A salesperson's response to the RFP is to give the prospect further information on how your company's offerings provide the solution, and the approach your company will take in implementing the solution. After the prospect has received responses to the RFP from all interested vendors, a few will be asked to compete for the final bid.

Presentation/Demonstration

In working toward winning the final bid, the salesperson will often have to prepare and present information about your offerings, as well as give technical demonstrations when necessary. This step gives the prospect a better understanding of how your products will address the issues being faced.

Product presentations are often taken from a library of standard presentations, perhaps stored in a marketing encyclopedia, and modified by the salesperson to address the particular circumstances of the prospect. Technical demonstrations, at least those of a generic nature, are also often collected in a library and are available to the salesperson.

Requirements Specification

As a part of the Request for Proposal the prospect will have listed many specific requirements that the prospect would like to see in any solution purchased by that company. Additional requirements may come up as your salesperson and salespeople from competing vendors make presentations and demonstrations, and as the prospect becomes familiar with the range of possible solutions.

The salesperson will need to identify and track all the requirements stated by a prospect, and ensure that they are all addressed in the final proposal presented to the prospect.

Site Visits

During the course of the sale the prospect may want to visit your company's facilities to inspect your manufacturing operations, or to meet your company's executives. The prospect may want to conduct a client site visit; that is, visit one of your current customers who is using the products that the prospect is considering. There is clearly a lot of value in taking a customer on such a visit, especially if the visit is to a client who is very satisfied with your company and is willing to say so.

In this step the salesperson is responsible for ensuring that all the appropriate personnel are notified and available, and the visits go smoothly.

Opportunity Management

During the course of the sales cycle there will be many interactions, many commitments made to the prospect, and tasks assigned to different sales team members and other personnel in the company. As mentioned earlier, a salesperson's role is much like the project manager's, keeping on top of all the deliverables and time lines in the project. The ongoing activities associated with managing all the little (yet crucial) details, the management of the opportunity, can take up a lot of time.

This is a very important part of the sales cycle, as many sales are lost as a result of poor opportunity management. The impact of Sales Force Automation can be very high in opportunity management.

Consulting and Training

Complex sales, especially those of technology products or high-ticket items, often involve the sale of some consulting and training services. These services are essential to ensure the customer can make full use of the products being sold; otherwise the customer's original issues will not be fully addressed and you will have a dissatisfied customer. A good salesperson will call out consulting and training needs when they are not specified in the customer's requirements, or review and verify the ones that are. The salesperson should also ensure that the services are available, and make arrangements for them to be delivered to the customer. This may mean adding on consulting and training to the sales order, or it may mean introducing the prospect to third parties that can assist in this area.

This is an important step in the sales cycle for companies that realize a significant portion of their revenues from the sale of consulting and training.

Sales Configuration

All the requirements the prospect specified in the original RFP, and those that have come up during the sales cycle, should guide the salesperson to a solution that meets those requirements, and can be proposed to the prospect. The process of translating those requirements into offerings your company sells, and ensuring that the set of offerings is complete and accurate, is called sales configuration. This process is nowadays often automated, especially in the sales of complex orders that have hundreds or thousands of line items that must all work together.

Getting the sales configuration correct is absolutely essential, as revenues, and more importantly customer satisfaction, are dependent on a properly configured and delivered order.

Closing the Sale

While working the sales cycle, the salesperson is actually addressing any uncertainties and questions the prospect has. As the uncertainties decrease and all the questions are answered, the salesperson can start to close the sale.

Economic Model

The first step in closing the sale is to help the customer develop and build the case for the sale. While many customers have already thought through what the purchase of a solution will do for the business, the salesperson can help the prospect build a case that makes your company the best choice to provide the solution. The economic model of the sale is a tool the salesperson can use to help close the sale.

The economic model will consist of both a business justification for purchasing your products, and a financial analysis of the purchase and its impact on the business of the prospective customer.

Proposal/Quote

The sales configuration developed during the sales cycle is an essential input into the economic model, as different configurations are probably priced differently. The sales configuration is also essential input into the proposal and quote developed for the customer. The proposal is the overall document, the bid, and the quote is that part of the proposal that quotes the pricing and payment terms. Preparing the proposal and quote can be a very time-consuming task, especially as last-minute contract negotiations tend to change sales configurations and pricing, thereby necessitating new proposals and quotes.

Proposals and quotes are often based on templates that are standard in the company. Like the product presentations described earlier, proposal and quote templates may be made available in a library of such templates.

Contract Negotiation

Contract negotiations can be either very brief if the prospect has been involved all along in the sales cycle and has given the okay on many of the items being proposed, or they can be very long if the individuals the salesperson has been working with are not the key decision makers. Be that as it may, there will be some work to do to finalize all the legal terms surrounding the sale.

After contract negotiations the prospect may at this point make the purchase, or not. If the sale is made, you have a new customer. If not, you may undergo further contract negotiations or lose the sale to a competitor.

Postmortem

Both wins and losses should be reviewed to see what was done well in the sales cycle, and which areas need to be improved. Remember, you can learn as much from wins as you can from losses.

In a postmortem the salesperson, appropriate members of the sales team, and sales managers will analyze the key elements of a loss (or win) and try to identify exactly what, if anything, could have been done differently. In the case of a loss, the goal is to avoid such losses in the future. In the case of a win, the goal is to identify ways in which to increase sales effectiveness and improve sales efficiency. This may mean, for example, that you develop a list of *best practices* that may be used by other salespeople in your company. Another benefit of analyzing wins is to use the information in competitive situations in the future.

Managing the Customer Relationship

Closing the sale does not mark the end of the sales cycle. If anything, it marks the beginning of a customer relationship and the prospect of future sales. The salesperson will want to take an active interest in the success of the customer in getting, installing, and using the purchased products, because a satisfied customer may be used as a reference for other prospects, and may be a good customer with more purchases in the future. The activities undertaken by the salesperson in ensuring customer satisfaction is what we call *Managing the Customer Relationship*.

Order Processing

The first step is to convert the contract and the quote into an order. The order that is submitted for processing must exactly match that which is agreed to in the contract negotiations. Not only must each line item match, but the pricing and delivery commitments must also be honored. Otherwise you run the risk of making a bad impression on the customer, and may even run into contractual disputes.

To ensure sales orders are accurate, a sales automation system often provides a means to incorporate the final product configuration and quote directly into the order processing system.

Shipment

The salesperson must be kept up to date on the shipment status of the order. Not only should the salesperson be notified when an order has shipped, but the salesperson should also be informed of any potential or actual schedule slips. This kind of notification allows the salesperson to contact the customer and verify the receipt of an order, or notify the customer of any delays in the shipment. Such proactive customer relationship management can go a long way toward creating and maintaining a satisfied customer.

A sales automation tool will often provide for shipping information to be incorporated from the company's manufacturing and logistics systems.

Installation/Consulting

Once the products have been received by the customer, the salesperson will want to ensure that the products can be installed and operated with no problems. Any consulting and training that is required is also scheduled and completed at this time.

During this period the salesperson will keep in constant contact with the customer. Other company personnel may work with the customer on delivering the installation and consulting services. The sales automation system should provide a means for tracking all activities and the current status of each.

Post-Sales Service

During the installation process, as the customer is deploying your products and after the products are in use, there will no doubt be situations where the customer will need technical assistance. This assistance will typically be provided by the Technical Support Organization of your company. The customer may also have other service needs, such as requesting additional documentation or checking on the current status of shipments. These service needs may be addressed by your company's Customer Service Organization.

These two organizations must be able to recognize the customer as a customer, and must know what the customer has purchased and installed. The sales automation system must be able to provide this information to the applications used by the Technical Support and Customer Service Organizations.

Account Management

A good account manager will periodically review all interactions anyone in your company has with the account. As described previously, many of these interactions will be by technical support and customer service personnel. In many companies these interactions are logged and recorded into so-called *customer interaction systems*.

But other people in your company may also have interactions with the customer. For example, a product marketing manager may want to use the customer as a reference account for a particular product or market segment. The interactions between the product marketing manager and the individual(s) in the customer's organization should also be logged and made available for review by the salesperson.

This periodic review of interactions with the customer gives the salesperson a lot of information to manage the account.

Selling into the Installed Base

The benefit of having all customer information available to the salesperson is that the information can be leveraged into improving customer satisfaction and increasing sales to this customer. For example, a salesperson may notice that the number of interactions a customer has with the technical support organization has increased in the past few weeks, and most of the interactions have to do with performance problems in a particular product area.

In a periodic review of the account with the customer, the salesperson could bring up this observation and ask if there is anything that the salesperson could do to assist the customer. In some cases the customer may not need any assistance, but in others the customer may decide that the real solution to the performance problem is to purchase additional products from the salesperson. In this situation the customer is once again a lead that is raw material for the sales process.

SALES FORCE AUTOMATION TOOLS

The preceding section covered a typical process involved in a complex sale, and discussed the actions that a salesperson would normally take in each step of the process while working toward closing the sale. It also mentioned how automation could assist the salesperson by providing more information in a timely manner, and reducing the time spent on administrative tasks. It alluded to the specific functions that must be performed by the sales automation tools, and how they would enable the sales process. We now turn to the key tools that make up a Sales Force Automation system.

You should remember that the purpose of tools is to make the salesperson more effective and efficient, and to improve customer satisfaction. While tools cannot replace the experience and expertise of a salesperson, they can provide a structure and means for the salesperson to get the job done. For example, a good Sales Force Automation system should implement the particular sales methodology that your organization uses, and guide the salesperson in the usage of that methodology.

In addition to making the salesperson's job easier, sales automation tools should also be easy to use. The disruption or cost of using the tool should be minimized, and in any event be much lower than the value that the *salesperson* realizes. This is important. The value of the tools must be perceived by the person using the tools, and enough value must be perceived by the user to overcome the effort and cost of using the tool. Often a tool is mandated for use by the sales organization because sales management wants to get better visibility into what salespeople are doing, but the salespeople that have to use the tool perceive no value from using the tool. Any such tool will not be successful in increasing your effectiveness, efficiency, or customer satisfaction.

Some of the tools that can be of great benefit to salespeople and therefore sales management, are described in the following sections.

Opportunity Management System

An Opportunity Management System (OMS) is the term given to the tool (or set of tools) that allows your salespeople to track and manage a sales lead all the way through the pipeline until it becomes a customer account with booked revenues. It is the backbone of any integrated Sales Force Automation system, and is what we term a *process tool* because it facilitates the operation of the sales processes.

An effective OMS will seamlessly integrate all of the functionality listed in the preceding sections on *Capturing the Lead* and *Managing the Sales Cycle*. The functionality is summarized here.

- Create and maintain leads
- Integrate with telesales and telemarketing applications
- Associate leads with sources or campaigns
- Rate and prioritize leads
- Route leads based on user-specified criteria
- Convert leads to opportunities
- Create and manage information on key players and buying influences
- Track the status of the competition for this opportunity
- Create, assign, and manage tasks and subtasks associated with an opportunity

- Create and assign teams associated with a particular opportunity or territory
- Create a notification and escalation system that implements user-specified business rules
- Create personal and team schedules
- Log interactions with opportunities
- Route opportunities and tasks

A good OMS will support team selling, in which many people from your organization (and partners) may have to undertake activities to make the sale happen. The OMS will allow a salesperson to specify the skills needed to make a sale, and search through the skill sets of all resources available to the salesperson to identify which resources would make the best sales team members for a particular sale. The OMS should also be able to schedule the resources as needed.

The *workflow engine* is an essential part of the OMS (see Figure 3.2). The ability to track leads, create and assign tasks and

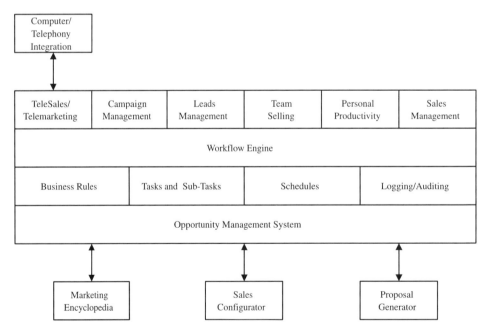

FIGURE 3.2 Opportunity management system.

subtasks, and implement a notification and escalation system all require the workflow engine. The workflow engine also allows a user to log all actions and updates and interactions associated with a particular opportunity, and keeps an audit trail of all the changes made in the course of an opportunity. The audit trail provides a means to go back and see what happened during the course of a sale, and is especially valuable in the postmortem.

An OMS should also provide tight integration with all the other tools used in the sales organization. For example, a salesperson should be able to use a proposal generator and a sales configurator from the same environment as the OMS, rather than having to run three different applications.

Commercially available OMSs offer all of the functionality previously described, and often more. Additional information on the functionality needed in an OMS can be found in Chapter 10.

Marketing Encyclopedia System

Another key component of a good Sales Force Automation system is a Marketing Encyclopedia System (MES). A MES provides a way to consolidate all marketing and sales-related information in one central repository (in a Web-based MES the repository may be physically distributed over many different locations, but it appears to the user to be located in one virtual location).

Marketing collateral for a company can consist of many different types and forms. Examples of these types are annual reports, corporate brochures, fact sheets, company profiles, price sheets, product configuration guides, product brochures, article reprints, press releases, and CD-ROM product demonstrations. Added to this list are the materials needed by your sales organization, such as corporate presentations, competitive analyses, product demonstration scripts, feature/ benefits lists, reference accounts lists, discount price schedules, and contracts.

When you look at the volume of material that needs to be maintained, printed, and distributed, it is a costly and time-consuming task. Typical problems that arise are:

- Over budget on printing
- Out of stock; new shipment not received

- Overstocked on outdated material
- Corporate logo/colors change
- Constantly updating pieces (i.e., new revised price list)
- What material is currently available

Earlier discussions covered the importance of having current versions of standard presentations and demonstrations, and how it was critical to have the latest information on all products. The consequences of not having all the latest information include:

- Lose a deal because you can't show newest enhancements
- Can't explain a feature because you don't have newest product presentation
- Limited time, so you can give demonstrations only to a selected few, leaving other prospects to purchase from competitors

A Marketing Encyclopedia System addresses all these issues by providing a consolidated information repository, and reduces costs because not only does the collateral and other information not have to be printed and distributed, but there also is no need to *remainder* the inventory of outdated material.

A good Marketing Encyclopedia System will provide a way to get information from many different sources in many different formats, and publish it into the encyclopedia (see Figure 3.3). Sources may include content created by company internal personnel, news and stock quote feeds, and industry research publications. The publishing process is important, because an unregulated system will result in information in the encyclopedia not being in a consistent form, or worse, conflicting with other information already in the encyclopedia. For example, different product managers may each use a unique style to publish competitive information in the encyclopedia. While creativity is certainly to be encouraged, a salesperson will be more effective if all competitive information is presented in a consistent manner.

Along with a publishing process, a marketing encyclopedia should provide a means to keep profiles of its users, and invoke business rules specified by a user when certain information is added to the encyclopedia. For example, a salesperson working

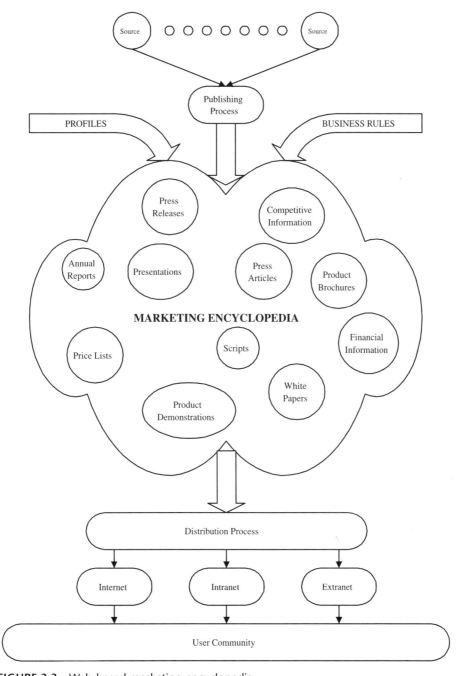

FIGURE 3.3 Web-based marketing encyclopedia.

in a particular territory will maintain a profile with the encyclopedia that details the salesperson's territory, product responsibility, preferred notification method, and so on. If working on an opportunity, the salesperson could set up a business rule that would cause a high-priority notification to be sent to the salesperson if there is any new product press release from any of the vendors against whom the salesperson is competing, or if the stock price of the prospective customer falls below a certain level.

This type of distribution effectively implements a *subscription model*, in which a salesperson can selectively subscribe only to information of interest on a regular basis, yet have access to all information in the encyclopedia when necessary. A Web-based MES can be accessed by your sales force at any time, and if you establish good processes for content creation and publishing, your sales force and even your customers will have access to the latest information.

Chapters 11 and 12 give examples of technologies that can be used to implement a Web-based Marketing Encyclopedia System.

Sales Configurator

Putting together a sales configuration that is accurate is of paramount importance in a sale. The sales configuration drives the proposal and the quote; these in turn drive contract negotiations that eventually result in a sales contract and revenues. An error made in a sales configuration can have a significant impact on actions that use the sales configurations. For example, a survey of sales executives commissioned by Calico Technology found that inaccurate sales configurations can cost as much as 2 percent of revenues. Not only are costs incurred in handling the returned material, correcting the configuration, and reshipping the correct configuration, but there also is a significant impact in the intangible cost of customer satisfaction.

For complex sales an order may be very complicated, with many dependencies on some products, and constraints on other products with which some products may not work. It is possible to manually create an accurate order, but it is a process fraught with perils. You may therefore want to consider a tool known as a *sales configurator* (sometimes also called a *product configurator*).

A sales configurator is conceptually very simple, in that it takes as its input the requirements of a sale, proposes a configuration, matches it against an offerings catalog, and enforces dependencies and constraints about the interoperability of the offerings listed in the proposed configuration (see Figure 3.4). In practice a sales configurator is a complex piece of software, because for all but the most trivial configurations the possibilities for errors are high, and the configurator must work through all possible constraints and rules. This is especially a problem in industries that have short product life cycles and a high degree of mass customization.

In a manufacturing environment it is vital that the sales configurator can make use of the parts structures used in manufacturing (e.g., a Bill of Materials in a manufacturing application). This eliminates the need to manually enter data about dependencies and constraints. A good system will also provide a means to create, edit, and selectively apply rules to configurations. For example, you may offer a special promotion that throws in extra widgets if a customer purchases your products during the promotional period. The sales configuration system

FIGURE 3.4   Sales configurator.

should not only propose the promotion when the salesperson makes a selection that could qualify, but it should also enforce the rules about availability.

A sophisticated configurator will suggest alternatives to configurations that are incorrect, and may even present a corrected configuration to the user. Other sophisticated configurators guide the salesperson through the configuration process, and based on the offerings selected at any point allow only valid offerings (including substitutes if your company does not make a particular product) to be added to the configuration. Chapter 13 discusses a sophisticated sales configurator that also supports quoting (see the following section).

Web-based configurators are gaining popularity, and more and more companies are allowing prequalified customers and partners to purchase products by directly placing an order over the company's Web site. Sales configurators are also used in these *Interactive Selling Systems*, but they are beyond the scope of this book and are not discussed here.

Proposal/Quote Generator

Proposal and quote generations are similar to sales configuration. In this case a proposal or a quote is being configured, not a sales configuration. Quotes and sales configurations are very similar in that a quote contains pricing information based on the sales configuration and a price list. We make the distinction because you may be able to apply different price lists to a particular configuration. Proposals and sales configurations are similar, in that both are made up of smaller building blocks.

A complete proposal will often use standard proposal templates edited by the salesperson to meet the specific needs of the prospect. Similarly, a quote will be prepared using standard price lists, and discounts will be applied to the price list based on customer criteria. For example, if the proposal and quote are for a prospect who came in through a specific marketing campaign, there may be some specific discounts applicable to this quote. The process to generate a proposal and quote is shown in Figure 3.5.

Quote systems are often incorporated into product configurators, and the resulting (priced) configuration is used to prepare

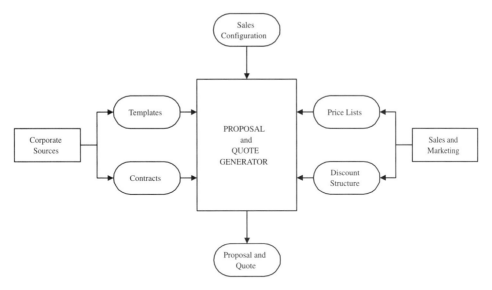

FIGURE 3.5   Proposal and quote generation.

the proposal. Essential functionality for any proposal/quote generator includes:

■ Support for multiple price lists
■ Ability to define and apply complex discounting structures
■ Support for multiple currency quotes and accurate conversions
■ Integration with forecasting tools used by sales management

Sales Management and Analysis System

The last set of tools together make up what we call the Sales Management and Analysis System. In reality these tools are often provided within the umbrella of the tools previously discussed. Most reports used in this kind of system are often created by the user, because of the unique circumstances and requirements of each company. For the sake of completeness, however, here are the essential functions required from these tools:

- Support for *ad hoc* queries on any data elements in the entire SFA system
- Support for *canned* queries
- Ability to display analysis results in graphical form
- Ability to extract and aggregate data for roll-up reporting
- Ability to track activities and performance of salespeople, opportunities, and territories
- Support for a forecasting function or tool

Chapter 14 discusses a report-writing tool that can be used to implement many of the functions listed in the preceding.

SUMMARY

This chapter discussed the steps needed to close a complex sale, and covered some of the tools that can enable salespeople to be more effective and efficient in the execution of the steps.

The next five chapters will cover these steps in some detail, and show how they can be automated using Web technologies.

Sales Processes and Models

Change the environment; do not try to change man.

Richard Buckminster Fuller in Design Science, *1969*

Capturing the Lead

4

How you generate, qualify, distribute, and manage sales leads into your sales channels are critical factors in the success of your company. After all, leads are the raw materials for your sales processes, the processes that will turn these raw materials into finished goods: satisfied customers and booked revenues. Clearly, the more leads you can turn into satisfied customers the more revenue potential your sales organization will have. One way you can increase the quantity of leads that get converted into customers is by playing the numbers game: Simply increase the number of leads you get in, and hope the larger number of leads will result in more customers. The downside of this approach is that the number of leads that do not result in sales also goes up. The net effect is that your salespeople will spend proportionately more time following up on poor leads. In other words, the productivity of your sales organization will remain the same or decline.

A better way is to improve the quality of leads you get in, and also the quality of your leads qualification process. This way the only leads that enter your sales process are those that have a good likelihood of becoming customers. In most companies the marketing organization is typically tasked with creating the programs to generate the quantity of leads necessary to meet your

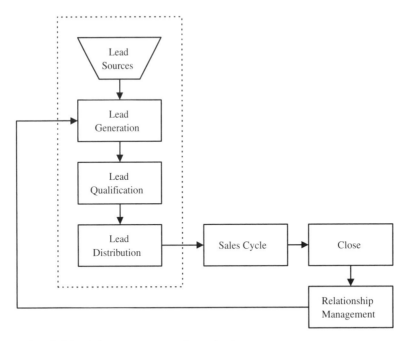

FIGURE 4.1   Sales process overview—leads.

company's revenue goals, and the sales organization (or sometimes the marketing organization) is responsible for qualifying and following up on these leads, and turning those leads into satisfied customers.

This chapter will examine leads from the perspective of what they mean to the sales process, how to generate them, and how to qualify leads and pass them on to the sales force. The first part of the sales cycle from Chapter 3, as shown in Figure 4.1, highlights the generation, qualification, and distribution of leads, which will be the focus of this chapter.

LEAD GENERATION

The step of actually acquiring a sales lead is called lead generation. In most companies the marketing organization is tasked with implementing sales promotion, advertising, and other programs that create awareness in the minds of the target customer base. The expectation is that this awareness will result in the target base contacting the company for additional information on products, and possibly sales. A contact made with the company may be considered a potential lead, and once acquired a lead may eventually result in a sale. The event initiated by marketing to generate leads is the *marketing campaign.*

Marketing Campaigns

The marketing campaign is designed first and foremost to generate leads. Market research, industry trends, and previous campaign successes dictate where to promote your products and services to maximize the potential lead return. A formal marketing campaign is developed and entered into your SFA system using a Web form, as shown in Figure 4.2.

As this form shows, the campaign is set up with a name, designated budget, target product and audience, duration, manager, and sponsor. The name, type, and cost data are key fields for several reasons:

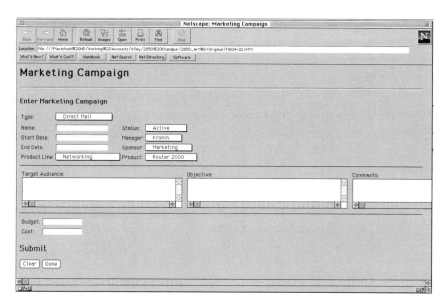

FIGURE 4.2 Marketing campaign form.

- The campaign name is linked in your SFA system with every incoming lead that it generates.
- The actual cost field is used in performing your campaign analysis, which we will see later in this chapter.
- Campaign and lead analysis are both summarized by campaign type.

Once the marketing campaign has been entered, you are set up to receive leads directly into your SFA system, which can then be linked to any marketing campaign.

Most leads and inquiries come from several areas:

Trade Shows	Direct Mail	Web
Seminars	User Groups	Referrals
Advertising	Current Customers	Purchased Lists
Public Relations	Press Tours	

These leads are the primary input to the sales funnel, as shown in Figure 4.3. Regardless of the source, the incoming leads initiate an evaluation process that qualifies the leads, then an escalation process that forwards the leads to sales.

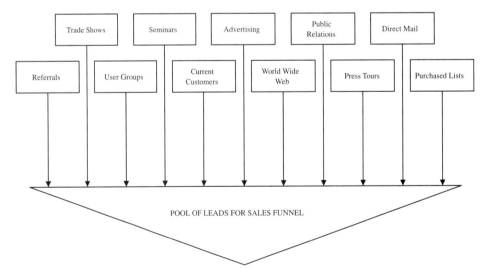

FIGURE 4.3 Leads as input to sales funnel.

A measure of the effectiveness of your sources to produce leads is in analyzing the leads by marketing campaign. This will also help marketing in planning future campaigns. Once your leads are in a central database (using the data model shown in Figure 4.15, discussed later in this chapter), you will be able to summarize this data to determine the source of the lead, as well as the distribution of these leads to your sales force. A typical report is shown in Figure 4.4. This report can be set up to run right from your intranet, with report output formatted as a Web page.

This report shows how many leads were generated by each marketing campaign in a quarter for each salesperson. By having a count of the total number of leads a salesperson received in a quarter, you can analyze if leads were distributed equally across all salespeople, in addition to understanding which marketing campaigns provided the greatest number of leads.

The next few subsections discuss the different sources of leads.

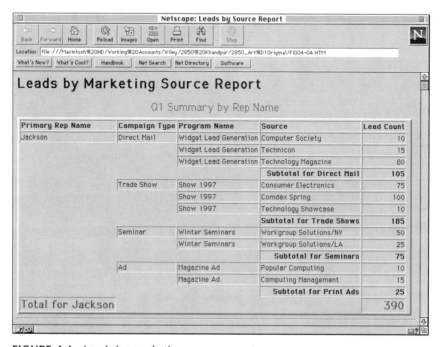

FIGURE 4.4 Leads by marketing source report.

Trade Shows

Trade shows are excellent forums for companies to demonstrate their products at industry-specific shows. Many companies will use this opportunity to introduce new products or make press announcements concerning the company or its products.

Many attendees will stop at a company's booth. The gathering of information about attendees can be done by gathering their business cards or taking imprints of their show badges. In addition to that information, you should also gather data about their needs, time frames, whether budgets are approved, and scope of projects. What do you do with this information? Companies spend large sums of money on their trade show budgets often without formalizing plans or strategies for what to do with the leads from those shows. Not only does a company's SFA system need to be set up to receive these leads, but an efficient manner to enter and prioritize those leads is also necessary.

One of the possible ways to reduce the paper flow from trade shows is to allow direct entry of information. This entry can be done through a Web application that captures the data, as well as allows

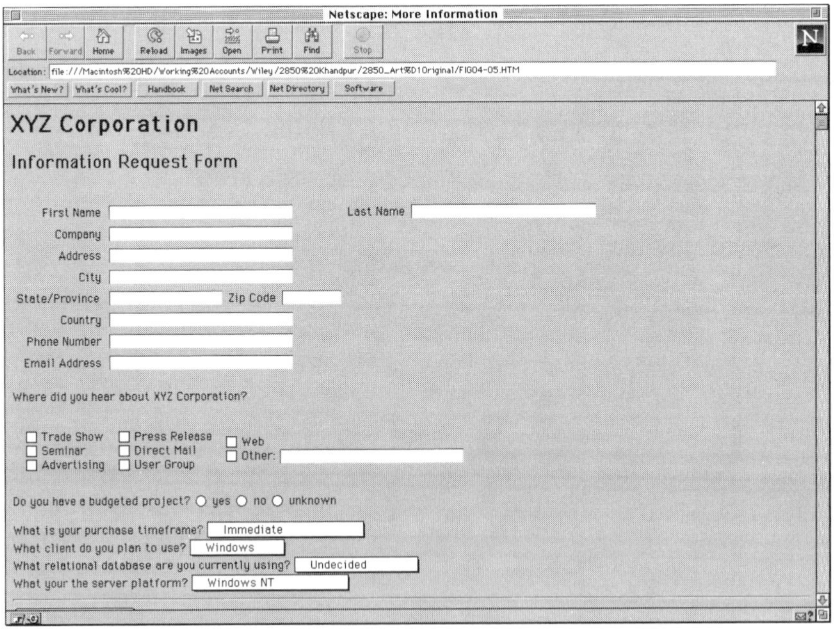

FIGURE 4.5   Web lead form.

the prospect to request any desired additional company or product information. Using this method reduces the need for data entry and ensures timely entry of the information. Your telemarketing group is then able to quickly follow up on the trade show leads.

A Web page can be set up with the lead form dialog like the one in Figure 4.5 to facilitate the lead data entry process. Whether this Web page is live to your site or stand-alone, the data can be easily transferred to your corporate information system, reducing any potential errors by having to retype this information. Depending on the type of badge system used at the trade show, use of bar coding or magnetic readers can assist with filling out the Web lead form without having to type anything.

Work Area for Trade Shows

We have identified many sources for lead generation. As input to your working functional requirements document, refer to the "Leads" section of this document on the CD-ROM, and provide answers to the following:

■ Which shows should your company participate in? (Where do you get the highest-quality leads?)
■ Have you provided online registration to attendees?
■ Have you provided online requests for additional information to attendees?
■ Have you defined a standard set of questions that enables you to qualify attendees?
■ Have you assigned responsibility for who will follow up on which leads?
■ Have you labeled all leads entering the SFA system, with the trade show name as its source?
■ Have you defined what the follow-up step will be (letter, e-mail, call)?

Seminars

Seminars are marketing activities that many companies use to generate interest in their product, or to move the prospect along in the sale cycle. The logistics for a seminar program can be quite extensive. The tasks range from establishing a seminar schedule, mailing invitations, registering attendees, confirming attendees, creating attendee lists for each location, obtaining lists of actual attendees, creating evaluation forms, and following up with attendees and nonattendees.

Typically, a seminar program will have many people involved with the seminars being held in different geographic locations. How do all those people communicate and maintain accurate and current data about all of the events? Your SFA system must have a seminar module that allows you to maintain all information about each seminar as well as about the people who have registered for that seminar. As you near the scheduled date of a seminar, accurate and current data is critical. This data can consist of:

- Size of room
- Number of people registered
- Number of people on waiting list
- Number of people confirmed
- Number of seminar information packets needed
- Roster of confirmed attendees, with their name tags

Marketing Seminar Summary Report

Q1 1997 Summary by Month

Seminar Date	City	Qty Mailed	Actual Reg.	Expected Reg.	Actual Reg. Rate	Expected Reg. Rate
1/4/97	Los Angeles	5968	272	119	4.6%	2.0%
1/8/97	San Francisco	5025	170	101	3.4%	2.0%
1/15/97	Las Vegas	5976	205	120	3.4%	2.0%
	January Totals	**16969**	**647**	**340**	**3.8%**	**2.0%**
2/2/97	New York	2819	40	56	1.4%	2.0%
2/15/97	Atlanta	6000	23	120	0.4%	2.0%
2/23/97	Boston	3645	2	73	0.1%	2.0%
	February Totals	**12464**	**65**	**249**	**0.5%**	**2.0%**
3/3/97	Dallas	2421	35	48	1.4%	2.0%
3/11/97	Detroit	5380	149	108	2.8%	2.0%
3/22/97	Chicago	3952	168	79	4.3%	2.0%
	March Subtotals	**11753**	**352**	**235**	**3.0%**	**2.0%**
Q1 Totals		**41186**	**1064**	**824**	**2.6%**	**2.0%**

FIGURE 4.6 Marketing seminar summary report.

Once all seminar information is captured in your SFA system, you will be able to summarize this information into an intranet report, as shown in Figure 4.6. This report shows for a given quarter the dates and locations of your seminars, the response rate for your invitations mailed, and the actual registration rate for each city. This information can be used to evaluate in which cities you may want to focus future seminars, and how effective were the direct mail pieces used.

After the seminars are completed a follow-up procedure needs to be executed, describing what actions need to be taken regarding the people who attended (telephone follow-up, thank you note), as well as the action for those who did not attend.

Work Area for Marketing Seminars

We have identified the logistics for organizing seminar programs. You must now define the seminar process and owners for each task. Here are the questions from the "Seminars" section of the functional requirements document:

- Who handles site logistics and where is that information available?
- What are the qualifications for attending an event?
- What are all the paths for issuance of invitations?
- What is the optimum number of attendees, and where is that information stored?
- What is the attrition rate of preregistrants to attendees?
- What factors influence the attrition rate (e.g., telephone or mail offer, type of confirmation, etc.), and what actions could/should be taken?
- How do you register actual attendees at the event?
- What attendee information needs to be captured?
- What is the process for getting this information back into the SFA system?
- How do you get the list back of attendees and nonattendees to the SFA system?
- What is the next step for attendees?
- What is the next step for nonattendees?

Advertising

Many companies place advertisements not only about their products but also corporate advertisements to establish a market presence. In that advertisement there can be several ways for the prospect to contact the company. The contact methods can include telephone number, e-mail address, Web site, response card, and business address. Any leads that come from advertisements need to be put into the SFA system for follow-up and qualification. Information that needs to be entered into the system should include which advertisement generated the lead, and all qualifying data available.

Work Area for Advertising

Document your advertising strategy as part of the functional requirements process. This will help determine what type of data needs to be tracked in your SFA system, as well as analysis and reporting requirements. The following questions should be answered in your functional requirements document.

■ Is your advertising corporate or product focused?
■ Which magazines do you advertise in, and why?
■ How frequently is the advertisement run?
■ How do you evaluate if an advertisement was successful?
■ How do salespeople know when and which advertisements are being run?
■ How do you follow up on responses to your advertisements?

Public Relations

The traditional way of releasing company press releases has been augmented through the use of e-mail and the company Web site. Many companies now put their press releases on their Web site. Not only does it provide the latest information about the company, but it may also act as a catalyst for that person to want more information about your company or product. It is extremely important to provide easy access to additional information, as well as capture information about the person who wanted that information. Any inquiries from public relations should be considered a lead and put into the SFA system.

Your Web page should contain product information, corporate profile, corporate contact information, location and addresses of all offices, and an information request form. The information request form should be e-mailed either to an appropriate individual at the company, or directly to a fulfillment house for literature requests.

Work Area for Public Relations

To help define and document your public relations objectives, you must think about and answer the following questions from your functional requirements document for each page on your Web site that may contain a press release that could generate an inquiry:

- How are press releases created in your company?
- How does the sales organization hear about press releases?
- How do salespeople find out about press releases?
- Do you need to identify which press release caused each inquiry?
- How will you follow up on inquiries resulting from press releases?
- What information must you capture from these inquiries?

Direct Mail

Direct mail pieces can be used for seminar invitations, offers for product enhancements or upgrades, a special demonstration offer, or for prospects to request additional information. These prospects should be able to call, e-mail, mail, or access your Web site after receiving a direct-mail piece. All pertinent information concerning who that person is, which direct-mail piece was received, and all qualifying questions must be entered into the SFA system.

Often in your company various individuals or departments will need direct-mail campaigns put together for them by marketing. Gathering all the relevant information needed to produce the campaign has often proven difficult in the past. There was no formal process to submit the request, nor a method to accomplish it. Through the use of intranet, requests for direct-mail campaigns can be submitted. This method allows consistent format for submitting requests, and ensures all required data is provided by the requester.

A campaign request form could contain the following:

Campaign Name:

Campaign Sponsor: (Who is requesting this program?)

Sponsor's Business Unit: (Is it product marketing? Is it a sales region or channel?)

Description: (Is the campaign for seminars? Is the campaign for presenting a product offer?)

Objective: (What is the objective for running this campaign?)

Key Message: (What is your primary message?)

Benefits: (What is the benefit to the respondent?)

Offer: (What are you offering to the prospect? Free CD? Free seminar? White paper?)

Target Audience: (Who are you trying to reach? What are the titles of the people you want to reach?)

Drop Date: (When is the initial drop of your campaign?)

End Date: (When does your campaign end?)

Communication Vehicle: (What are you using to communicate your message? Letter? Tri-fold?)

Quantity Mailed: (How many pieces are you sending?)

Estimated Response: (What percentage reply do you expect?)

Source Codes: (How will you identify the different mailing lists you are using?)

Special Instructions:

Since a company will often use multiple mailing lists for a single mailing, it is important to understand where you have your greatest qualified responses. An analysis of the leads in the SFA system will provide you with the information to better utilize your marketing budget by showing you which lists provided the highest quality and quantity of leads.

Work Area for Direct Mail

To help define and document your direct-mail objectives, you must think about and answer the following questions from your functional requirements document for each direct-mail piece that will be sent out:

- What is the target audience of your direct-mail piece?
- What is the offer?
- How many pieces are you mailing?
- What is the drop schedule for the mailing?
- How will fulfillment be handled?
- What is the follow-up to these leads?
- What qualifying questions are included on the piece?
- How is sales notified of the When, What, and Who of this direct-mail piece?
- How does this information get entered into the SFA system?

Web Site

A company's Web site can be an excellent source of leads for your company. It is critical that your Web site incorporates the functionality to capture data about prospects if they choose to download white papers and demonstration or trial software, or register for an event. Most Web server software provides some audit-trail functionality so you can track the various pages on your Web site that were viewed by each prospect.

White Papers

Many technology companies have a section on their Web sites that contains a collection of technical articles about products and their usage, so-called *white papers*. Prospects often browse this section of the Web site to learn more about the products. These prospects tend to have a higher inclination to purchase, and so can be very good leads.

Your Web site can capture identification information of people who visit your site, as well as which pages in your site they visit. Therefore, if the White Papers link is chosen, this information is stored in your Web access log file automatically by your Web server software. The access log file can be easily used as input to a Web access report so you can assess the effectiveness of your White Papers section.

Demonstration or Trial Software

It is also quite common for software companies to have a section on their Web sites that contains demonstration or trial versions that a user can download and try. This software is (often) of reduced functionality, or is otherwise limited, but it gives a user a chance to sample the product.

As with white papers, the audit trail of a visitor to your site is captured also when demonstration or trial software is downloaded. If you have multiple versions of the software (Windows 95, Windows NT, Windows 3.1), your access log file can record which version the visitor downloaded.

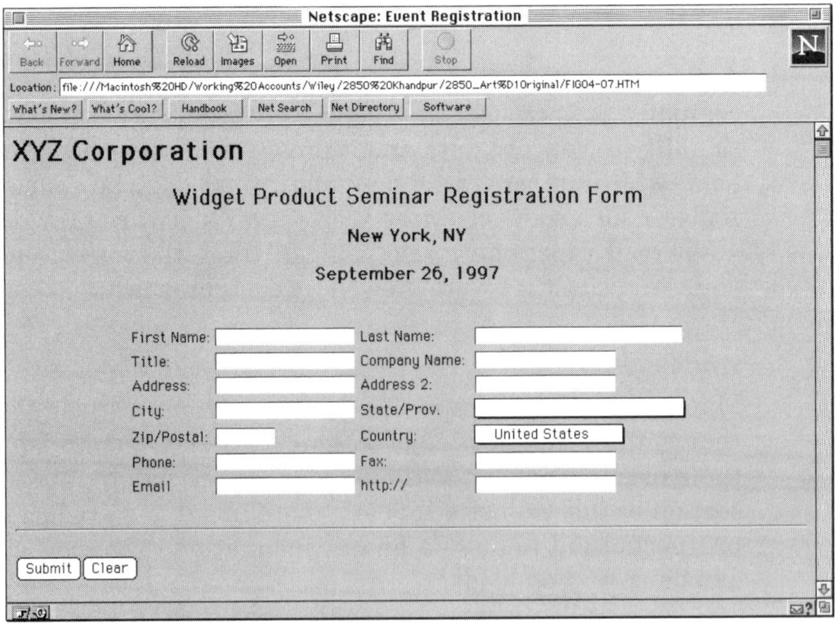

FIGURE 4.7 Web event registration form.

Companies that make other products may set up a request form for a demonstration or trial product, which is then sent to the requester. In either case, enough information can be captured about the requester to follow up at a later time.

Register for Event

By providing an online registration form for an event you are planning, you can capture a significant amount of data that simply is not captured in your access log. Figure 4.7 shows a sample Web registration form, and as you can see much detail is captured here. This information is either e-mailed to a designated e-mail address right from the Web form, or can be inserted right into your corporate database.

Work Area for Web Site

Some of the questions you must answer when thinking about generating leads from your Web site are:

- What are the technical documents you can share with the general public?
- Will those documents assist in the eventual sale of your products?
- Where will these documents come from?
- Who will be responsible for maintaining the accuracy of these documents?
- Do you already have demonstration or trial versions of products?
- If so, how do you distribute them now?
- If not, is it feasible to have them?
- Who will create and maintain the demonstration or trial versions?
- How will those versions be supported?
- Should you register everyone who requests or accesses technical information or demonstration or trial versions of your products?
- What will you do with the information you collect?
- Who will be responsible for following up on the information?

Referrals

Quite often the best leads come from current customers and prospects. Asking those people if they know of any other individuals who may have a need or interest in your product is an excellent way to find quality leads. It is important to include in questionnaires a field for referrals, as well as have a way to capture which leads came from referrals in your SFA system. You may actually choose to give a bonus to your telemarketing representatives for the referrals they obtain.

The report in Figure 4.8 shows how many referrals each telemarketing representative acquired. The information in this report would come out of your SFA system.

This report would extract out all leads coded with a *source = Referral,* and subtotal the lead count by telemarketing representative. The telemarketing manager can use this report as a basis for a referral bonus program.

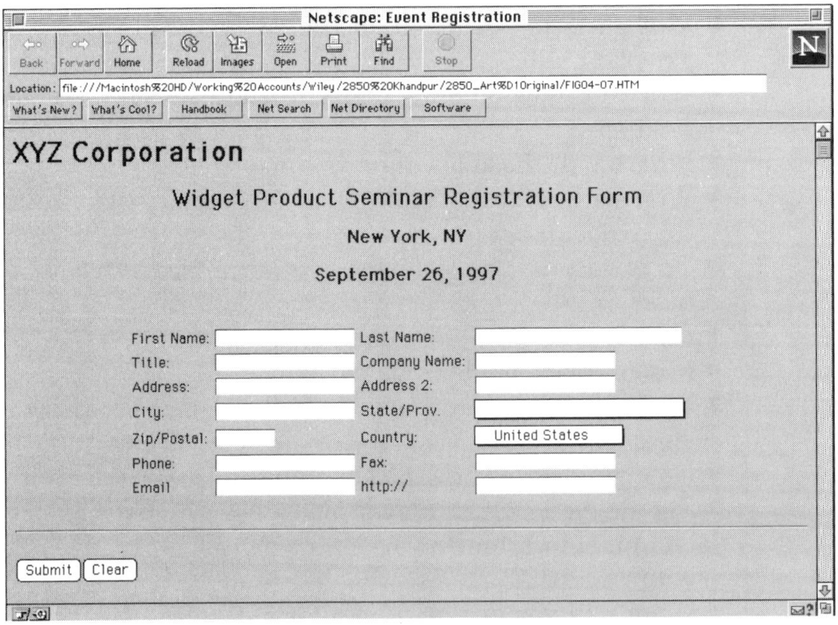

FIGURE 4.8 Referral summary report.

> **Work Area for Referrals**
>
> Before planning how to automate your referrals program, some of the questions you must answer include:
>
> - How do you handle referrals today?
> - Are referrals actively solicited, or do you wait for customers and prospects to give them to you?
> - Do you need to identify the source of each referral?
> - Do you need to provide an incentive to potential sources of referrals?

LEAD QUALIFICATION

Once the leads have been received by your company, each lead must go through its own process before the qualified lead can be given to sales. Typically a company may do all or some part of this process based on the resources and procedures the company has in place. The more effective and efficient this process, the greater productivity you will receive from your sales force. To achieve this goal a well-defined process and system of lead management must be in place.

Consider the following steps in developing or documenting your company's lead qualification process (we will examine each process in detail):

- Process for receiving leads from various sources
- Literature fulfillment for all types of leads
- A system of rating all leads
- A process for escalating *hot* leads
- A process for remarketing to *lukewarm* leads
- A process to provide additional qualification of the leads

Process for Receiving Leads

A company will often have leads coming in from various sources and in various forms. The forms can range from bingo response cards, business cards, lists, Web inquiries, seminar registrations, general inquiries, and trade show attendees. Each type of lead may have different information gathered about that lead. So not only must you address how you will handle each form of lead, but also how you will capture the different data that may exist for each type.

Your IS department often needs to build different interfaces to the outside vendors that may be initially processing these leads for you. If you are entering these leads yourself, data entry screens must be developed that are easy to use for your SFA system. The Web lead form shown previously in Figure 4.4 is one example of such a data entry screen.

Literature Fulfillment

Inquiries often seek additional information about your company and products. The traditional way to satisfy those inquiries was to mail a packet of information about your company to that person. This method proved to be costly in many cases, and very time-consuming. The inventory management of your collateral and the cost associated with production are often headaches for your marketing department. People often need information immediately and mailing would be too slow for them.

Faxing of marketing material has become very popular. Individuals can now fax from their own PC the information the prospect may want. This does require the marketing department to ensure that the latest and newest material is available and known by your salespeople. The distribution and announcement of this new and updated collateral often proves a problem for companies. The intranet provides a means to ensure that the most current material is available to all in your company. Not only will this current information be available on the intranet, but your company Web site can also allow prospects to view and download this information. Through the use of faxes and the Web, your prospects can receive the most current marketing information in an expedient manner.

System of Rating Leads

Not all leads are created equal. Yet how does your company decide which leads are good and which leads may not be worth following up on? Unless your company has developed a rating system for its leads, the quality leads could get lost in the volume of leads.

The rating system can be based on various factors ranging from time frame to purchase, dollar amount of the deal, budget approval, number of units, or other factors. Once this rating has been established, the goal is to have all marketing programs capture this information on each lead. When each lead is rated your sales people can prioritize their activities based on that information. This lead rating will also help your marketing department to understand where the highest-quality leads are coming from. This information will help them better decide where to spend their marketing budget in the future.

Lead Rating System Example

Implementing a lead rating system is a critical step in the lead management process. Without such a system, no amount of analysis can be performed to determine the quality of your incoming leads. Use of a company-accepted Lead Rating System will enable your company to:

- Easily prioritize lead follow-up
- Track all prospect activities and results, both by prospect and campaign
- Move prospects through sales cycles

The scale shown in Table 4.1 is typical of a lead rating system, and is used in our sample reports. Each lead must be evaluated and assigned one of the codes shown.

Once leads have been rated, a monthly summary report can be run from your SFA system as an overview of the type and quantity of your incoming leads.

By generating a report, as shown in Figure 4.9, of the rating of all leads received, you can understand if the quantity of

TABLE 4.1 Lead Rating System Example

Rating	Description
A	Intends to purchase within 30 days.
	Prospect's management has approved purchase.
	Compatible with company's technical requirements.
	Prospect expects to speak immediately with a salesperson.
B	Intends to purchase in 31 to 90 days.
	Compatible with company's technical requirements.
	Prospect can identify when the contact wishes to speak with a sales representative.
C	Intends to purchase in 3 to 9 months.
	Compatible with company's technical requirements.
R	Remarket: Intends to purchase in more than 9 months.
	Compatible with company's technical requirements.
	Retain/add to mailing list: possible future potential.
X	Remove from mailing list.
I	Insufficient information to rate lead.

qualified leads is enough to support the revenue goals of your company.

Process for Escalating Leads

When and how do you escalate a lead? After the lead has been received and an initial rating has been assigned, who is responsible for the follow-up? A process must be defined that explains how the lead information is sent to the appropriate salesperson in which sales channel. In the past the methods for communicating the lead included voice mail, fax, and e-mail. These methods were particularly true if the receiving person was not at the corporate office. This situation was one of the catalysts for wanting your sales force to have remote access to your SFA system. Through the use of remote clients and intranet access, salespeople can now have access to valuable lead information in their territories.

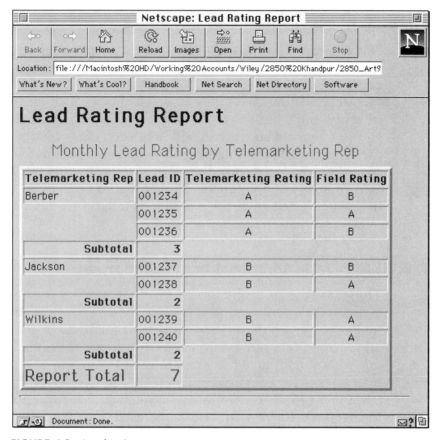

FIGURE 4.9 Lead rating report.

Consider the following in documenting your lead escalation process:

- Is this a hot lead?
- Does this lead cross multiple sales channels?
- Should your SFA system have an automatic notification mechanism for user-defined events, such as escalating a lead?
- How do you determine if a remote salesperson is on vacation?
- How do you determine a backup salesperson if the appropriate one is not available?

Process for Remarketing Leads

Not all leads that come to your company have an immediate need. In the future the potential for a prospect to need your product may be there, and therefore you would like to maintain contact with that prospect. How do you identify which leads fit this category, and what do you do with them once they are called *remarket?* Your rating system will help you define whether a lead fits remarket. Marketing programs must be designed for these remarket leads to ensure that they are continually reminded of your company and products. These programs can take the more traditional forms of direct mail and seminars, or you may start to utilize e-mail in those programs.

Process to Provide Additional Lead Qualification

The leads your company receives will come with various degrees of qualification information. It is important that a process is established that enables these leads to be qualified to a level that allows appropriate disposition of these leads. Ideally all incoming leads would have the same minimum amount of qualifying information. An effective lead qualification process will produce leads that have been examined for quality, as well as determine the best distribution strategy to be used. Quality can be determined by:

- Company's revenues and financial health
- Number of employees
- Line of business
- Business need
- Time frame to make a decision
- Budget allocated
- Compatibility with your technology or product
- Number of units needed
- Decision maker is known
- Competitors are known
- Products the company is currently using

Qualification data that was received from written responses may need to be requalified. The initial data will produce a preliminary lead rating that can be used to help prioritize which leads need to be requalified. Typically you will pursue the highest rated leads for requalification. This process can be accomplished by your telemarketing group. All new information and all revised data received from this qualification call must be captured in your SFA system. A revised rating may be entered at this time. With this new information you can decide if this lead needs to be forwarded to your sales organization, and which sales channel will receive it.

LEADS DISTRIBUTION

Who receives which leads? Does your company have a definition of which leads go to which sales channels? Or do leads go to multiple sales channels? These important questions must be answered by your company. As you map out your lead-flow process, a definition of what type of sales each sales channel is responsible for is required. At this time you must also determine the sales territories to which leads will be distributed. In all cases you must define the rules for leads distribution (i.e., unambiguously state where every possible qualified lead should go). Once this analysis has been done, this logic can be embedded in your SFA system. Once that is done, qualified leads can be distributed based on that criteria.

Figure 4.10 shows an example of leads that have been distributed to the different sales regions. From this report you can quickly see what the company names are, what the lead rating is, where the company is located, and which marketing campaign generated the lead. All of this information is helpful in understanding how many leads are distributed across the different geographic regions or sales channels, as well as the quality of those leads.

Leads may also be sent on to a reseller or partner for further action. To see what has been sent to each reseller, you may run the report shown in Figure 4.11.

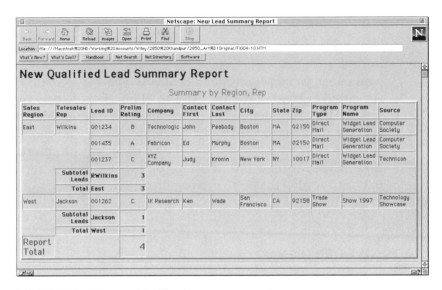

FIGURE 4.10 New qualified lead summary report.

Reseller Lead Report

Summary by Reseller

Reseller Name	Date Notified	Company	Contact First	Contact Last	State	Zip	Phone	Lead ID	Products	Prelim Rating	Timeframe	Units
Western Pacific	3/7/97	XYZ Roberts	John	Peabody	CA	95112	415-555-1212	001234	Widget Software	C	6-12 months	1-5 Units
	3/5/97	Trellicon	Bob	Archer	CA	95097	408-555-1212	001235	Widget Software	A	1-3 months	5-10 Units
	3/8/97	IK Research	Ken	Wade	CA	95068	510-555-1212	001236	Widget Software	B	1-3 months	1-5 Units
	3/4/97	R&R Sound	Karen	Nelson	CA	92122	619-555-1212	001237	Widget Software	A	1-3 months	5-10 Units
	3/1/97	Agent Manufacturing	Ed	Murphy	CA	90210	714-555-1212	001238	Widget Software	A	1-3 months	25-100 Units
Reseller Subtotal		5										
C&C Distributors	3/3/97	Telephonics	Mary	Lazenby	CA	92308	702-555-1212	001240	Widget Software	B	1-3 months	5-10 Units
	3/6/97	Pacific Northwest	Judy	Kronin	CA	92101	808-555-1212	001239	Widget Software	B	4-6 months	10-25 Units
	3/2/97	Lakehouse Components	Paul	Anderson	CA	92308	818-555-1212	001241	Widget Software	B	1-3 months	5-10 Units
Reseller Subtotal		3										
Report Total		8										

FIGURE 4.11 Reseller lead report.

LEAD ANALYSIS

How do you know if your lead qualification process is working? Often the feedback comes in the form of verbal comments or impressions that individuals have made. It is extremely important that tangible, quantifiable data is available to evaluate your success. Your SFA system must capture the data necessary to create these metrics, and you must develop useful reports in order to analyze this data.

Lead Status

The report in Figure 4.12 shows how many leads each telemarketing representative is working on or has distributed to the sales channels. This report shows you the number of leads that each sales channel received. From this information you can determine which channels have the most leads, and if your tele-

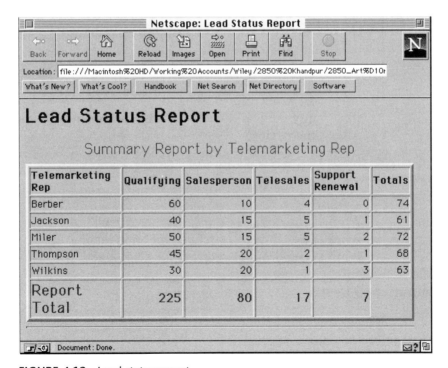

Telemarketing Rep	Qualifying	Salesperson	Telesales	Support Renewal	Totals
Berber	60	10	4	0	74
Jackson	40	15	5	1	61
Miler	50	15	5	2	72
Thompson	45	20	2	1	68
Wilkins	30	20	1	3	63
Report Total	225	80	17	7	

FIGURE 4.12 Lead status report.

marketing representatives are equal in the number of leads they can process.

Another example of a report that can be used to check the status of leads, especially the last action taken on that lead, is shown in Figure 4.13.

Lead Metrics

Both the marketing and sales organizations will want quantitative data about the leads. The following metrics are just a few of the additional measurements you may wish to track:

- Marketing will want information on:
  What is the number of new leads for a particular time period?
  What marketing campaigns were these leads generated from?
  What is the lead rating for these leads?
  What is the response rate for direct-mail campaigns?
  What is the number of attendees per seminar?
  How many leads were generated from a particular trade show?
  How many requests for information did your company receive on their Web site?
  How many downloads of your products occurred on your Web site?
- Sales will want information on:
  How many leads did each salesperson receive for a particular time period?
  What is the distribution of leads across the different sales channels?
  Which marketing campaigns are the best leads generated from?
  What is the dollar potential for each lead?
  What is the time to purchase for each lead?
  What is the product interest for each lead?

Unmatched Leads

Another measure of quality is to track how consistent your telemarketing representatives are in rating leads compared to other representatives, or compared to other marketing campaigns. The report in Figure 4.14 shows you the leads where the preliminary and current ratings differ.

Lead Action Analysis Report

Leads by Action

Action	Telesales Rep	Company	Reseller	Reseller Notification Date	Lead ID
Closed	Berber	Traycor Test Equipment	Mountain Manufacturing	4/1/97	001261
	Subtotal: Closed	1			
Converted to Opp	Jones	TNJ Roberts	Western Pacific	4/5/97	001293
	Berber	XYZ Company	Northwest Monitors	4/2/97	001263
	Subtotal: Converted to Opp	2			
Passed to Reseller	Krone	Zilcon	Northwest Monitors	4/3/97	001267
	Miller	Rubicon	Northwest Monitors	3/31/97	001268
	Miller	MNX Bicycles	Pacific Distributors	4/1/97	001260
	Thompson	Calico	Lighthouse Manufacturing	4/1/97	001284
	Subtotal: Passed to FS	4			
Working	Smith	Technologic	C&C Distributors	4/3/97	001234
	Berber	Fabricon	C&C Distributors	4/2/97	001265
	Jackson	Kellco	Lighthouse Manufacturing	3/31/97	001247
	Miller	ACME Manufacturing	Industrial Consolidators	4/1/97	001245
	Jones	M&M Technology	Lighthouse Manufacturing	4/3/97	001248
	Kent	Kryptonite Media	Western Pacific	4/2/97	001249
	Subtotal: Working	6			
Report Total		13			

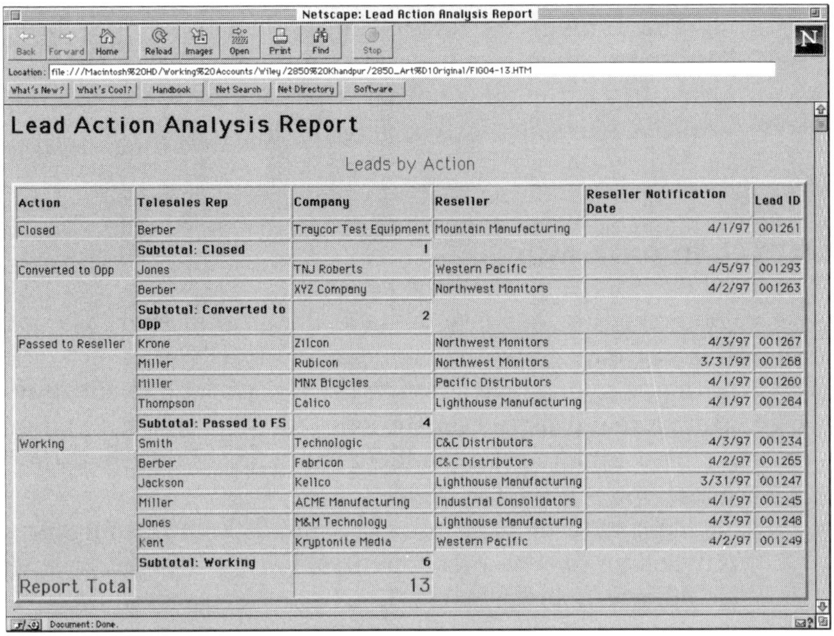

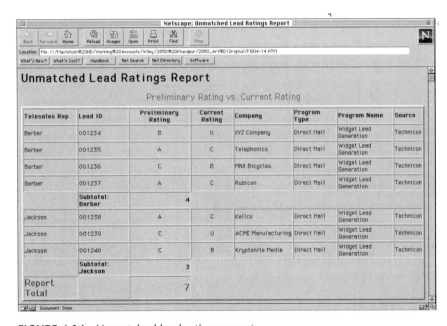

FIGURE 4.13 Lead action analysis report.

Unmatched Lead Ratings Report

Preliminary Rating vs. Current Rating

Telesales Rep	Lead ID	Preliminary Rating	Current Rating	Company	Program Type	Program Name	Source
Berber	001234	B	U	XYZ Company	Direct Mail	Widget Lead Generation	Technicon
Berber	001235	A	C	Telephonics	Direct Mail	Widget Lead Generation	Technicon
Berber	001236	C	B	MNX Bicycles	Direct Mail	Widget Lead Generation	Technicon
Berber	001237	A	C	Rubicon	Direct Mail	Widget Lead Generation	Technicon
	Subtotal: Berber	4					
Jackson	001238	A	C	Kellco	Direct Mail	Widget Lead Generation	Technicon
Jackson	001239	C	U	ACME Manufacturing	Direct Mail	Widget Lead Generation	Technicon
Jackson	001240	C	B	Kryptonite Media	Direct Mail	Widget Lead Generation	Technicon
	Subtotal: Jackson	3					
Report Total		7					

FIGURE 4.14 Unmatched lead ratings report.

The manager of telemarketing can use this information to determine if certain marketing campaigns are consistently being incorrectly rated, or whether a particular telemarketing representative is consistently rating the leads incorrectly.

SALES LEAD DATA MODEL

The preceding discussions have shown that there is a lot of data that you may collect about leads so that you can use the information to take a lead through the process and eventually convert it into a real prospect for the sales force. Figure 4.15 shows a simple yet complete data model of the types of information you may collect about a lead.

This data model shows that leads come from contacts who may belong to sites in companies. For each contact we will want the following data:

- Company information, such as industry, SIC, size, revenues
- Site information, such as division, line of business
- Contact information, such as name, title, decision-making authority
- Contact address and other contact information
- Qualifying questions, such as a statement of the business problem, proposed application
- Lead rating, as described previously
- Fulfillment information, such as what material has been sent to this contact
- Scheduled follow-up, such as what commitments have been made to this contact
- Notes area, to record additional notes
- Marketing source, as described earlier
- Assigned salesperson, who will manage this contact, or the current status
- Reseller information for this contact, if applicable

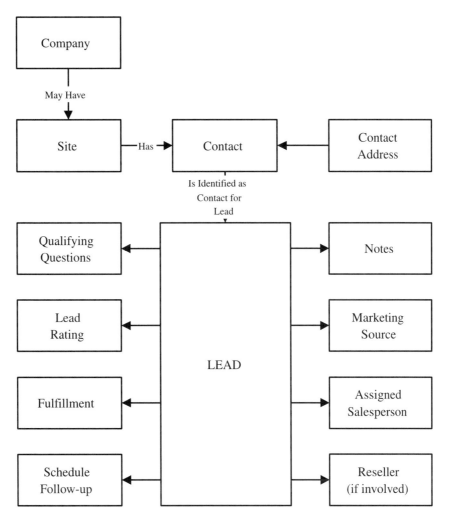

FIGURE 4.15 Sales lead data model.

From a systems viewpoint, the leads will flow from marketing campaigns through different media into the Sales Force Automation database, and upon qualification to the different sales entities. This is shown in Figure 4.16.

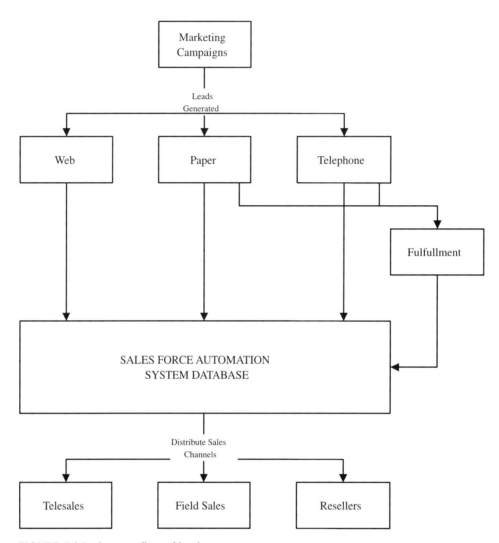

FIGURE 4.16 Systems flow of leads.

SUMMARY

It is extremely important to have a Sales Force Automation system that will enable you to capture pertinent data about each lead as it processes through the qualification cycle. We have seen how the Web form can be used as a data entry device to capture and update lead information, and act as an analysis and reporting medium to view critical metrics on your leads.

Often you may have received some of the data when a prospect responded to a marketing campaign. This data must be fed automatically into your SFA system, and the lead updated as additional information is gathered. Once a lead profile has been completed, an action is taken with that lead. Possible actions for a lead are:

- Send to sales
- Continue lead qualification
- Remarket—include in future marketing campaigns
- Eliminate from list—not a viable lead for your company

All of these possible actions must be captured by your system for an analysis of how many leads were processed and which category they fall into. This analysis will help marketing better understand how effectively they spent their marketing budget. Because you have captured in your SFA system which marketing campaign each lead came from and what action was taken, you are able to evaluate which marketing campaigns were most effective for your company.

If a qualified lead is passed to the sales channel, the salesperson is able to review and analyze all the gathered information about that lead from the SFA system. This ability to provide the sales channel with accurate, current information about the lead ensures the salesperson with the information to continue the sales process.

Now that a lead has been generated, qualified, and passed on for sales action, the next chapter will cover what a salesperson does with a qualified lead.

Managing the Sales Cycle

5

At this point in the overall sales process, leads that came in to your company have been inspected, and qualified leads have been sent on to the sales organization. But how is a lead converted into a customer, and also into booked revenues? What will it take, and who will do it?

In a complex sale it takes many steps to get from a lead to a customer. The individual steps taken and the sequence in which they are executed will depend on the strategies and tactics used in your sales organization, and your organization's preferred sales methodology. In some companies even complex sales are handled entirely by individual salespeople; in other companies every sale requires the involvement of a sales team. In our experience no two organizations have exactly the same sales processes. Indeed, given the variations in companies, products, channels, cultures, and people, that is hardly surprising.

Having said that, this chapter presents a generic sales cycle that covers the key steps taken in most complex sales situations. This generic process is used to describe what happens during a sale, and to give examples of how using Web technologies can improve your organization's effectiveness, efficiency, and customer satisfaction.

The sales process to achieve your sales goals will vary, depending on your sales cycle, market awareness of your product, product offerings and pricing, technical complexity of your product, and contractual requirements. The process shown can easily be adapted to the specific needs of your organization. You may discard some steps and introduce others. No matter—the discussion in this chapter is for illustrative purposes, and is intended to help you design your own sales processes.

The sales steps in Figure 5.1 include the most common steps that can occur in a sales cycle. It is not necessary, however, that a sale follow all steps exactly. For example, a lead can drop off the cycle at the Verify Lead Qualification step if the salesperson deems the lead dead due to budgetary constraints, product in-

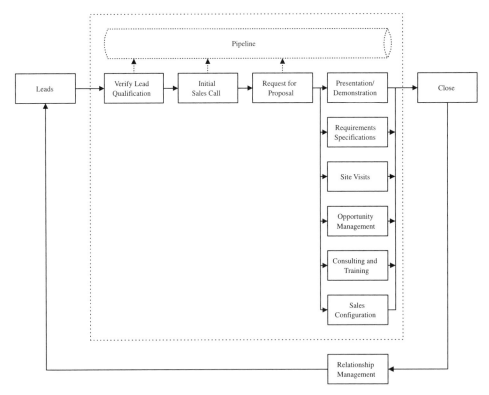

FIGURE 5.1 Sales cycle overview.

terest, or timing. On the other hand, a lead can drop right into a forecast from the lead qualification stage if the customer has:

- Budgeted dollars for the project
- An immediate purchase need due to end of fiscal year spending requirements
- Adequately sized the product, consulting, and service components of the sale

In this case, the salesperson is fortunate enough to bypass the majority of the sales stages and can proceed directly to the contract negotiation stage of the sale.

VERIFY LEAD QUALIFICATION

The amount of qualification that is done before a lead is presented to a salesperson will vary from organization to organization. In some sales organizations a lot of work goes into qualifying a lead before a salesperson gets involved. This may include an analysis of the lead's company, its position in its market segment, and its financial health, among other things. In some other sales organizations the qualification is somewhat less thorough, and it is up to the salesperson to perform some of the qualification. We believe that the less a salesperson has to do in qualifying a lead, the higher the quality of the lead qualification process. This is because less of a salesperson's time is taken away from selling activities.

Figure 5.2 shows a simple process for verifying a sales lead. In some organizations the process may be very formal, in others very informal; however, the activities and their sequence remain essentially the same.

In most sales organizations a salesperson will contact a qualified lead to get more information about the potential sale. Before actually talking to the lead, the salesperson knows that the information provided by the lead suggests that there is potential for a sale. A Web-based sales automation tool can give the salesperson not only information supplied by the lead, but also all the research and analysis done by other people in the sales organi-

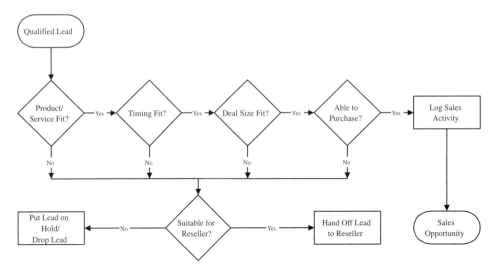

FIGURE 5.2 Verify lead qualification.

zation. Armed with this information, the salesperson can have a very informative discussion with the lead.

It is important to note at this point that no matter how much information is logged into the sales automation tool, the experience and expertise of the salesperson is absolutely essential in deciding if the lead is in fact an opportunity worth pursuing, and if so what it will take to make the sale.

Upon receiving a lead from telemarketing, a salesperson will typically verify the information about the lead and make a determination of its sales potential. This step often consists of calling the prospect and rechecking the basic qualifying questions, as well as establishing the needs and urgency of the prospect. Qualifying questions that are typically asked include:

- Is there a need within your company for our products?
- What is the business problem you are trying to solve?
- How are you currently addressing this problem?
- What is your time frame to make a decision?
- What is your time frame to implement?
- Are budget dollars allocated for this project?
- Who are the decision makers?
- What is the decision process?

- Who is the competition?
- What products are you interested in purchasing?
- How many units do you intend to purchase?

If the salesperson verifies that the lead has real revenue potential, it may at this time be converted into a sales opportunity and enter the sales pipeline. On the other hand, if the salesperson determines that a qualified lead does not in fact have a good potential for resulting in a sale, the salesperson could put the lead on hold and follow up at a later time; or reassign the lead to the telemarketing group for follow-up. In some cases a reseller may be a better match for the sale, so a reseller may be handed the lead.

Because all the information that telemarketing collected is in the SFA system, the salesperson has easy access to that data and can update information about the lead once this initial call has been made. The sales lead form in Figure 5.3 gives an example of

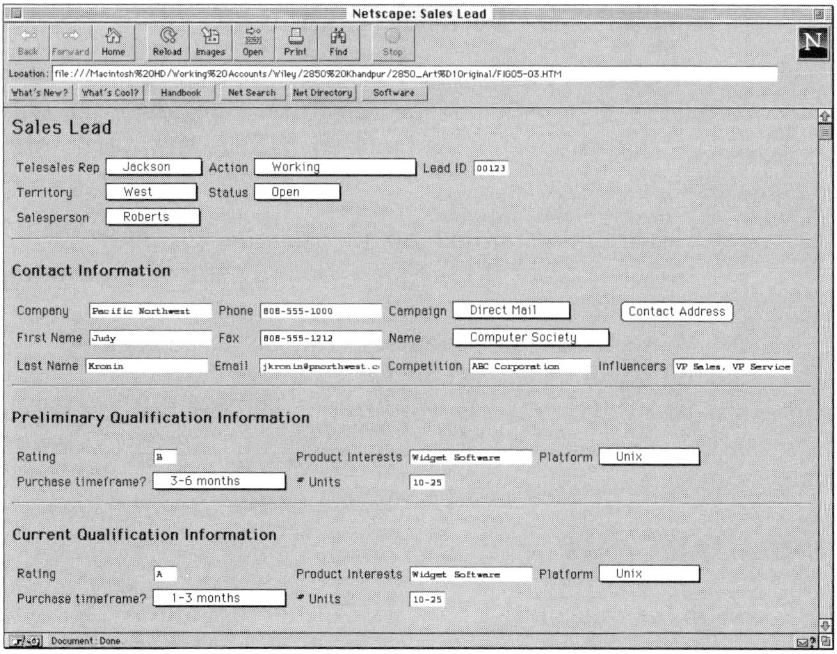

FIGURE 5.3 Sales lead form.

the fields the salesperson will be updating prior to converting this qualified lead to an opportunity. In this example, the initial rating for the lead is B, but after verifying the lead the salesperson has upgraded the rating to A. The salesperson has also updated the purchase time frame, and verified the product interest, the platform, and the number of units the lead intends to buy.

By having a centralized database of all lead information, your company can maintain current, accurate data about all leads. This is particularly helpful when more than one salesperson is working on a lead, because all the involved parties have access to the same information. This allows the individuals to know exactly what has happened and who is responsible for what. In addition, if salespeople left your company, the SFA system would provide you with all the sales activity that is occurring in their territory.

Once a qualified lead is deemed a viable sales lead, the initial sales call can be scheduled.

Work Area for Verifying Qualified Leads

The following are some questions to answer when thinking about the steps a salesperson in your organization will take to verify a qualified lead passed on from the marketing organization:

- How reliable is the lead qualification process?
- How long does it take for a lead to get from marketing to a salesperson?
- What are the key elements that must be verified?
- Who will do the verification?
- What data must be captured in the verification process?

INITIAL SALES CALL

With the information that was gathered while verifying the sales lead, the salesperson can develop a strategy for how to handle this opportunity, and what the goals should be for the initial sales call. The steps involved in the initial sales call are shown in Figure 5.4. As preparation for this call begins, the salesperson may need the most current information available in several areas:

- Company information
- Product availability information
- Competitive information
- Information of the latest products

A Web-based Marketing Encyclopedia System can provide much if not all of the information a salesperson may need to make the initial sales call. If the marketing organization has provided all of the information in the MES, and keeps it up to date, your salespeople will have access to a powerful resource. By providing Web access to the MES, your salespeople don't have to track down the individual in your company to get the most recent competitive information prior to a sales call. The marketing organization need only update the one source on your corporate intranet, and this information is instantly available to your entire sales force. A salesperson can download relevant information to a local system (a portable computer or a workstation in a sales office), and customize the information for the specific opportunity. This is an example of how streamlining the information flow in an organization can increase productivity within the sales organization. A salesperson has already saved valuable time prior to the sales call with one trip to the company's intranet Web site.

After customizing the information and making the sales call, the salesperson will need to log what happened during the sales activity. Logging the initial sales call into your SFA system will provide visibility to the rest of the sales organization on the activity associated with this company. Figure 5.5 shows a sales activity form that can be used to log the initial sales call.

The data logged for this initial sales call can include:

- Date and time of call
- Attendees

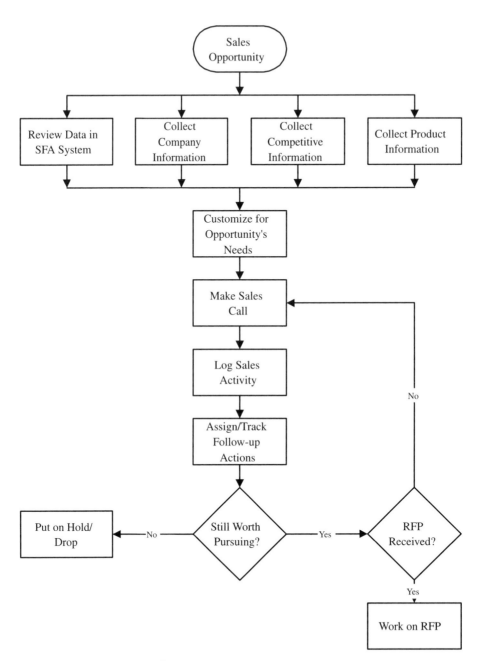

FIGURE 5.4 Initial sales call.

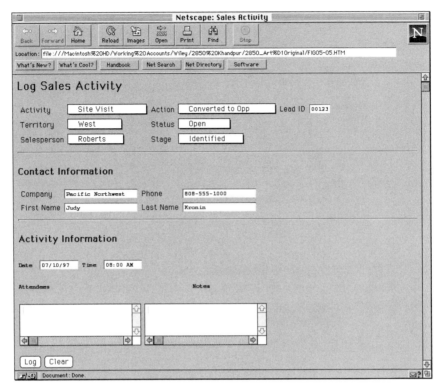

FIGURE 5.5   Sales activity form.

- Notes
- Follow-up actions (log commitments with due date and description)

Online access to this information is critical in team selling environments, where commitments can be allocated to other members of the sales organization. Since everyone has access to a Web-based SFA system, all members of the sales team can view the activity form as soon as it is updated, and view any commitments that may be assigned to them.

Once the salesperson has gathered additional information regarding the potential sale, the corresponding opportunity in-

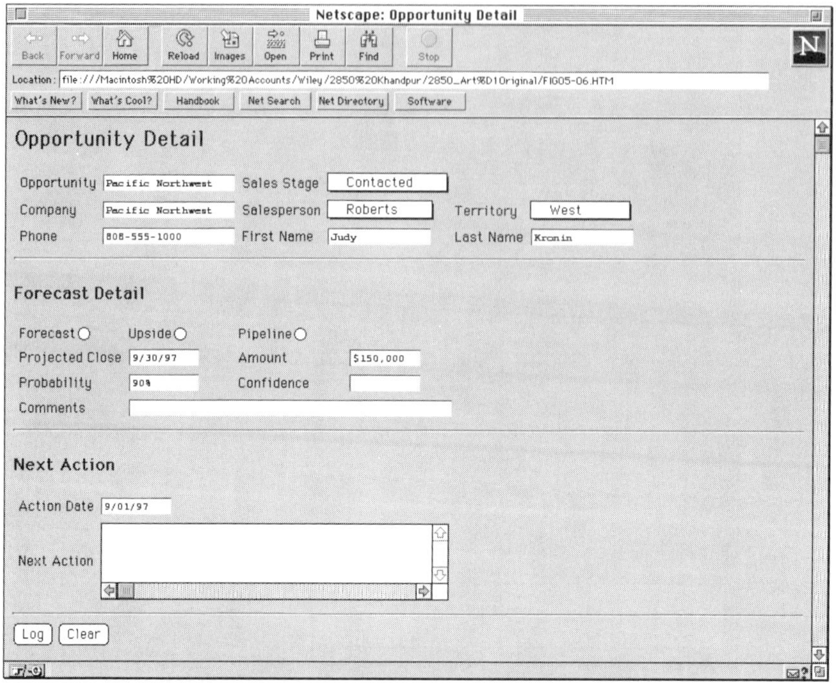

FIGURE 5.6 Sales opportunity form.

formation is logged, as shown in Figure 5.6. In this example, the salesperson can indicate whether the opportunity falls into the forecast or the pipeline, make an estimate of the revenue potential, and judge the probability and confidence levels in the sale. This form also provides a means to log actions that must be performed to advance the opportunity in the sales cycle.

The lead form and the opportunity form are the foundation for your Sales Force Automation system. All forecasts, pipeline projections, and postmortem analyses are done from the information gathered on these forms. For example, you can use the information from these forms to track the current stage of this opportunity, potential closing date, and projected revenue (see Figure 5.7). In this example report, a sales manager can see the

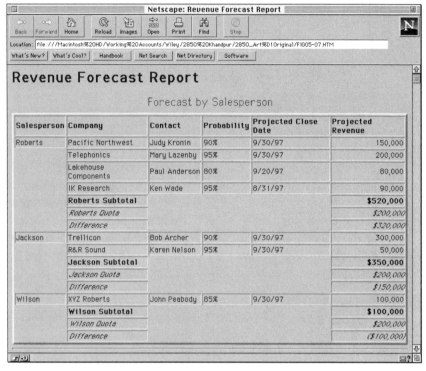

FIGURE 5.7 Revenue forecast by salesperson.

current state of opportunities in a territory, and the performance of each salesperson relative to sales quota (clearly Wilson needs some assistance to come up to quota).

This forecast report can be run weekly, monthly, or quarterly; it will give you an accurate, up-to-date revenue projection for each salesperson against quota for the period. In addition, you may want to generate variations on this report, grouped by the following parameters:

■ Forecast by account
■ Forecast by period
■ Forecast by product family
■ Forecast by territory

Another advantage of automating this information is to provide a system of checks and balances against the data that are collected. For example, the SFA system could automatically calculate the forecast/pipeline/upside flag by using the following two fields from this form:

- Anticipated close date
- Stage of sales cycle

For example, if the anticipated close date is set to occur in the quarter following the current quarter, then the flag would be set to *Pipeline* instead of *Forecast*. Also, the SFA system would require the salesperson to set the stage of the sales cycle to something more complete than *Identified* in order to categorize this opportunity as a *Forecast*. This is a way of using the system to enforce process standards using *business rules*.

Work Area for Initial Sales Call

The following are some questions to answer when thinking about the steps a salesperson in your organization will take during the sales call:

- What information will the salesperson have when starting to work on an opportunity?
- What additional information will the salesperson need?
- Who will provide this information?
- How accurate and current is that information?
- Is all the information in the same format and style?
- How much customization will the salesperson be able to do?
- Does the salesperson have the tools to do the customization?
- What information about the initial sales call should the salesperson log into the SFA system?
- How will this information be used?
- How will the salesperson assign and track actions?
- How will people who have been assigned actions be notified, and how will they indicate completion?

Business rules can also be used to enforce particular sales methodologies. For example, your sales methodology may require that the buying influences be identified, and a weekly update be made by the salesperson on the status of interactions with each influence. If no update is made for a week, then the system could automatically notify the salesperson that the buying influence needs to be contacted, and the status of the communications with that influence updated to reflect the interaction.

After the sales activity form has been completed, the salesperson will make a further determination on the potential of the opportunity; if it is still worth pursuing, the salesperson's next task is to receive a Request for Proposal from the prospect.

REQUEST FOR PROPOSAL

After the salesperson's initial meetings with the prospect, and agreement has been reached that your company's product offering could provide a possible solution for the prospect, your company's name will be included to receive the Request for Proposal (RFP). Many companies use the RFP to evaluate and select the vendor with which they would like to do business.

The RFP will normally give considerable detail on the business opportunities or issues confronting the prospect, and the approach the prospect wishes to take to address the opportunities or issues. The RFP could, however, contain very high-level questions with no technical details, so the requirements specification stage of the sales process becomes all the more critical. The RFP will request a formal response from the salesperson by a specific date. A salesperson will typically identify all the items that need a response, assign tasks to relevant sales team members, gather the information needed to respond to the RFP, and then consolidate the information and prepare a formal response (see Figure 5.8). The tasks that need to be done can be tracked using the Sales Opportunity Form shown earlier.

A salesperson in your company may be working with several prospects, each of which may require a response to an RFP. The complexity of each response will vary, as well as the information

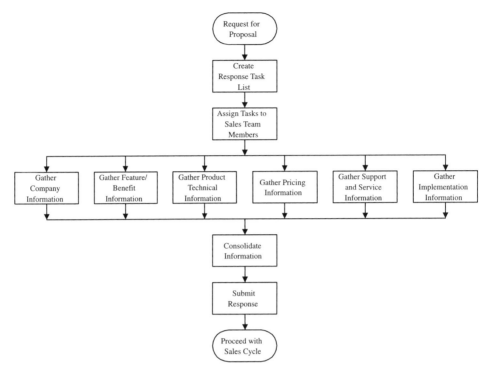

FIGURE 5.8 Request for Proposal.

requested, depending on the nature of the opportunity and the completeness of the information in the RFP. More information about the content of an RFP can be found in Chapter 10.

Because a salesperson may be working on more than one RFP at a time, as well as managing all other prospects in the various stages of the sales cycle, the time a salesperson has to work on a particular RFP is often limited. This is why many sales organizations have standard template responses to typical RFP questions. These template responses, and other information, can be placed on your corporate intranet for use by your sales force. The advantages of having this information on your intranet are:

- Improves the salesperson's efficiency
- Ensures accurate responses to questions

- Provides a single point of reference for the salespeople
- Updates only a single location with the most recent information

Since an RFP often requests information that has been used to answer another RFP, you can develop a set of corporate-approved responses that are developed and maintained by someone on the corporate intranet. This information could include:

- Company information
- Product descriptions
- Product availability
- Product releases and update schedules
- Product pricing
- Technical requirements for product
- Feature/function of your products and associated benefits
- Support services and policies
- Training information and schedules
- Consulting services and pricing
- Implementation process and typical schedule

These standard responses can be organized in a structured manner on your Web site, or accessible via a searching tool on your Web site, enabling the salesperson to quickly find the desired standard response. This allows rapid completion of the formal RFP response, guaranteeing a quick turnaround for your prospect. Figure 5.9 illustrates the results of a search that may be used to find standard RFP responses, with the *company information* keywords used to initiate the search.

Turning in the formal response is not the end of the sales cycle. Note that in some cases the RFP may be given to the salesperson very early in the sales cycle, and in other cases it may not be given until the prospect is close to making a final selection. For discussion purposes, we will assume that an RFP is issued only to vendors who have demonstrated in the initial sales call that the products they offer can address the customer's needs. The responses to the RFP will be used to narrow down the vendor list to a few vendors, and then additional sales effort may need to be undertaken before the prospect makes a final decision.

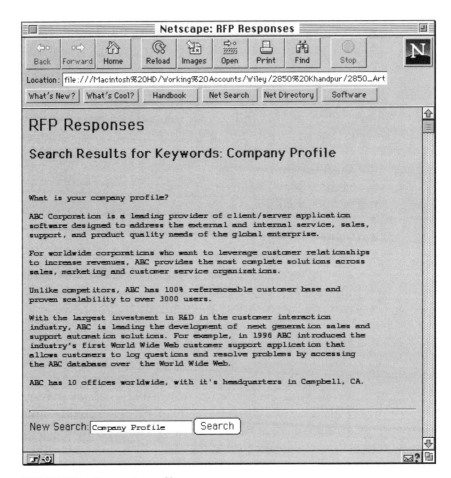

FIGURE 5.9 Corporate profile response.

PRESENTATION/DEMONSTRATION

As an opportunity moves through the sales cycle, the salesperson often must do a product presentation or demonstration for that company. The presentation could be before a few people or many people in many different locations.

Work Area for Request for Proposal

The following are some questions to answer when thinking about preparing a response to an RFP:

- How does an RFP typically come in to your organization (hard copy, electronic form, etc.)?
- How is the RFP routed to the appropriate salesperson?
- How does a salesperson track all the items needing a response?
- How does a salesperson assign and follow up on RFP preparation tasks?
- In all the responses your organization has prepared in the past three months, how many had a large degree of duplication?
- Did your salespeople create new responses to questions, or did they use and modify previously used responses?
- How easy is it for your salespeople to access previously used responses?
- How many standard response templates does your organization currently use?
- Are all of these templates easy to find and use?
- What are the usage statistics for these standard response templates?

At this stage in the sales cycle there are essentially two types of presentations:

- Product presentation
- Technical demonstration

The preparation a field salesperson does for each of the two types of presentations requires slightly different kinds of resources. Figure 5.10 shows the basic process in getting ready for a presentation or demonstration.

Product Presentation

Product presentations often require the gathering of existing marketing information about the product to present a customized, organized presentation addressing the prospect's interest and concerns about your product. This is quite similar to the presentation given during the initial sales call, but may have a greater level of detail in it because the prospect is already familiar with the high-level features of your products.

As before, if you have your most current product marketing information on your corporate intranet, a salesperson can quickly gather that information and be assured that it is the latest available. The intranet can also be used by the salesperson to ask product-specific questions of the technical resources within the company (such as sales engineers, support engineers, research and development personnel). This may be done by e-mail, but also in discussion threads or through groupware.

Technical Demonstration

The other type of presentation a salesperson may need to present is a technical product demonstration that is heavily customized to show specifically how your company's products will address the prospect's requirements. In the extreme case, your organization may even have to create a prototype of the prospect's anticipated solution to assure the prospect that your products will meet all the requirements specified in the RFP.

Technical demonstrations can occur when your prospect wants to see your product in actual use. In this case the salesperson is not only gathering and organizing product information, but also arranging with technical resources to present your product. This technical presentation often requires the customization

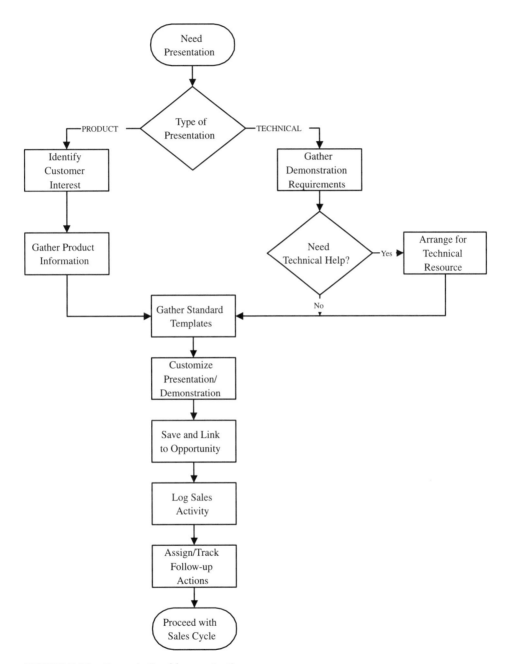

FIGURE 5.10 Presentation/demonstration.

of your product. If you have a demonstration copy of your software on your intranet, the individuals involved in this presentation can jointly be developing this technical presentation. In cases where the audience is located at different sites, having the ability to let them see the demonstration through Web access is critical to keeping the cost of sales down. Not only does this eliminate the need to do the technical demonstration several times, obviously a resource drain, but it also allows you to keep the sales cycle short.

In both cases, the presentation or demonstration should be saved and linked to the opportunity. The first action ensures that the customized presentation is available to other salespeople if they should need something similar. The second action provides an audit trail of what was actually presented to the prospect.

As part of the Marketing Encyclopedia System, your corporate intranet could become a presentation and demonstration repository, containing the latest copies of the following materials:

- Detailed presentations about products
- Industry-specific demonstrations ready for downloading
- Customer-specific demonstrations used
- Standard demonstration scripts

After the presentation or demonstration, the details surrounding the presentation should be recorded as sales activity against this company, as shown in Figure 5.11.

During the course of the sales cycle a salesperson may give a number of different demonstrations to the prospect. A good Sales Force Automation solution will provide the capability to organize and index the different demonstration material used, and record the attendees at each demonstration and the key issues that came up during the course of the demonstration. The product demonstration form is tracking the following information:

- Products/versions shown
- Presentations used
- Functionality shown
- Attendee list

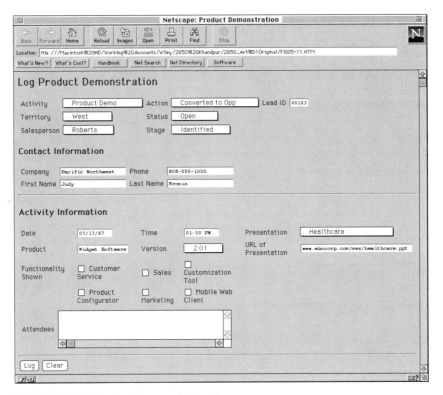

FIGURE 5.11 Product demonstration form.

Once the product demonstration is logged against this company, the sales activity history is updated to show the date of the product demonstration, as shown in Figure 5.12.

Note that not all demonstrations will require the salesperson's presence. Your products may be such that you can create a set of standard (or even custom) demonstrations that can be sent to customers for trial purposes. A Web-based solution will allow your prospects to access and download these demonstrations, and keep track of the demonstrations used by each prospect. For example, many companies will place a demonstration version of their products on the corporate Web site, and allow registered users (leads or prospects) to either download the demonstration or run it on the company's systems over the Internet.

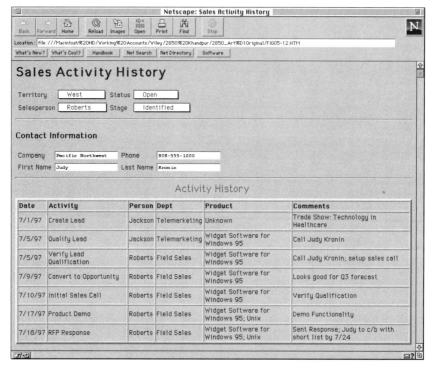

FIGURE 5.12 Sales activity history.

Work Area for Presentation/Demonstration

The following are some questions to answer when planning your presentation and demonstration material:

- Do you have standard presentations and demonstrations?
- Are they available for all products, application areas, and industry segments?
- How is the material kept up to date?
- How do salespeople have access to the material?
- Do salespeople keep track of material they customize?
- Is material available to customers without the intervention of a salesperson?
- Do you track direct access by customers?
- Do salespeople keep track of all attendees, and follow up with them? Should they?

REQUIREMENTS SPECIFICATION

From the prospect's Request for Proposal, the salesperson can gather initial information to size the individual components of the potential sale. However, there are often other requirements that come up over time, some of them specifically stated by the prospect during meetings with the salesperson, others based on the salesperson's experience and assessment of the situation. Requirements could also be missing from the RFP (in those instances where the RFP is focused on high-level issues), which need to be completely defined in the requirements specification stage. During the course of the sales cycle, and especially during and after product demonstrations and prototyping, the salesperson will identify additional requirements and perhaps need to alter requirements identified earlier.

A sales automation solution can be used to manage these requirements by providing the capability to record the requirements, actions associated with each requirement, and the current status of work being done to address the prospect's requirements. The tool can also notify the salesperson that certain requirements are still outstanding if the salesperson attempts to change the status to indicate that a proposal is complete before all the requirements have been addressed. An example process for consolidating all requirements is shown in Figure 5.13.

Some examples of additional information that must be gathered and that can be tracked in your SFA system include:

- Customer environment:
  Hardware type
  Operating system version
  RDBMS version
  Communications protocol and version
- Training requirements
- Size of consulting requirement (hours required)
- Type of consulting skills required
- Size of deployment effort
- Project team makeup
- Project team skills

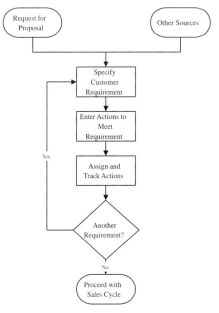

FIGURE 5.13 Requirements specification.

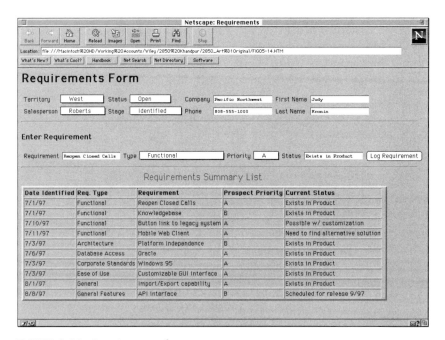

FIGURE 5.14 Requirements form.

An example of a requirements form that can be used in a Web-based sales automation tool is shown in Figure 5.14.

Work Area for Requirements Specification

The following are some questions to answer when thinking about the steps a salesperson in your organization will take to collect and consolidate all the requirements for a particular sale:

- How does a salesperson identify and track customer requirements?
- How does a salesperson ensure that all requirements are met?
- Have you lost sales because not all customer-specified requirements were met? If so, why were the requirements not met?
- How are customer requirements mapped to the sales configuration?

SITE VISITS

During the course of the sales cycle there will be many interactions between the salesperson and the prospect. Good salespeople keep detailed notes of each interaction, recording who participated in the interaction, the details of the interaction itself, and any action items arising from the interaction. In a complex sale different members of the sales team may contact many different people in the prospect's organization, so it is critical to log the site visit activity. Figure 5.15 shows an example of the process involved in preparing for a site visit. After the need for a site visit is identified (for example, by request of the prospect), the salesperson will define the goal of the visit, and prepare the agenda. Then, depending on the nature of the visit (see following discussion) the salesperson will either identify and notify other company personnel who will need to participate in the visit, or identify a client to host the visit and get permission from that client.

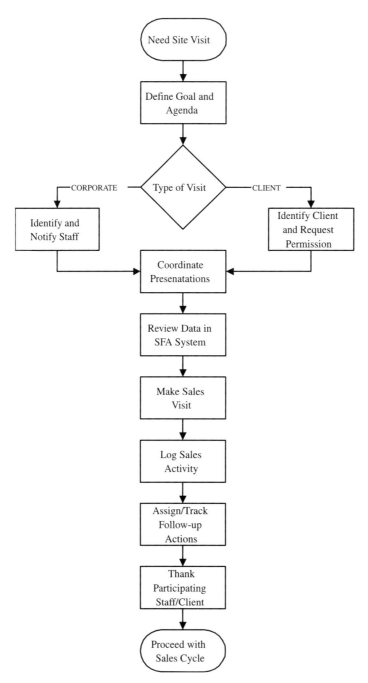

FIGURE 5.15 Site visit.

Site visits typically fall into two categories:

- Corporate site visit
- Client site visit

Corporate Site Visit

Corporate site visits require the coordination of executives from headquarters to present a personalized presentation based on the prospect's needs. The intranet can be used by the salesperson to communicate the goals of the meeting, define the roles individuals will play, provide pertinent information needed about the prospect, and to review each person's presentation before the scheduled visit. Therefore, it should be a requirement that all parties associated with the corporate visit put their presentations on the intranet so that the salesperson can review them for consistency and ensure there is no duplication across presentations.

The types of corporate site presentations that can be available as part of your marketing encyclopedia can be categorized as:

- Corporate
- Product
- Technical

Client Site Visit

The client site visit allows your prospect to see your product in action at one of your client sites. In preparation for such a visit, the salesperson will visit the intranet, which should contain a current list of referenceable customers sorted by the industry type, environment, number of users, and so on. This way you can quickly locate an appropriate client for your prospect to visit.

For example, your prospective customer may be in the healthcare industry, and may only want to visit a client using the product in a healthcare-related application. Another example could be prospective customers interested in using your product with 1000 users. You wouldn't want to send them to a client with only 50 users in production.

After information has been collected by the salesperson and the visit arranged, the salesperson will typically review the collected notes in the tool database to come up to speed on the status at the account before actually conducting the visit. This kind of preparation gives the prospect the impression that the sales team is working well, and can raise the prospect's comfort level in doing business with your organization.

After the visit itself, the salesperson will want to log the activity. As described earlier, a Web-based Sales Force Automation solution can provide a standard way to capture the nature and details of each interaction so that the salesperson (the project manager for the sale) can keep track of all communications and be informed when additional actions are required. For example, the site visit form in Figure 5.16, once filled out, can also update the sales activity history for that prospect.

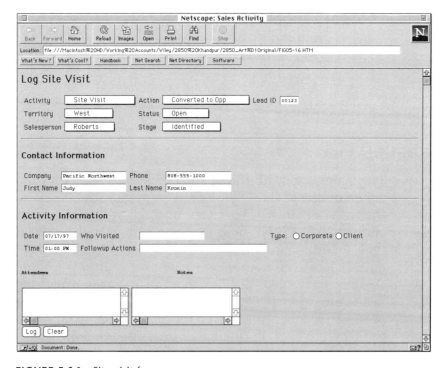

FIGURE 5.16 Site visit form.

The typical information logged for each visit includes:

- Who visited (the attendees)
- Nature of discussion
- Follow-up actions

A sophisticated sales automation tool can be used to identify who attended the visit, who helped put it together, and if a client site was used for the visit; and then create messages (or remind the salesperson) to thank all those who participated.

Work Area for Site Visit

The following are some questions to answer when thinking about planning automation for site visits:

- How many site visits does your organization conduct each year? Client or corporate?
- What are the common elements of each visit?
- How does a salesperson identify internal resources to assist with site visits?
- How is their time scheduled?
- How does a salesperson find clients willing to participate in site visits?
- How much time is spent by the salesperson in arranging site visits?
- How does a salesperson identify and track actions arising from a site visit?

OPPORTUNITY MANAGEMENT

In this context, opportunity management has to do with the actual ongoing management of the activities of the sales team in driving toward the close, including:

- Identifying and contacting key players
- Bringing in sales executives as needed
- Developing strategies to close the sale

- Assigning and coordinating tasks
- Redirecting and redeploying resources needed to close the sale
- Keeping the prospect customer current on new developments
- Tracking all assigned tasks and open issues

In addition to the salesperson managing the activities of the sales team involved in making the sale, sales managers will want to keep track of the current status of each sale so that issues can be resolved in a timely manner. An experienced sales manager may be able to identify potential issues before the salesperson, and can offer advice and assistance on how to proceed. A sales automation tool must provide the ability to produce not only periodic reports, but also the ability to create and run *ad hoc* queries, and interrogate the sales databases for the details of each sale.

Work Area for Opportunity Management

The following are some questions to answer when thinking about sales management activities:

- What are the key indicators a salesperson uses to manage an opportunity?
- How does the salesperson know when to bring in additional resources?
- What resources does the salesperson use to develop sales strategies and tactics?
- How does the salesperson get hold of these resources?
- How does the salesperson know when to escalate an issue?
- How does a salesperson know if the sales methodology is being followed?
- What information does a salesperson need to better manage an opportunity?

Many sales organizations also use standard sales methodologies, such as those from Kappa or Miller-Heiman. The methodologies essentially dictate the process that a salesperson must follow, and provide specific steps to take and forms to fill out. If your organization uses a standard sales methodology, your sales automation tool should enforce the methodology and provide a capability for sales mangers to be notified when key elements of the methodology are not being followed, or when their intervention is necessary.

Opportunity and sales management activities are discussed in greater detail in Chapter 8.

CONSULTING AND TRAINING

A complex sale may involve not only the sale of products, but also some consulting and training services to help the customer be successful in the use of the products you sell. The consulting and training services may be provided either by your own organization, or by third parties affiliated with your company, such as training and implementation partners. The services may be of different types, such as business consulting, sales methodologies, application implementation, technology training, tools training, and so on.

For example, if your company sells a complicated system (such as an enterprise Sales Force Automation solution), the salesperson will have to consider whether the customer will need any consulting services to develop sales processes, analyses, and programming services to implement the system; and training services for the application programmers, system administrators, and the end-user salespeople in the prospect's organization.

A sales automation tool will provide the ability for the salesperson to identify consulting and training needs, and be able to arrange whether they will be provided by your company or by someone else. The process is essentially similar to that used during requirements specification, but may need to involve an external partner. An example of a process to gather consulting and training requirements is shown in Figure 5.17.

The requirements for consulting and training will either be stated in the RFP, or developed during sales calls, and site visits, product presentations, or technical demonstrations; in short, at some point during the sales cycle. If your company has a separate consulting and training organization, these requirements may be passed off to the person in that organization, who will be re-

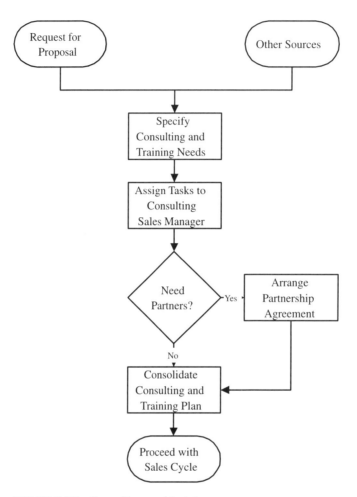

FIGURE 5.17 Consulting and training.

sponsible for putting together the consulting and training part of the sales proposal, and perhaps even pricing it. If your company does not (or cannot) deliver the actual consulting and training services, the salesperson or the consulting sales manager may have to identify a third party that can fulfill these requirements, and either hand off the business to the third party or subcontract the third party to deliver the services. Third parties that may be preapproved and prequalified to bid with you may have access to your Sales Force Automation system over an extranet.

Work Area for Consulting and Training

When automating this process, here are some questions you will want to think about:

■ How are proposals for consulting and training services prepared?
■ Who prepares them?
■ What are the information sources needed to prepare the proposals?
■ Does your company have in-house resources or do you typically use a third party?
■ Do you have existing relationships with third-party providers?
■ What are the steps taken to arrange a third-party proposal?
■ How is such a proposal incorporated into your own proposals?

SALES CONFIGURATION

A proper sales configuration is essential for many reasons, the most important being customer satisfaction and sales quality. An incorrectly configured sales order can result in products being sent to the customer, which when installed will not work together, or worse, will not address the customer's requirements. This can result in the customer returning the products, or your organization not realizing the full value of the sale.

Sales configuration is conceptually very simple. The first step is for the salesperson to analyze the prospect's requirements and needs, and make selections from what you sell that will address those needs. The second step is to ensure that all the selections work together. For example, a prospect may want to purchase a high-performance, sporty sedan with fat tires but equipped with a trailer hitch. Your salesperson can first select from your offerings a list of high-performance cars, sedans, fat tires, and trailer hitches, any one of which will meet individual requirements. The next step is to combine all the requirements to come up with those sedans that are high-performance, can handle fat tires, and are able to handle a trailer hitch.

It sounds easy, but developing a configuration for a sale can be a very tedious and error-prone process if your offerings are even slightly complex. As mentioned in the preceding example, there are two hurdles: product configuration and selection compatibility. Many products come in different versions, sizes, and packages, and may have different operating requirements. This can make configuring a particular product very time-consuming. In complex sales a sales configuration will often contain a long list of products. However, many products, especially technology products, have dependencies on other products. For example, Widget B version 2 may require Widget X version 3 or higher to be installed; Widget X in turn may have dependencies on other products, and may not run if Widget Z is also installed. As new offerings get added to your catalog, the possible combinations of products can increase exponentially, and no salesperson can realistically be expected to easily develop a configuration for even a simple product sale.

The problem is compounded during the sales cycle, because proposed sales configurations can change almost daily as the prospect views product demonstrations and changes requirements. A sales automation tool should allow a salesperson to dynamically develop a sales configuration at the customer's request, and save copies of all configurations that are created so that they can be reused if necessary. A simple solution will make the catalog available over the Internet, and give the salesperson a complete and current catalog to work with. A more sophisticated system will assist the salesperson in developing a configuration, and enforce rules and constraints on what a salesperson can configure (see Figure 5.18).

If your company sells software products, an example of another level of complexity to the product configuration is the compatibility with the relational database management system (RDBMS) on the target machine and machine operating system. These third-party compatibility issues are critical in ensuring your product will run in the customer's environment. You want to avoid a situation where the customer has purchased the latest

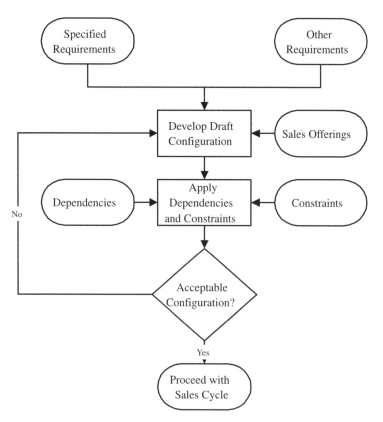

FIGURE 5.18 Configuration.

version of your product and finds it won't run on the RDBMS version they have. Simply upgrading their RDBMS version may not be enough. We have seen situations where upgrading the RDBMS version required also upgrading the operating system version; however, the latest operating system version was not compatible with the customer's legacy manufacturing and finance systems. The customer ultimately had to purchase another server to run the ABC product.

Figure 5.19 gives an example of a compatibility matrix for the following configuration: ABC product version 1.0 and XYZ Computer version 2.0, showing which RDBMS versions and operating system versions are compatible and supported.

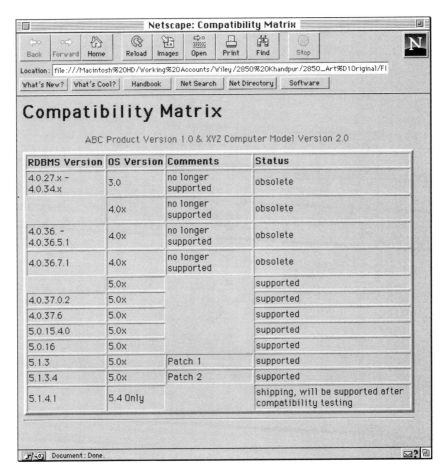

FIGURE 5.19   Compatibility matrix example.

Your organization must supply such third-party compatibility matrices for all possible configurations of your product. Maintaining this information within your SFA system ensures access to the most up-to-date supported configurations, and reduces the time the salesperson has to spend tracking down this information in the engineering or quality assurance groups. This is just another example of how applying automation in another segment of the enterprise can indirectly cause increased productivity within the sales organization.

Work Area for Sales Configuration

The following are some questions to answer when analyzing how configurations are prepared in your organization:

- How much time does a typical configuration take to prepare?
- How many draft configurations does a salesperson typically prepare before a final configuration?
- Do your products have a large number of possible configurations?
- Do your products have many dependencies on third-party products?
- Are you losing sales because your policies and tools do not allow you to offer custom configurations?
- What tools exist to help a salesperson prepare a configuration?
- How are third-party dependencies updated and communicated to the sales force?
- Is it easy for your salespeople to reuse configurations they have prepared in the past?

SALES OPPORTUNITY DATA MODEL

The primary goal of a sales organization is to produce revenue. How that revenue is generated can be achieved through various strategies, such as focusing on:

Targeted or named accounts	Education
Vertical markets	Geographic territories
Specific products	Size of account
Government	Resellers

Each of these strategies can affect the type of data tracked, and how you want to capture that data. This in turn can influence the Sales Force Automation system you implement. Before implementing an SFA system, therefore, you identify the data elements you want to track for your sales opportunities. A simple representation of a data model for sales opportunities is shown in Figure 5.20.

This data model shows that the information at the top—on the company, the site, and contact information—is essentially the same as for a lead, and in fact may use the same data tables as those used to store leads data.

If a reseller or partner is involved in the sale, there should be a link between the opportunity and the name of the reseller. In the reseller data model, there could be many more data elements to describe the reseller, but at this point we are interested only in knowing if a reseller is involved; and if so, who it is. In a sophisticated Web-based SFA tool that is implemented on an extranet, the reseller may be able to view and even update data for those opportunities that involve the reseller.

Also associated with the opportunity is the competition your organization faces in this deal. This part of the data model can be used to record who the competition is, what they are offering, their pricing, and other notes and actions that your salesperson may take to address the competition. This element could be linked to a separate competitive database that a salesperson could peruse.

Another element in the model is the prospect's product interest. This may be filled in during the lead qualification process, but may continue to get updated if the salesperson discerns an opportunity for additional sales.

As discussed earlier in this chapter, there will be many activities that will be performed before the sale is closed. Some of those activities will involve following up with customers and other people in the organization. This data element can be used to keep track of the schedule of commitments, so a sales team member can immediately see what needs to be done for this opportunity, and when.

In the course of the sales cycle, the salesperson may prepare many draft configurations for review by the prospect. These draft configurations may be rejected at first, and then accepted by the prospect. This data element allows the salesperson to track which configurations were prepared and presented, and reuse earlier configurations as necessary.

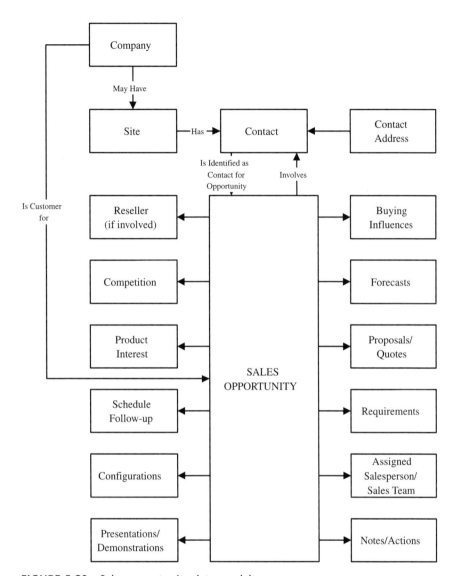

FIGURE 5.20 Sales opportunity data model.

The same goes for product presentations and technical demonstrations. The data model could point to the location of the material actually used so that if any questions come up long after a presentation has been made, there is a record of what was actually presented.

Another key part of the sales opportunity data model is a list of buying influences for that opportunity. These may be additional contacts for this prospect, or other people in the company that are key to closing the sale, or even third parties such as consultants and references that can significantly affect the sale. Associated with this data element are all the actions taken by the sales team to influence the buying influences.

The revenue associated with an opportunity and the time frame for the sale are essential input to your company's sales forecast and planning model. Linked to each opportunity, therefore, you should keep track of all pipeline and forecast information, including changes in the outlook and reasons for the changes.

As the opportunity moves toward a close, the salesperson will be submitting proposals and quotes. These should be tracked just as configurations and presentations are, for the same reasons. Versions of proposals and quotes used earlier in the sales cycle will prove especially useful in the contract negotiations.

As discussed earlier there will be many requirements listed in the RFP, and thereafter, that need to be met to close the sale. A list of current requirements associated with the sales opportunity make up the next key element of the sales opportunity data model.

Obviously there must be a salesperson, and sometimes a sales team, associated with an opportunity. This information identifies who is working on that opportunity, and is used in the preparation of reports, escalations, and notifications.

Finally, there will be many events that happen during the course of a complex sale, and many actions that arise as the salesperson moves the sale along the pipeline toward the close. Associated with each sales opportunity, therefore, you will want to keep track of the history of the opportunity, and the actions that were taken to close the sale. This information will be helpful to you even after the sale closes (or if you do not get the business), because analysis of this information can help you improve your sales processes.

SUMMARY

This chapter discussed in detail the steps that are taken during the sales cycle, and covered some examples of processes and Web pages you can use to implement these steps in your Sales Force Automation system. We took a qualified lead, and by working it through the sales cycle we have come to the point in the sale where we are ready to start closing the sale.

The next chapter will cover the steps and processes involved in actually closing the sale.

Closing
the Sale

6

Up to this point the salesperson has been managing the sales cycle. The salesperson has taken a qualified lead passed on by the marketing organization, verified that it is in fact a qualified lead, and made an initial sales call. A response has been prepared to the prospect's Request for Proposal (RFP), and all questions arising from that RFP have been answered to the customer's satisfaction. More recently, the salesperson has been working with other company personnel (the sales team) to prepare and present detailed information about your products to show how the products will address the prospect's business needs, and may even have shown the prospect product demonstrations and prototypes. All the requirements listed by the customer (and some that were not) have been addressed, and the salesperson has worked with the prospect to develop the configuration for the sale. Many site visits have been made, buying influences identified and sold. Surely this must come to an end.

As the salesperson works the lead through the sales cycle, and as the uncertainties about the sale are resolved, at some point it will be time to close on the sale. The salesperson will need to pull together a formal proposal, complete with the proposed configuration and a price quote. This will undergo some negotiation, and eventually the sale will be either made, or not (see Figure 6.1).

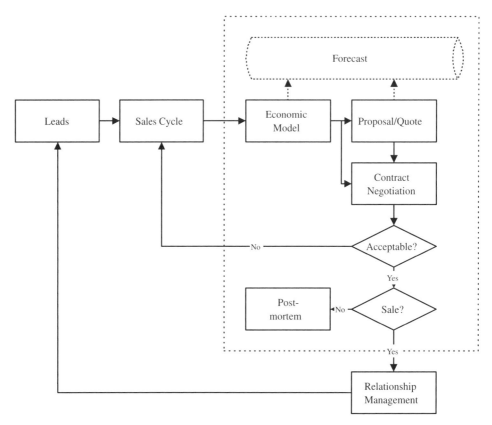

FIGURE 6.1 Closing the sale.

This chapter discusses the steps taken to close the sale, and how a Web-based application can make those steps easier to take.

ECONOMIC MODEL

In many complex sales the primary contact at the purchasing company will need to make a business case for selecting a particular vendor. This may be something that the prospect does only for the benefit of the small team making the selection, or it may be a full presentation to senior executives of the purchasing company. A salesperson can help the prospect in making this business case.

An economic model of the sale is developed by the salesperson as a justification tool to help with closing the sale. The economic model gives the salesperson further leverage by providing a business and financial case to customers in justifying how they will see both benefits and a return on their investments as a result of their purchase with your company.

Your company has specific industry knowledge, and because you compete in particular market segments you have a good understanding of the costs and benefits of your products. The salesperson can draw on this knowledge, as well as specific information from the prospect, and help the prospect develop the business justification for the purchase (see Figure 6.2). These are specific impacts your products will have on the prospect's business operations.

In a complex sale there will have been many sales configurations created and modified, and many requirements stated, retracted, and modified. The final sales configuration that is proposed for the customer will determine the cost side of the economic model. Included in the cost side of the economic model will be the costs of the purchase itself, the costs of implementing the

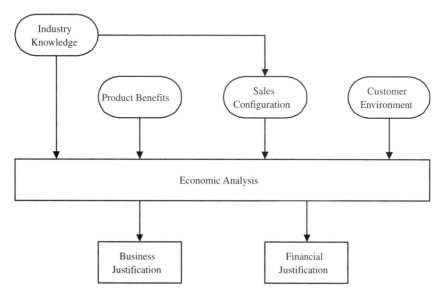

FIGURE 6.2 Economic model.

products, and the costs to the customer of running and operating the products during their life cycle.

The financial benefits side of the economic model will be driven by the current situation at the customer site (as specified in performance metrics), and also the estimated impact on those metrics if your company's products are purchased. The incremental revenues or savings that result from the purchase can then be assessed against the costs, and the salesperson can complete the economic model.

The return on investment on the purchase can be categorized in both business and financial terms. To illustrate this, consider the following scenario with a fictitious prospect, the XYZ Corporation.

Business Justification—XYZ Corporation

Your company makes, sells, and integrates customer support software that a customer can use to automate customer support functions in a company. Your experience in this market has given your company a good understanding of the impact your products can have on customer support business operations, and the salesperson knows how to assess and quantify the impact.

The prospect, XYZ Corporation, currently has 50 customer support representatives (CSRs) on staff, who use a home-grown application to track customer support requests. There is no application available to help the CSRs actually resolve problems; all problem resolution is done manually, and because there is no record of problem resolutions the time to resolve a customer's support request is quite high.

The long time to resolve customer issues has led to significant decreases in customer satisfaction, which has manifested itself in a 30 percent drop in support contract renewal rates. In other words, many customers are now simply not renewing their support contracts because they are dissatisfied with the time it takes to get a response. Since most of XYZ's support revenues come from support renewals, the drop in contract renewals is having a material impact on profitability.

Your company's experience and the salesperson's analysis of XYZ's operations say that by implementing your customer support software, XYZ can reduce the time to resolve a customer support request and expect a productivity increase of 25 percent per CSR. Each CSR can now not only resolve customer support requests quicker, but also handle more support requests. This improved performance in turn is expected to produce an increase in customer satisfaction, and the increase in satisfaction is expected to increase support contract renewals by 20 percent.

As an added benefit, using the automated customer support solution will allow XYZ to design, sell, and provide new support offerings that feature additional levels of service, something it is not currently equipped to offer. XYZ will be able to offer standard and premium plans, with varying service levels that will be tracked closely with the online call tracking system. This again should have a significant impact on support revenues as customers select the exact offerings that best meet their needs.

A template showing the results of a benefits analysis are shown in Figure 6.3. The items listed on that template could

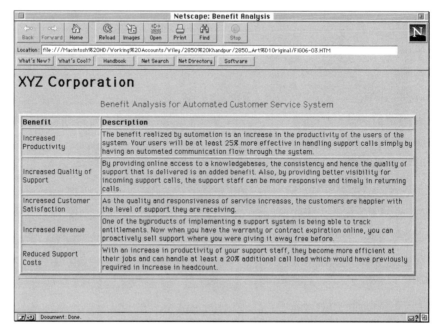

FIGURE 6.3 XYZ Corporation benefits analysis.

have been gathered from a database of specific benefits, stored in the marketing encyclopedia.

Financial Justification—XYZ Corporation

The financial model used to justify the investment in technology is the Return on Investment (ROI) analysis. The ROI model analyzes the current financial situation against the savings the prospect would realize as a result of implementing technology, measured against the investment costs to produce the return on the investment. The financial model is typically projected over a five-year period, with increasing returns by the fifth year of your investment. Figure 6.4 shows a sample ROI analysis for the first eight quarters (two years) after XYZ Corporation's purchase of your customer support software.

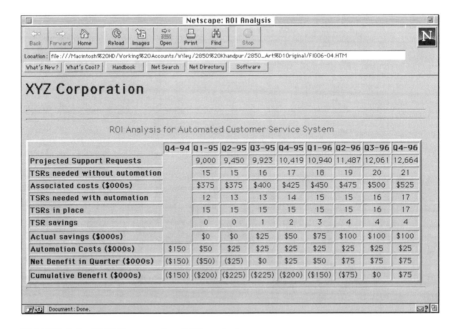

	Q4-94	Q1-95	Q2-95	Q3-95	Q4-95	Q1-96	Q2-96	Q3-96	Q4-96
Projected Support Requests		9,000	9,450	9,923	10,419	10,940	11,487	12,061	12,664
TSRs needed without automation		15	15	16	17	18	19	20	21
Associated costs ($000s)		$375	$375	$400	$425	$450	$475	$500	$525
TSRs needed with automation		12	13	13	14	15	15	16	17
TSRs in place		15	15	15	15	15	15	16	17
TSR savings		0	0	1	2	3	4	4	4
Actual savings ($000s)		$0	$0	$25	$50	$75	$100	$100	$100
Automation Costs ($000s)	$150	$50	$25	$25	$25	$25	$25	$25	$25
Net Benefit in Quarter ($000s)	($150)	($50)	($25)	$0	$25	$50	$75	$75	$75
Cumulative Benefit ($000s)	($150)	($200)	($225)	($225)	($200)	($150)	($75)	$0	$75

FIGURE 6.4 XYZ Corporation ROI analysis.

(From *Delivering World-Class Technical Support* by Navtej (Kay) Khandpur and Lori Laub, published by John Wiley & Sons, Inc., 1997.)

The ROI analysis was prepared using the information that had been previously collected by the salesperson regarding XYZ's current operations, and the market and product information in your marketing encyclopedia. Using the customer's particular metrics, estimates of savings and benefits were translated into monetary amounts and used in the model. In this situation the additional information that was combined with the information in the marketing encyclopedia included:

- Number of support representatives
- Call volume
- Costs per customer support representative
- Call duration

Work Area for Economic Model

The questions to consider when planning to automate your economic modeling function include:

- Do you have industry studies about products in your market segment, including yours?
- Is this information available to your sales force?
- What specific knowledge do you have about the performance of your products in customer situations?
- Do you understand how your products impacted customer performance?
- Is that performance repeatable in other situations?
- Have you developed a causal relationship between product features and customer performance?
- How often do prospects seek assistance in developing an economic model?
- What kinds of assistance do they seek?
- What kinds of information do customers provide about their current operations and performance?
- Do your salespeople use this information?
- What tools do your salespeople use to develop economic models?

PROPOSAL AND QUOTE

After configuring a sale and working through an economic model, the salesperson will need to put together a formal proposal and a quote for the proposed sale. This should be relatively easy, since all the information necessary to prepare the proposal and quote has already been created in earlier steps during the sales cycle, and is available to the salesperson over the corporate intranet. The information that will be used to prepare the proposal and quote includes:

- Sales configuration
- Product availability
- Shipment schedule
- Current pricing
- Discount schedule
- Tax schedules
- Payment terms

Figure 6.5 shows an example of a template for an online quote, which can be converted to an order once the customer has final financial approval.

Doing all the paperwork to pull together the proposal can be very time-consuming, because the elements of the proposal are often in different places. A sales automation tool that can reduce this time can dramatically improve the salesperson's productivity. As discussed in Chapter 3, proposals and quotes can be based on standard templates, and can automatically include much of the work done during product configuration and economic modeling. Some of the information in a proposal may be kept in the marketing encyclopedia, or another repository on the intranet.

Proposal generators and quoting tools are often tied closely to the sales configuration tool. In fact, many sales configurators provide the capability to create not only sales configurations, but also quotes. Many also provide a feature to export the sales configuration in a format that can be used by a word processing package. Preparing the proposal then becomes a cut-and-paste exercise, with some minor editing.

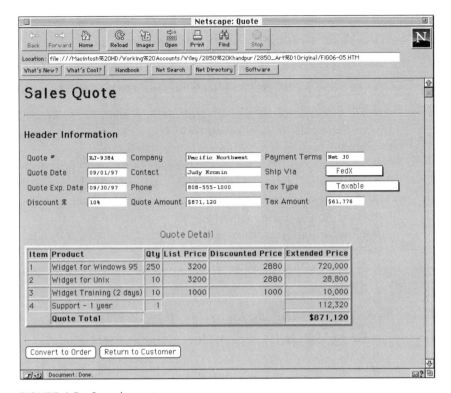

FIGURE 6.5 Sample quote.

In many companies all proposals and quotes have to be reviewed by a sales manager before they can be presented to a prospect. The purpose of the review is to verify the accuracy and completeness of the information in the proposal or quote. In some companies this is a necessary step (for reasons ranging from product complexity to untrained salespeople); in other companies this step introduces a delay that can make the difference between a win and a loss. We recommend that you analyze the value gained in the proposal and quote review, and suggest there may be ways to achieve accuracy and completeness in sales proposals and quotes without subjecting each proposal or quote to an extensive review process.

Work Area for Proposal and Quote

Some questions that may come up when planning to automate your proposal and quoting function include:

- How much of a typical proposal is standard and can be made available as a template?
- How much is available in template form?
- Is it easy to find, access, and use templates for proposals?
- Is there consistency in the style and format of the proposals?
- How do salespeople convert sales configurations into quotes?
- How do they incorporate quotes into a proposal?
- How much time does a salesperson spend on preparing a proposal?
- How much time does a salesperson spend on preparing a quote?
- Do salespeople have the ability to reuse proposals and quotes prepared earlier?
- Do proposals have to undergo an approval process?
- Why?
- How long does it take to approve a proposal?
- What are the bottlenecks?
- How often is a proposal rejected or not approved?
- If proposals were to be based on preapproved standard templates would they still need to be approved?

CONTRACT NEGOTIATION

Once the proposal has been presented to the prospect there will in all likelihood be some contract negotiation. The prospect may ask for some changes, and the salesperson may have to develop a new proposal, quote, or configuration. At this point it is helpful to have access to the sales configuration tool, and use it in developing the new proposal and quote. In some extreme situations, contract negotiations may break down and the sale put back to a point earlier in the sales cycle for more work. This sequence of events continues until a sale is either made, or not.

In addition to the proposal and the quote, the key elements in the contract should include:

- Support renewal agreement
- Consulting contract and agreement
- Licensing agreement

Your corporate attorneys will designate areas of your contracts that are negotiable. It is good practice to build up an encyclopedia of contracts in your SFA system for several reasons. First, this is a good reference for new sales to see how a particular negotiable section has been reworded for other customers. Second, any additional sales to this customer may need to follow any discount schedules outlined in the original contract. For example, XYZ Corporation may have negotiated in an earlier sale a 20 percent discount on all products for an indefinite period of time. This information should be easily accessible to your sales personnel and the quoting tool when preparing a quote for any future product purchases by XYZ Corporation.

Figure 6.6 shows an example of some information that could be accessed from a customer record.

One click from the main customer record will bring up this window, which lists all supporting documentation associated with an order. By clicking on the hyperlink for each of these documents, the document will be opened as an HTML page for your viewing. The download and upload buttons allow you to bring a copy of the document to your local PC, modify and upgrade the revision number, then upload back to the encyclopedia as a revised version associated with an additional order.

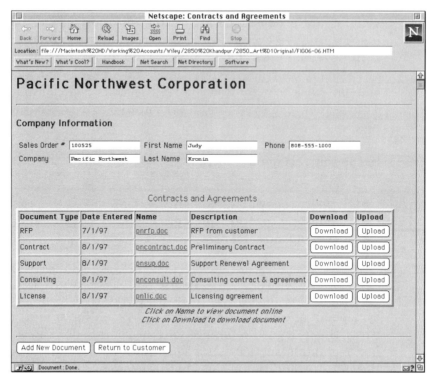

FIGURE 6.6 Customer contracts and agreements.

Work Area for Contract Negotiation

The questions to consider when planning to automate the contract negotiation function include:

■ How long does a typical contract negotiation take?
■ How many revision cycles does a typical contract undergo?
■ How many of those cycles could be eliminated if the salesperson had access to preapproved contract sections?
■ How much of a salesperson's time is taken up by the negotiation process?
■ How can this be reduced?

FORECASTING

As mentioned earlier, the uncertainties about the sale are resolved as the sale moves through the sales cycle, and a salesperson begins to gain confidence about the likelihood of a sale. In other words, the salesperson's estimate of the probability of the sale actually happening increases the further along the cycle the sale is. At some point sales managers start including some or all of the potential revenues from a sale in the revenue forecast for the sales organization. The point at which a sale gets included in a forecast and the actual methodology used in the forecast varies from company to company, but the basic task is done in almost all sales organizations.

The key requirement for a good forecast is accurate and up-to-date information. A good forecast will be based on the configuration being proposed to the prospect, pricing and discounting schedules, delivery schedule, payment terms, and confidence the salesperson and the sales manager have in the likelihood of the sale (see Figure 6.7). A sales automation tool should provide the ability for all of these inputs to be considered in a timely manner when developing a forecast. For example, in Figure 5.6 we showed a template that a salesperson would use to record information

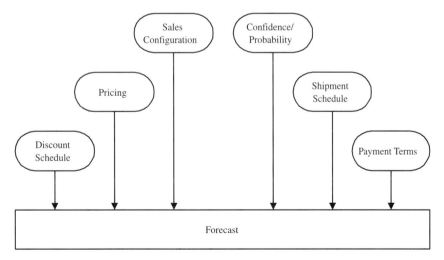

FIGURE 6.7 Inputs to forecasting system.

about an opportunity. Included in that template were places for the salesperson to enter the salesperson's estimates of the confidence in the sale, and the probability of it occurring. That information could be reviewed by a sales manager, and modified by the salesperson or the sales manager, as warranted.

Work Area for Forecasting

Some questions to consider when planning to automate the forecasting function include:

- How is forecasting done today?
- How reliable are the forecasts produced by your forecasting system?
- What needs to be done to improve the forecasts?
- What additional sources of information should be considered when developing the forecast?
- Can the forecast be generated from information routinely collected by the salesperson?

CLOSING

How do you know when the deal is finally closed? Each company recognizes deals with varying levels of documentation from the customer. What constitutes a close for one company may be very different for another company. The nature of your business and your business practices dictate how much information is required to close the sale. The following items are the most complete representation of a close, but you may decide that a signed contract is simply enough to declare the deal a sale:

- Signed contract
- Purchase order
- Letter of intent
- Credit approval (D&B rating)
- Credit card or check for initial payment

If your sales typically involve financing, you may wish to provide the associated credit applications on your Web page for the customer to download easily and quickly. The form could then be sent back by electronic mail or fax to your company, thereby reducing the total time involved in processing the transaction. You should also have available to you the credit data collected during the lead qualification process.

In addition to securing the order, the actual close of the sale also involves setting the expectations for the customer for product delivery. This may have been specified in earlier proposals and quotes, and perhaps in the sales contract itself. Figure 6.8 shows a new order that has been converted from the previous quote. On the order screen, you can have access to finished goods inventory levels, as seen by the Product Availability button on this window.

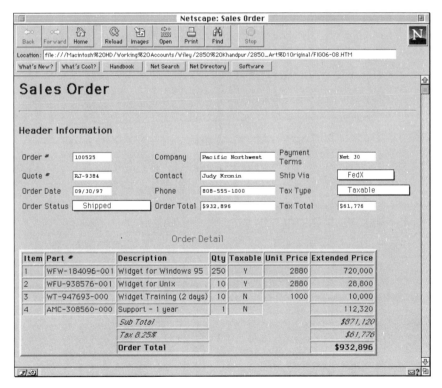

FIGURE 6.8 Sales order.

If your SFA system has online access to product availability, as shown in Figure 6.9, you can allocate this inventory to your customer, which reserves it from being taken out of inventory for anyone else. In this case the SFA application is interacting with the application used by your logistics organization.

This screen allows you to designate the order number with which to associate this inventory. You should have the option of choosing the physical location from which to pull this inventory. For example, if your customer is on the east coast, you may wish to allocate inventory from the east coast warehouse or fulfillment center so that the shipment will arrive in a timely manner. If, however, the east coast locations are out of inventory, you can check which other locations in the country cur-

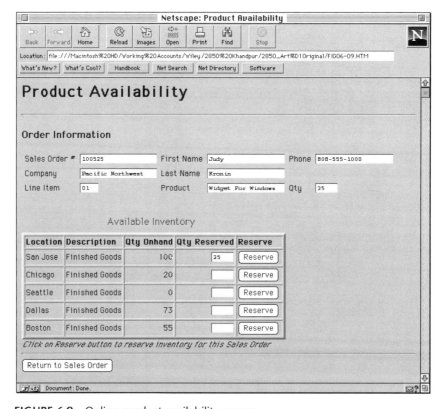

FIGURE 6.9 Online product availability screen.

rently have the product in stock, and choose to allocate that inventory.

If you are selling a software product, the best form of distribution may be to provide online access to the software via your Web page. Your customer could download the latest release of the software, and with a numeric *key* obtained by customer service can turn the limited-use version of the software into the fully functioning product.

Once the order is complete, the order information is used as input to your financial bookings reports. These reports will be used by different members of your management team for different reasons, including revenue recognition, product revenue allocations, and the calculations of sales commissions. Figure 6.10 shows an example of a bookings report.

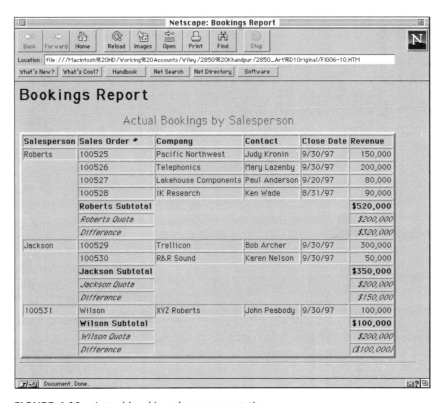

FIGURE 6.10 Actual bookings by representative.

This same data can be formatted into any of the following reports:

- Actual bookings by region
- Actual bookings by representative
- Actual bookings by product family and line
- Actual bookings by platform

This report can be used by sales managers and VPs to determine the bookings for a particular month and quarter, strictly in financial terms. A product manager, however, may use this report to determine which products are selling, and trace the sale back to the marketing source to see which campaigns are the most effective.

Work Area for Closing

Some questions that may come up when planning to automate the close process include:

- What are the criteria that determine when a sale is closed?
- Who is responsible for declaring a sale closed?
- What are the data elements that must be present to make the close?
- What happens after the close?

POSTMORTEM

There is always the possibility that a sales effort will not result in a sale. The salesperson may lose the sale to a competitor, or the prospect's financial or business situation changes and the sale is no longer feasible or necessary. Whatever the reason, it is important for salespeople and sales managers to follow up on each lost sale, and try to identify why the sale was not won. This analysis should result in good information that can be used to prevent future sales losses. For example, if the prospect's business environment changed during the sales cycle, perhaps your lead qualification process could have done a better job in qualifying the prospect, or the salesperson could have been more observant during sales calls and spotted the telltale signs of a changing business climate.

The value of a Sales Force Automation system in conducting a postmortem is that the system can provide a detailed account of all the activities that went into the sales effort. This information can help identify what needs to be done differently in the future.

Figure 6.11 shows some information that you could track for opportunities in which you competed but did not win.

In some companies a postmortem is conducted for all sales, the wins and the losses. While the reason for examining the

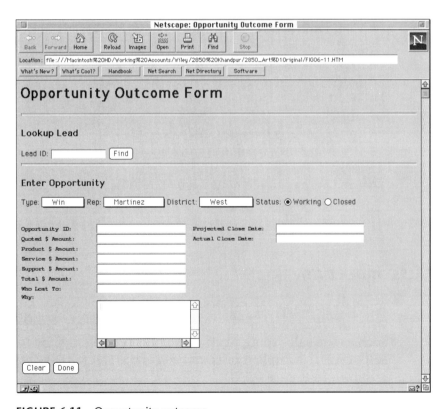

FIGURE 6.11 Opportunity outcome.

losses is obvious, you may also learn a lot about your sales processes by examining the wins. For example, you could find out the key factors that led to the win, and try to replicate those factors in other sales cycles. The data in your sales automation database for both wins and losses can be a very valuable training tool.

Work Area for Postmortem

Questions to consider when planning for a postmortem include:

- Were all commitments made to the customer met on time and completely?
- What key factors led to the outcome of the sale?
- Were any of these factors a surprise?
- Could and should these factors have been identified earlier in the sales cycle?
- Was the sale a good fit for the customer?
- Is the customer satisfied with the outcome?
- What is the customer feedback on the outcome of the sales process?
- Are there any changes indicated in your sales processes?
- Are there any changes indicated in your sales methodologies?
- Are there data elements you should be capturing that you are not currently capturing?

SALES ORDER DATA MODEL

As discussed earlier there are many data elements associated with an order once the deal has been finalized. Much of the data, such as the sales configuration, is collected before and during the sales cycle. A sample representation of the sales order data model is shown in Figure 6.12.

This data model shows that starting with a sales order we can navigate our way into many of the data elements described

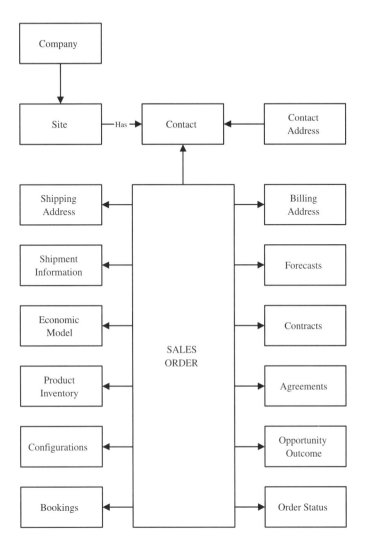

FIGURE 6.12 Sales order data model.

in earlier chapters. For example, the information about the contact would have been collected during the leads process. The site and shipping addresses may be collected during the sales cycle. The link to product inventory is established when the salesperson reserves inventory. Shipment information is usually specified when the order is filled out by the salesperson.

There may be additional data elements associated with a sales order in your company; the preceding example illustrates the fact that data collected at all points in the sales process is used many times in other points in the process.

SUMMARY

This chapter covered the different steps involved in moving from the sales cycle to actually closing the sale. We explained how a salesperson could create an economic model using a Web-based tool, and then discussed the preparation of a formal proposal and quote; and showed how input from the sales configuration tool, coupled with preapproved proposal templates, could be used to pull together a proposal. Finally we covered the work that goes on in negotiating the contract, and closing the sale. We also discussed how you could use the Web to record the reasons for the outcome of the sales cycle.

The next chapter will cover the next set of actions a salesperson must perform to make the new customer a source of a future revenue stream by closely managing the customer relationship.

Managing the Customer Relationship

7

All the hard work during the sales cycle has finally paid off. Your products and services meet requirements, the competition has been held at bay, negotiations are complete, both parties are in agreement, and the sales contract has been signed. You have a new customer! Congratulations!

Given the effort your salesperson, indeed the entire sales organization and company, put into making the sale, it is extremely important that the salesperson follow through on the sale and wrap up all the little details that come up in any complex sale. The salesperson must ensure that the order is processed and shipped to the customer, and installation and consulting services delivered. The salesperson then must manage the account and follow through on new sales opportunities with this customer (see Figure 7.1).

Making the sale by no means marks the end of the sales cycle. It marks the beginning of the relationship between your company and the customer, and if managed well, this relationship will be the source of much revenue and profit in the future. This chapter will cover the activities involved in managing the customer relationship after the sale has been made.

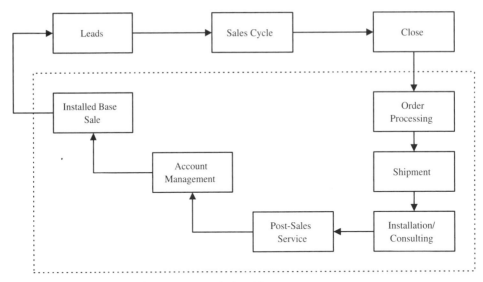

FIGURE 7.1 Managing the customer relationship.

ORDER PROCESSING

The first step is to convert the signed contract into an order that can be processed by your sales operations personnel. This order must contain all the line items necessary to ensure that the contracted-for goods and services are listed so that your company personnel know what must be delivered to the customer. The order should also contain stock numbers and pricing information, information on the discounts that have been applied by line item or on the total amount, as well as tax schedules and payment terms. The order should also contain the agreed-to shipment dates and delivery locations. An example of a screen that shows such an order was given in Figure 6.8 in the last chapter. Figure 7.2 shows an example of the detailed shipping information related to that order.

Order processing systems are often not a part of a Sales Force Automation system; however, in well-designed SFA system, the sales configuration system would feed into the quoting and proposal generation tools, which in turn would feed into a separate order processing system (see Figure 7.3). The order pro-

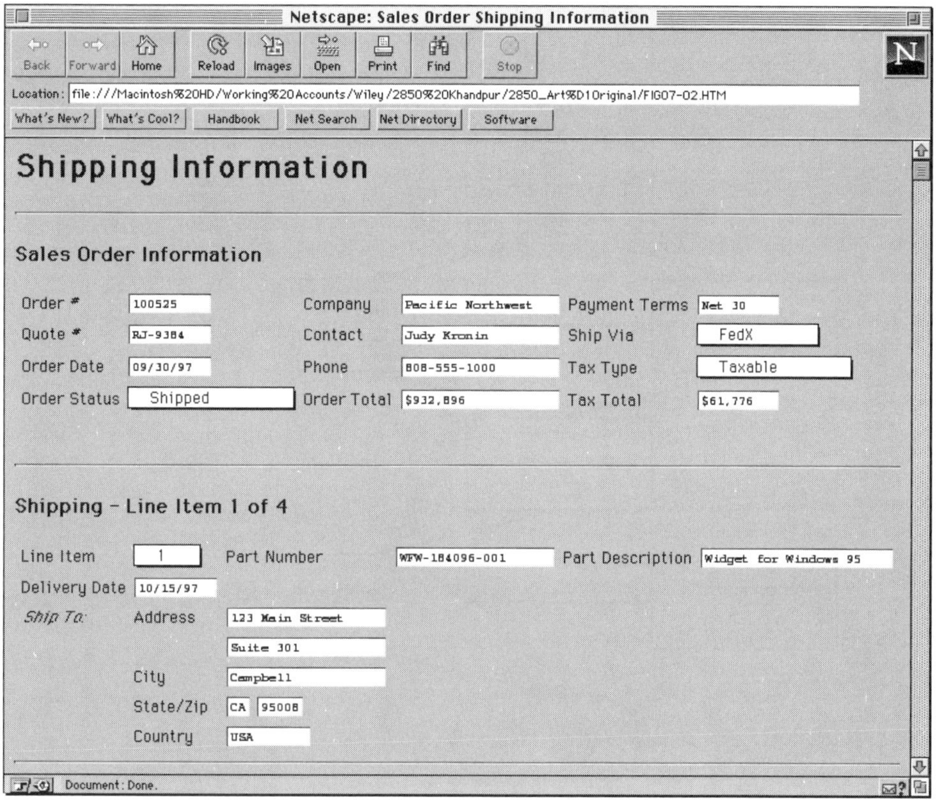

FIGURE 7.2 Sample order form.

cessing system in turn creates work orders for the manufacturing and logistics organizations in your company.

Many commercially available order processing systems are integrated with so-called *back-office* applications (discussed later in this chapter), but they provide an Application Programming Interface that you can use to feed the system data from another application. So, for example, the sample screen shown in the previous figure can be used to verify the complete order, and then sent to the order processing application when everything on the order appears to be correct.

A Web-based system can also be used to track subcontracted orders, or orders that will be fulfilled by other vendors who are

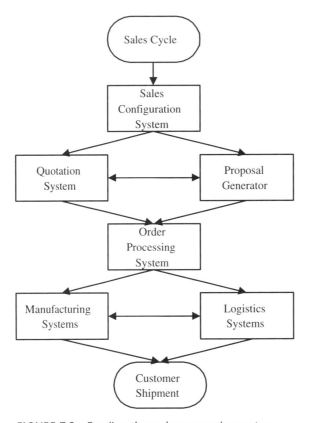

FIGURE 7.3   Feeding the order processing system.

your partners. For example, in a large and complex sale your organization may be the primary bidder on the sale, and have subcontracted with some of your partners to deliver additional products and services. Rather than have the customer negotiate and manage parts of the sale with the other vendors, your salesperson is the primary point of contact for the customer, and all subcontracted work flows through your organization. In this case, when the salesperson reaches an agreement with the customer on the terms of the sale, and an order is created in your order processing system, the salesperson must also have a means of sending work orders to the partners. This may be accomplished through the order processing system, as shown in Figure 7.3, which may result in a purchase order being generated and sent to the partner. Or you may have a separate screen in your sales automation tool to manage the work to be done by previously approved partners. On this screen you can specify what work is to be done by the partner, and when complete send the order to the partner by electronic mail. Alternatively you could give your trusted partners to the sales automation tool over an extranet, and issue an alert to the partner when the partner's attention is needed. An example of such a screen is shown in Figure 7.4.

Getting all the details right on an order is essential. What gets put into the order form is what will determine not only what is shipped to the customer, and how much the customer is charged, but also the salesperson's commission. To ensure satisfaction all around, your SFA system should be designed in such a way that there is little or no rekeying of data entered somewhere else in the system.

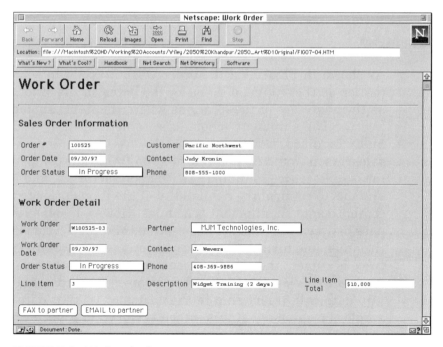

FIGURE 7.4 Work order for partner.

Work Area for Order Processing

Some things to consider when automating the link between your Sales Force Automation system and the company's order processing system are:

- How are orders currently entered?
- How much integration is there between the tools used by the salespeople, and the order processing system?
- How much data is manually rekeyed to create an order from a sales configuration, proposal, or quote?
- What is the error rate on orders?
- Have you lost customers as a result of mistakes in order processing?
- How many times do you have to hand off orders or subcontracts to partners?
- How is this done today?

SHIPMENT

As shown in Figure 7.2 the order will also contain some information on the shipment dates for the items on the order, as well as the addresses of the locations where the items should be delivered. The shipment schedule is something that would normally be discussed during the contract negotiations, and the salesperson would rely on information from your company's Enterprise Resource Planning (ERP), manufacturing, and logistics systems to confirm the availability of the items prior to making commitments on shipment schedules. However, some time may pass between the contract negotiations and the actual signing of the order, and further delay may occur between the time the contract is signed and the order entered. The salesperson should therefore check to see that items promised for shipment by a certain date will in fact ship to the customer by that date. An example of a shipment status screen is shown in Figure 7.5.

Notice that some items on the order may be fulfilled by your partners; as before, this can be implemented by having your partner notify the salesperson when an item has been shipped,

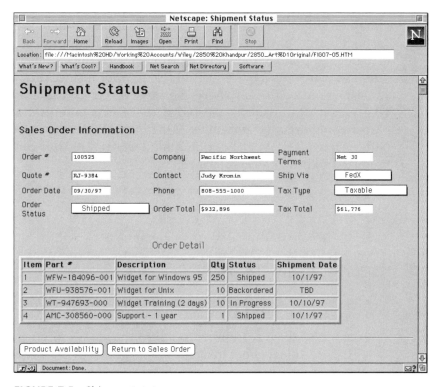

FIGURE 7.5 Shipment status screen.

and having the salesperson (or someone on the sales operations staff) update the shipment status. A better way would be to have an electronic mail interface so that a shipment status message from the partner could automatically update the status. The best way, of course, would be to give the partner access to the shipment status database, and have the partner's systems linked to yours so that the update can be made transparently with no manual intervention.

Your salespeople should be aware of the status of all shipments made or planned to all their customers. While this may sound like an administrative burden, it can be implemented very simply so that it takes very little of the salesperson's time. For example, one way to implement this would be to have the starting assumption be that all shipments will be made as scheduled on the original order. You could then write a small program to periodically compare the scheduled shipment date with the planned shipment date. If the planned shipment date is after the scheduled date, then the salesperson could be notified by electronic mail that there will be a problem with the shipment schedule, so the salesperson could take appropriate action. The salesperson would not therefore have to check the status on a daily basis, but will be alerted if there is a potential problem. Most commercially available Sales Force Automation solutions offer some kind of notification and alert system that can be customized to provide this feature.

Work Area for Shipment

Some things to consider when considering the link between your Sales Force Automation tools and the company's shipping and logistics systems are:

- Is the current shipment status of orders available to the sales force?
- Is it easy for a salesperson to find the status of an order?
- How do salespeople find out about parts of orders fulfilled by partners?
- Is there a way for a salesperson to be notified if an order is delayed?
- What kind of notification scheme is necessary?

BOOK REVENUES

This is probably the most gratifying part of the sales cycle, when the revenues from the sale are actually recognized by your company. We have shown this step to occur when the sales configuration is shipped to the customer. However, in practice the revenues may be booked at some other point in the sales cycle, depending on the revenue recognition and accounting policies in your company. For example, while many companies may recognize revenues when the sales items ship, other companies may be able to recognize revenues when the contract is signed (for example, if there is nothing to ship, such as a software support and maintenance contract), other companies may not recognize revenues until the order items are received by the customer, and yet others may not recognize revenues until the order items are installed and formally accepted by the customer. Clearly the later in the sales cycle that the revenue is recognized, the greater interest the salesperson has in getting to the revenue recognition point.

INSTALLATION/CONSULTING

Sales of complex products often require the vendor (or a partner) to provide some assistance with the installation of the product, and sometimes some additional consulting services to use the product in the customer's application. The salesperson has an interest in ensuring that the installation goes well, and that the consulting services are delivered as contracted.

For example, if you were to purchase an enterprise Sales Force Automation tool, the vendor of the tool would take great interest in ensuring that the tool was installed properly so that you could use it. As discussed in earlier chapters, all the elements that go into Sales Force Automation make its implementation and deployment a large undertaking. Merely having an installed product on their system may not be enough for your Information Technology organization to actually deploy it to your sales force. Few, if any, enterprise systems can be used without some customization. Your IT organization will in all likelihood need some assistance with understanding the sales automation product, the underlying assumptions, the technical requirements, and the customization methods. At a minimum this may require some classroom training; on the other extreme, the IT organization may outsource the implementation and deployment, and have either the vendor, a partner of the vendor, or a third party do all the work. If these additional services are part of the contract, then the vendor's salesperson will ensure that the work is done.

If your company makes complex products, your sales force will often rely on technical staff to install the product, and otherwise help the customer with technical issues. The nature, context, and content of every contact the technical staff has with the customer should be captured in your sales automation system so that it is available for review by the salesperson.

A sample checklist for installation activities for a complex hardware product is shown in Table 7.1.

In Table 7.1 two field personnel are responsible for installing the hardware and handing it over to the customer. As each task is completed, the field engineer can use a screen to update the status in the sales automation system, and record some special notes. An example of such a screen is given in Figure 7.6.

As with shipments, scheduled tasks should be monitored by the salesperson so that any potential problems can be addressed proactively before they affect the customers. Any delays in the schedule, such as the slip in installing the cable in Table 7.1 and Figure 7.6, can be brought to the attention of the salesperson. Not only can the salesperson follow the status of the installation, but the salesperson also knows that an additional cable should have been ordered but was not. This means that either the salesperson made a mistake, or the customer did not provide complete information during the sales process. Whatever the reason, the salesperson now knows that this particular configuration of products may have a problem with cabling, something the salesperson can address in the future with another prospect. If this was in fact a configuration problem, the installation report could be sent to the person responsible for maintaining the sales configuration tool so that the tool can be updated for future use.

TABLE 7.1   Checklist for Product Installation

Item	Task	Owner	Planned Completion Date	Status
1	Prepare room environment	B. Fallin	01SEP97	DONE 01SEP97
2	Install cabling	B. Fallin	04SEP97	DONE 05SEP97
3	Check boxes for damage	B. Fallin	09SEP97	09SEP97
4	Open boxes and remove equipment	B. Fallin	09SEP97	09SEP97
5	Run unit tests	B. Fallin	10SEP97	10SEP97
6	Integrate and run system tests	B. Fallin	12SEP97	12SEP97
7	Install software	J. Elwell	13SEP97	14SEP97
8	Run software diagnostics	J. Elwell	15SEP97	15SEP97
9	Hand over to customer	B. Fallin	17SEP97	17SEP97

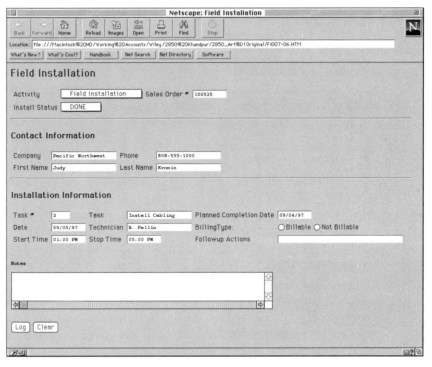

FIGURE 7.6 Field installation report.

Work Area for Installation/Consulting

Some questions to consider when tracking progress in installation and consulting are:

- What is the process by which your products are installed?
- Do personnel from your company get involved in installation and consulting?
- How are their activities initiated, coordinated, tracked, and managed?
- Is installation information and status available to a salesperson?
- What kind of quality review is done after the installation to assess the completeness and accuracy of the sales configuration?

POST-SALES SERVICE

Once the sale has been made and the customer is using your company's products, there will no doubt be some ongoing interactions between the customer's staff and personnel in different parts of your company. These ongoing interactions will generally fall into the following three categories:

- Customer support
- Training and consulting
- Customer service

Customer support interactions are those that are about product-related issues, that is, issues the customer is experiencing that are directly related to the products that the customer has purchased. Depending on the nature of your products, these interactions may be fairly mundane or extremely complex. For example, if your company sells office furniture, your customers may call to inquire about technical specifications that are not covered in the product documentation, or about using the furniture in nonstandard configurations. On the other hand, if your company sells internetworking hardware and software, your customers may have detailed questions about using your products in a particular environment, or about what appears to be a defect when the products are used in a particularly complex configuration. In general, customer support issues tend to fall into four categories:

1. Questions about usage, installation, and configuration
2. Reports of suspected defects in your products
3. Requests for new features in your products
4. Requests for assistance in using your products to solve a particular problem

Customer support interactions tend to be recorded in so-called *problem-tracking* applications, but the data can be made available to anyone in the company.

Training and consulting interactions are, as their name would imply, those interactions that come up during formal or informal training classes, or during consulting assignments. At a minimum a salesperson should have access to the company's training database to see which customer personnel have been trained, and which ones are still waiting for training. This information can be used to sell additional training services to the customer. Consulting interactions should also be recorded, and an effective salesperson will review notes of each consultant's interactions with the customer. This information can prove very valuable in identifying new product and service revenue opportunities. For example, a consultant may notice while at a customer site that the site is being visited by senior executives from another division of the customer's company, and that these visitors are thinking about purchasing your company's products. This other division may not yet have contacted your company, but the consultant can record what was observed, and the salesperson can review that observation. This in turn may result in another sale.

Customer service interactions are those interactions between the customer and your company that do not fall into the preceding categories. For the most part these interactions are initiated by customers who want to track down someone or something. For example, a customer may want to know when an order will be shipped. Another customer may want to know the next conference at which your company will be presenting. In many companies there is a separate customer service organization that handles customer service issues, though a customer service interaction may also be between a customer and the salesperson.

Whatever the nature of the interaction, your sales automation system should have a way of incorporating information about these interactions so that the salesperson (and sales management) has total visibility into what has transpired between the customer and the company. Figure 7.7 shows a form that can be used to record such customer interactions.

Your company may have separate systems for tracking the different types of interaction. The Customer Support Organization may have a specialized problem tracking application, the Training Group may have a home-grown registration and class management database, and the Customer Service Department may use the same sales automation tool as the salesperson. Your

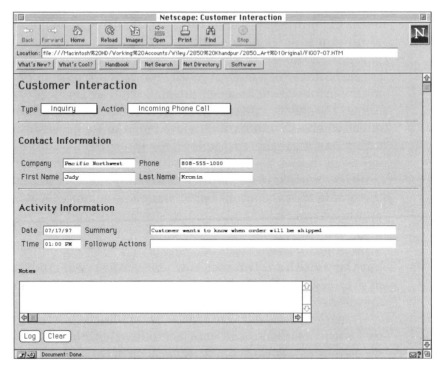

FIGURE 7.7 Customer interaction form.

sales automation tool should be designed so that a salesperson can see all the interactions with the customer.

Work Area for Post-Sales Service

Some things to consider when automating the links between your Sales Force Automation system and the company's other customer-related systems are:

- How much information is shared between organizations?
- How much information is shared between systems?
- How do the support and service organizations find out about new customers?
- Are salespeople aware of all customer interactions?

ACCOUNT MANAGEMENT

Ongoing management of customer accounts is an essential component of any salesperson's job. The relationship between the customer and your company is an important one, and like any other relationship it takes management and proactive actions to make it successful and beneficial to both parties. As discussed in Chapter 1, customer satisfaction is a contributor to customer loyalty, and customer loyalty is in turn a contributor to profitability. The assigned salesperson is usually the focal point for the customer; in some companies a *relationship manager* may be designated to manage the account. No matter who actually manages the account, the primary activities performed by the account manager fall into two categories:

- Reactive
- Proactive

Reactive activities are those that happen after an event has caused a disruption to the normal flow of activities, and require the intervention of the account manager to make things right. Account management in these situations may mean that the salesperson has to handle customer complaints and escalations about specific issues. For example, a customer may voice concern about the delay in receiving a promised bug fix to a software problem, or the shipment of a product upgrade has been delayed and is significantly affecting the customer's business. In these situations, the customer is interested primarily in having the underlying issue addressed by your company; and the salesperson, being the primary relationship manager, may have to coordinate actions within the company to resolve the customer issue. In our examples, this may mean that the salesperson has to have a conversation with the manager of the development team responsible for creating the bug fix, or follow up with the logistics organization to see what needs to be done to have the product upgrade shipped. Good account management in these cases would require the salesperson to first address the immediate issue, and then follow up with the customer and internal organizations after the fact to understand why the issue came up and what could be done to prevent such a situation in the future.

Proactive activities are those that the salesperson undertakes on a regular basis to prevent the need for reactive activities, and so ensure customer satisfaction. Account management in these situations may mean that the salesperson has regular account status meetings with key customer personnel to go over all interactions the customer has had with your company since the last meeting, and to review the status of all actions arising from that meeting. Through these meetings the salesperson can understand how your company's products are performing at the customer's site, what changes to the products the customer may want to see, what future uses the customer may have for the products already purchased, and, most importantly, what future plans the customer has that may be an opportunity for additional sales. The salesperson can assess the customer's satisfaction level, and if there is any potential for dissatisfaction the salesperson can address issues before they require reactive account management. In the preceding examples a good account manager would have known that the bug fix was late, and that the product upgrade had not been sent to the customer. In the first situation the salesperson could have found out about the delay and contacted the development team to find out the status of the bug fix, and either escalated the priority of the bug fix, or prepared the customer to expect a delay. In the second situation, the salesperson could have checked with the logistics organization, and given the customer a new shipment schedule. Customers by and large realize that unforeseen circumstances can make it difficult to meet all commitments, and appreciate it when they are given advance information of any changes so that they can adjust their own plans and schedules.

An example of discussion points for an account management meeting is shown in Table 7.2.

Preparation for an account management meeting may be preceded by an account team meeting, in which the salesperson reviews the current account status with representatives from the customer support, training and consulting, and customer service organizations of your company. The data required for this meeting can be generated from the sales automation application data-

TABLE 7.2 Account Management Meeting Discussion Points

General	Review current environment
	Gauge customer satisfaction
	Discuss customer-raised issues
Update	Review key customer interactions since last meeting
	Review all open action items
	Review changes in customer organization
	Identify new action items
Future	Discuss planned changes in existing environment
	Discuss new applications/opportunities
	Present new product information to customer

bases, and from the databases of the applications used in the other organizations.

Notes from the account management meeting will typically be logged by the salesperson into the sales automation system, using a screen similar to that shown in Figure 5.5.

Work Area for Account Management

Some things to consider when improving account management are:

- Who is responsible for managing the relationship with the customer?
- What account management activities do your salespeople currently perform?
- How frequently do salespeople talk to current customers if there is no sale pending?
- Do salespeople get involved in customer escalations?
- If so, how are they notified?
- What actions do they take?

INSTALLED BASE SALE

Frequent contact with the customer and good account management should give the salesperson visibility into opportunities for both incremental sales to enhance what the customer has already purchased, and new sales for new applications.

Incremental sales require very little additional selling effort. The customer at this point is already familiar with the products, and knows how they work and how they can be used. There is usually no need for many of the activities that are normally done during the sales cycle, such as product demonstrations and requirements specifications. There may be some work to be done in configuring the new sales order to ensure that the items ordered are compatible with the existing configuration, and a need to quote the customer a price. With the right tools this is an easy exercise for the salesperson. In fact many companies provide Web-based tools that enable existing customer to configure and purchase existing products, with no intervention from the salesperson. These so-called *interactive selling systems (ISS)* provide a sales configurator with a quoting system. Customers set up purchase accounts with the company, which allow selected customer personnel to access the ISS to configure and purchase any additional products they want. Orders are confirmed with the customer, and upon approval by the customer are processed and sent to the logistics organization for fulfillment. Upon shipment a notification is sent to internal accounting systems, and an invoice sent to the customer; or the customer's account is billed for the amount of the purchase. Since there is little or no manual intervention, selling costs are low and companies that provide an ISS to customers often offer products at a discount.

In addition to enhancing what has been purchased, satisfied customers may want to purchase additional products for use in new applications, or refer the salesperson to other parts of the customer's company that may benefit from the products. As you may imagine, selling costs for new sales for new applications to an existing customer are also often lower than selling into new accounts. There is generally no need for exhaustive lead qualification, as much of the information about the customer is already available as a result of the existing relationship. The sales cycle itself may require fewer steps. For example, selling to an existing customer may not require any identification of and relationship building with the buying influences (though there may be some work here if the prospect is another division of the customer's company). The initial sales call may be a part of a regularly scheduled account management meeting, as may product presentations and technical demonstrations. Site visits by the salesperson for the new sale may be combined with other visits that salesperson has to make to this customer, thereby saving some of the salesperson's time. The customer's credit background and history is already on record, so there is no need to spend time and money going over that again. As with account management, preparing for and closing a sale into an existing customer account requires the salesperson to have access to all customer interactions.

Work Area for Installed Base Sale

Some things to consider when looking at installed base sales are:

- How much of your business is from current customers?
- How many customers are you losing?
- Why?
- Is it easier for current customers to do business with you than new customers?
- Do the customers share your opinion on the last question?
- Where in the sales cycle does repeat business come in?
- Is the sales cycle for repeat business much shorter than the sales cycle for new business?
- Are your customers willing and able to use technologies to make their own purchases without the intervention of a salesperson?
- What would you need to change in your organization to make that happen?

SALES FORCE AUTOMATION IN THE ENTERPRISE

Many of the preceding sections have mentioned the need for your Sales Force Automation system to use information from, and provide information to, other applications in your company. One way to do this is to develop programmatic interfaces between the different applications used in your company, using so-called *Application Programming Interfaces (APIs)*. The advantage of this approach is that key data elements in an application can be used by other applications that need them. However, a major challenge in this approach is the complexity and cost of creating and maintaining all the interfaces. This problem is particularly severe when applications in different parts of the company were developed at different times, and there is little consistency in how the data elements are defined or used. As a simple example, consider how difficult it would be to interconnect a sales force tool with a customer support problem tracking system if the way the sales organization defines a customer is different from the way the support organization defines a customer. The sales organization's systems may define a customer as a corporate entity, and within the entity there may be multiple sites, and each site in turn may have a key contact. The customer support organization, on the other hand, may define a customer to be anyone who uses your company's products and has paid to receive support services from the customer support organization. Clearly it would be a huge task for a salesperson to identify which support customers are part of the sales customer, let alone identify all the support interactions with that customer.

For this reason many sales automation systems are nowadays part of a suite of enterprise applications, all of which use the same definitions and standards for all the data elements. A customer no longer belongs to the sales organization, or to the customer support organization. Rather, the customer belongs to the whole enterprise, and all references to the customer are consistent across all the applications in the enterprise suite. This concept allows your organization to utilize the customer data in each application, and more effectively manage the relationship with the customer. An example of an enterprisewide application suite is shown in Figure 7.8.

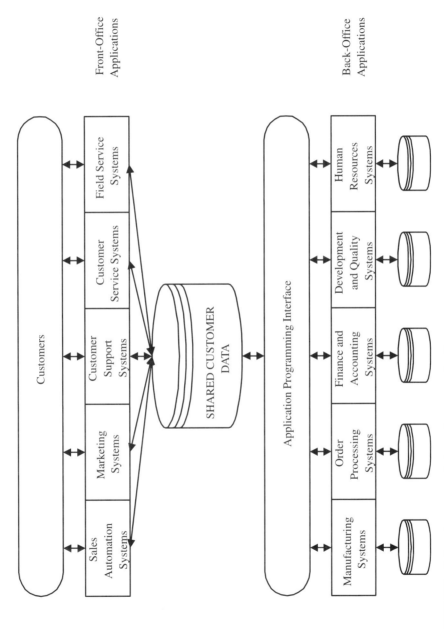

FIGURE 7.8 Enterprise approach to customer applications.

The model in Figure 7.8 shows the so-called *front-office* applications (which are used for customer interactions) all work off the same customer data, so any one application can see data that has been updated by another. The so-called *back-office* applications use their own databases, but to the extent they use customer data there is an API that makes the conversion between how the data are defined in the front-office applications, and how they are used in the back-office applications. For example, the order processing application in your organization could draw its primary input from the front-office applications, and after some processing share the data with logistics application and the accounting and finance applications through an API.

Benefits of an Enterprise Approach

The benefits of an enterprise approach to customer data are many, but the two key benefits are:

- Easy visibility into customer interactions
- Enterprise notification and workflow for customer interactions

Easy Visibility

An enterprise approach to the data model enhances both day-to-day customer relationship management and the ability to *mine* all the data to identify trends and sales opportunities. Day-to-day management is enhanced because anyone in the company who has an interaction with the customer can review the status of all recent interactions, and so be better informed in the current interaction. For example, a customer may call in to your company's customer support organization with a high-priority support issue, and needs a bug fix for a particular problem as soon as possible. Your company's support policies may require the customer support representative (CSR) to tell the customer that the bug fix will not be available until the next release; however, if the CSR can easily see through the enterprise database that the customer is currently considering significant additional purchases in the next few months, the CSR may decide to invoke an exception escalation and request that the development organization prepare the bug fix as soon as possible. This way customer satisfaction is enhanced, and the likelihood of closing the additional business goes up. In the same way a customer that calls in to request the status of a particular shipment can, if necessary, be told of the status of not only that particular shipment, but also all planned shipments. These extra little touches can go a long way toward increasing customer satisfaction.

Customer data shared among enterprise applications can also provide a rich resource for *data mining*, or the ability for interested parties to analyze the data and examine it for trends and sales opportunities. Of particular utility is the ability to analyze the relationships between data elements collected in different applications. This kind of analysis can answer such questions as:

- Do particular customers request more support than others?
- Is this related to the sales configurations they purchase?
- Do customers who have received training request support less than customers who have not?
- Is there an opportunity to sell training products to some customers?
- Are customers who have received training more likely to purchase additional products than those who have not?
- Do calls to the customer support organization reveal an opportunity for a training program, or value-added consulting services?
- Are there common features that customers have requested?
- Have you lost customers as a result of poor customer service?
- What percentage of shipments are late?
- Do late shipments result in an increase in the number of calls to the customer service organization?

Once all the customer data are consolidated, there are almost endless possibilities in the number of different types of analyses that can be run against the data.

Enterprise Notification and Workflow

Another benefit of the enterprise approach to customer data is the ability to notify company personnel when specific criteria are met, and to assign and track actions across organizational lines. An earlier example discussing proactive account management showed that a good account manager would find out about a slip in a shipment schedule, and take appropriate action. One way to implement this is to use a notification system that monitors the enterprise database, and applies *business rules* to notify selected personnel when data elements in the database meet certain criteria. For example, a business rule could be set up in a notification system so that if a shipment has not been sent by the scheduled date, the relationship manager for that customer is automatically notified of the slip in the schedule. Another business rule could notify the installation team when a shipment is sent so that appropriate installation personnel can schedule a site visit. Key accounts could be monitored by the salesperson by having the salesperson notified whenever any interaction with the customer is logged into the enterprise database.

Workflow across the enterprise is also facilitated by an enterprise database in two ways. Normal workflow capability is provided if the system allows actions related to customer transactions to be assigned to different company personnel. Exception workflow occurs when certain conditions are met in the enterprise database; business rules are triggered and the workflow system can assign actions to appropriate personnel. In the preceding example, the normal workflow may have been that a customer service representative had issued a shipment order and tracked the status of the action. When the due date for the shipment passed, the workflow system could have taken the shipment order off the list of pending shipments, and assigned it to the salesperson for follow-up actions.

SUMMARY

This chapter covered the importance of managing customer relationships, and the activities involved therein. We discussed the different actions that must be taken, and how sales to the installed base feed back into the sales cycle. We also showed how a Web-based sales automation tool, especially one that uses an enterprise approach to customer data, can significantly enhance your capabilities in managing customer relationships.

The next chapter will cover the activities involved in managing the overall sales process, and give examples of reports that you can use.

8

Transforming Sales Data into Knowledge

MANAGEMENT REPORTING

Traditionally there is no follow-through to determine which of the initial responses turn into sales. That means the success of a marketing program is not really being measured. It can mean that solid leads are not being followed up, while weaker ones are. It means that the best customers for a new release are not even contacted.

Up to now, we have outlined the various activities involved with each step of the sales cycle. We discussed how each activity could be automated via the Web to ensure a streamlined flow of customer information throughout the sales process.

Now that we have concluded the steps through the sales cycle, it is important to discuss the data that has been collected in your SFA system up to this point, and how you can distribute this information to all levels of managers in your organization using Web reports.

By providing Web reporting, you can provide access to critical data your management needs at any point in the sales cycle. You can give visibility to sales forecasts as they happen, as well as view valuable lead ratings and workload across your telemarketing organization to see if the leads are distributed equally.

The traditional approach to SFA automation tools provided reporting capabilities, but the report distribution to the appropriate individuals always seemed like a bottleneck. The reports are of no use in this case if they don't get into the right hands. By Web-enabling your reporting requirements, all information is sure to be current and available to any member of your management organization at any point in time.

POWER OF INFORMATION

The SFA reports are the main tool in managing the overall sales and marketing process, which we call Sales Knowledge Management. From these reports, all financial forecasting, bookings, lead qualifications, and so on, are determined. For this reason we have devoted this chapter to Sales Knowledge Management reports, which are essential to your sales operations at varying stages of the sales cycle.

The reports presented here are samples of what type of output you should expect from your SFA system, whether they be *canned* reports that come with the product, or additional reports that need to be developed in house. Not only are the reports themselves critical, but it goes without saying that the data collected is also essential as input to these reports. We have grouped the reports into the following two categories:

1. Marketing
2. Sales

Marketing Reports

Marcom and telemarketing managers will need to evaluate both the performance of the representatives and the performance of the product. Marketing data from your SFA system helps you understand your position in the marketplace.

Qualified Lead Count Summary Report

Chapter 4 talked about the importance of developing a lead rating system. Once this rating has been established the goal is to have all marketing programs capture this information on each lead. This lead rating will also help your marketing department to understand where the highest-quality leads are coming from. This information will help them better decide where to spend their marketing budget in the future. When each lead is rated, your salespeople can prioritize their activities based on that information.

As a telemarketing manager, I would want to understand from a summary all leads rated A and B from my group, as well as total number of leads per representative. This information will enable you to better manage your group and give you a sense of their productivity. Figure 8.1 shows a summary report by telemarketing representative.

As both a Marcom manager and telemarketing manager, the summary totals as a group will give you an idea of the distribution of ratings for that time period, which would help focus the group on which marketing campaigns they need to work with. Obviously, you would want to focus on the campaigns producing the As and Bs, so a variation on this report might include a column for campaign type and name.

Qualified Lead Count Summary Report

Summary by Telemarketing Rep

Rep	A	% A's	B	% B's	C	% C's	X	% X's	I	% I's	Total Leads	% Total Leads
Smith	2	20%	3	30%	3	30%	1	10%	1	10%	10	22.22%
Berber	0	0%	1	2%	2	40%	1	20%	1	10%	5	11.11%
Jackson	0	0%	1	100%	0	0%	0	0%	0	0%	1	2.22%
Krone	5	31.25%	4	25%	2	12.5%	1	6.25%	4	25%	16	35.55%
Thompson	1	25%	1	25%	0	0%	0	0%	2	50%	3	6.66%
Jones	3	30%	4	40%	1	10%	0	0%	1	10%	10	22.22%
Report Total	11	24.4%	14	31.1%	8	17.8%	3	6.7%	9	20%	45	100%

FIGURE 8.1 Qualified lead count summary report.

Lead Action by Telemarketing Representative Report

This report provides similar information as in the lead action analysis report seen in Chapter 5. As a telemarketing manager, the report in Figure 8.2 gives you a quick look at how many leads are in each stage category for each telemarketing representative.

The stage categories in this report are defined as follows:

- New: No one has touched them yet!
- Working: Touched, trying to maintain.
- Passed to Telesales, Field Sales, VAR Representative: What is being handed off.
- Remarket: Some potential, but no short-term potential.
- Dead: Not worth pursuing.
- Convert to opportunity: How many leads they worked on which were then converted to an opportunity.

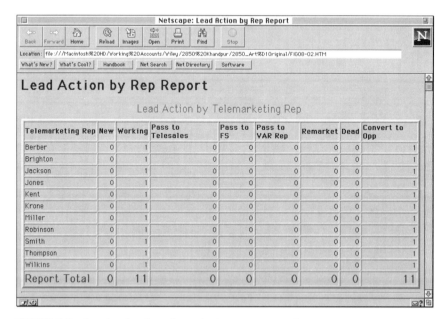

Telemarketing Rep	New	Working	Pass to Telesales	Pass to FS	Pass to VAR Rep	Remarket	Dead	Convert to Opp
Berber	0	1	0	0	0	0	0	1
Brighton	0	1	0	0	0	0	0	1
Jackson	0	1	0	0	0	0	0	1
Jones	0	1	0	0	0	0	0	1
Kent	0	1	0	0	0	0	0	1
Krone	0	1	0	0	0	0	0	1
Miller	0	1	0	0	0	0	0	1
Robinson	0	1	0	0	0	0	0	1
Smith	0	1	0	0	0	0	0	1
Thompson	0	1	0	0	0	0	0	1
Wilkins	0	1	0	0	0	0	0	1
Report Total	0	11	0	0	0	0	0	11

FIGURE 8.2 Lead action by telemarketing representative report.

By summarizing these categories of leads, you can determine the skill level of your telemarketing group at the qualification process. Consider the following scenarios:

- After a trade show you should expect to see a lot of new, incoming leads across the telemarketing group. If one representative gets stuck with 1000 leads while the others have only a few hundred, you would instantly know that the load level is unbalanced across the group. Therefore, in reviewing this report, look for one representative having too many leads over the others.
- If very few leads are in the remarket category, and most of the leads are tagged as dead, this should raise a red flag. This is considered *overqualifying* the lead by ruling out a lead due to incorrect or misinterpreted information, when in fact the lead is a possible Fortune 500 company. As an indication that the representatives are not really understanding the value of doing ongoing campaigns to the remarket group, they may be categorizing these leads as dead, which would drop them off any active campaign and would possibly get archived or purged from the database.

As you can see, this information can tell you if qualification and discernment skills need to be improved, and additional training should be provided.

Support Renewal Lead Report

This proactive report gives installed base sales a list of all customers whose support agreements are expiring in each month for the upcoming quarter. No longer do you have to offer free support because your manual support agreements haven't caught up with your customer service system.

Figure 8.3 tells us that of the three accounts which are due to expire in January, two have already been contacted and closed, and only one remains in a "Waiting for PO" stage. By the time the support agreements expire for these customers, a new, active support agreement will be in place, so the customer has no lapse in support coverage.

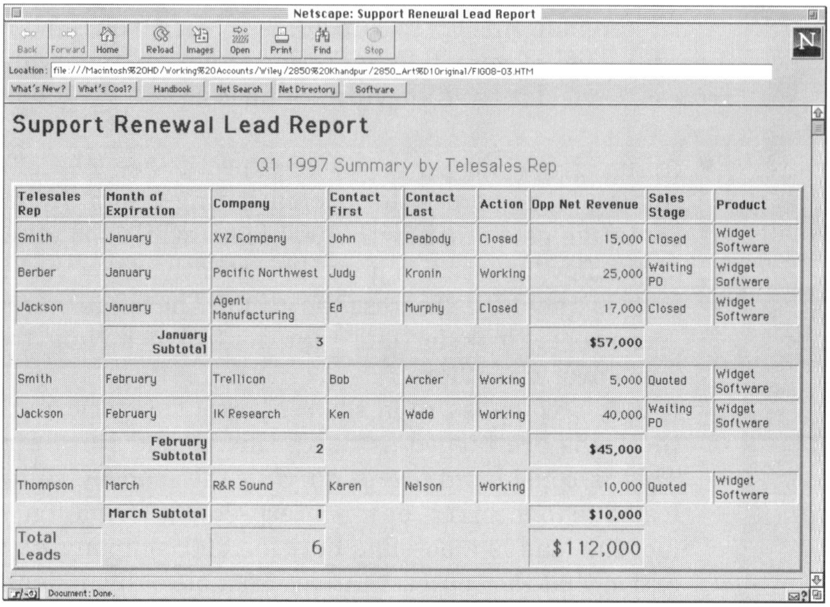
Netscape: Support Renewal Lead Report

Support Renewal Lead Report

Q1 1997 Summary by Telesales Rep

Telesales Rep	Month of Expiration	Company	Contact First	Contact Last	Action	Opp Net Revenue	Sales Stage	Product
Smith	January	XYZ Company	John	Peabody	Closed	15,000	Closed	Widget Software
Berber	January	Pacific Northwest	Judy	Kronin	Working	25,000	Waiting PO	Widget Software
Jackson	January	Agent Manufacturing	Ed	Murphy	Closed	17,000	Closed	Widget Software
	January Subtotal	3				$57,000		
Smith	February	Trellicon	Bob	Archer	Working	5,000	Quoted	Widget Software
Jackson	February	IK Research	Ken	Wade	Working	40,000	Waiting PO	Widget Software
	February Subtotal	2				$45,000		
Thompson	March	R&R Sound	Karen	Nelson	Working	10,000	Quoted	Widget Software
	March Subtotal	1				$10,000		
Total Leads		6				$112,000		

FIGURE 8.3 Support renewal lead report.

This report also gives sales a heads up on the support renewal side of installed base sales, which can be useful in forecasting.

Marketing Cost Analysis Report

The cost-per-lead measurement is a key component in determining the efficiency of your marketing programs. The report in Figure 8.4 provides an analysis of the data gathered in the marketing campaign and lead forms from Chapters 4 and 5.

From this report you can decide which campaign types are generating the greatest response of lower cost leads.

Win/Loss Analysis

The information on this report is derived from the Opportunity Outcome form in Chapter 6 to help analyze how and why you won or lost a deal. Figure 8.5 shows if a deal is lost and to whom it is lost. Knowing which competitor you lost to most frequently

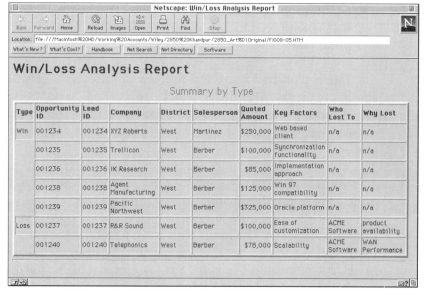

FIGURE 8.4   Marketing cost analysis report.

Marketing Cost Analysis Report

Summary by Campaign Type

Campaign Type	Program Name	Source	Lead Count	Cost of Program	Cost Per Lead
Direct Mail	Widget Lead Generation	Computer Society	10	1300	130
		Technicon	15	1500	100
		Technology Magazine	80	4000	50
		Subtotal for Direct Mail	**105**	**6800**	**65**
Trade Show	Show 1997	Consumer Electronics	75	5100	68
		Comdex Spring	100	7500	75
		Technology Showcase	10	3000	300
		Subtotal for Trade Shows	**185**	**15,600**	**84**
Seminar	Winter Seminars	Workgroup Solutions/NY	50	2500	50
		Workgroup Solutions/LA	25	3000	120
		Subtotal for Seminars	**75**	**5500**	**73**
Ad	Magazine Ad	Popular Computing	10	7500	750
		Computing Management	15	4200	280
		Subtotal for Print Ads	**25**	**11,700**	**468**
Report Total			**390**	**$39,600**	**$102**

Win/Loss Analysis Report

Summary by Type

Type	Opportunity ID	Lead ID	Company	District	Salesperson	Quoted Amount	Key Factors	Who Lost To	Why Lost
Win	001234	001234	XYZ Roberts	West	Martinez	$250,000	Web based client	n/a	n/a
	001235	001235	Trellicon	West	Berber	$100,000	Synchronization functionality	n/a	n/a
	001236	001236	IK Research	West	Berber	$85,000	Implementation approach	n/a	n/a
	001238	001238	Agent Manufacturing	West	Berber	$125,000	Win 97 compatibility	n/a	n/a
	001239	001239	Pacific Northwest	West	Berber	$325,000	Oracle platform	n/a	n/a
Loss	001237	001237	R&R Sound	West	Berber	$100,000	Ease of customization	ACME Software	product availability
	001240	001240	Telephonics	West	Berber	$78,000	Scalability	ACME Software	WAN Performance

FIGURE 8.5   Win/loss analysis.

could tell you that maybe the competition is engaging in underpricing. Conversely, if a deal is won, you can see where the best source of leads came from. Marketing campaigns need this type of feedback in order to determine success ratios.

This report will also be useful to sales. It helps to build new strategies, in the event the losses could be attributed to a new feature that the competition has developed, which is giving them a competitive advantage over your product.

Lead Disposition Closed Loop Report

Used by both Marketing and Sales, this data is what most companies strive for. Your ultimate goal is to trace every marketing dollar spent to either a win or a loss. This report tells you of all the marketing dollars spent on inquires, how many actually close and what is the revenue amount associated with each deal. These numbers capture the effectiveness of your marketing and sales organizations by giving you a sense of the following:

- Value of marketing dollars
- Length of sales cycle
- Dollar amount of sale, which, when tracked back to the marketing source, can determine the best lead source for certain products

The report in Figure 8.6 follows the life cycle of the lead to the opportunity. Qualified leads are passed to sales, which in turn passes back the opportunity feedback. The information that drives this report are the Lead and Opportunity Entry forms we saw in Chapters 4 and 5.

The first half of the report is sorted by district and program. The salesperson is responsible for providing the projected revenue figures for the second half of the report.

Typically run on a monthly basis, this report gives a summary by district of the leads that were passed on to sales, and the resulting feedback on the opportunities produced from these leads. As mentioned earlier, this report could be used by both marketing and sales managers.

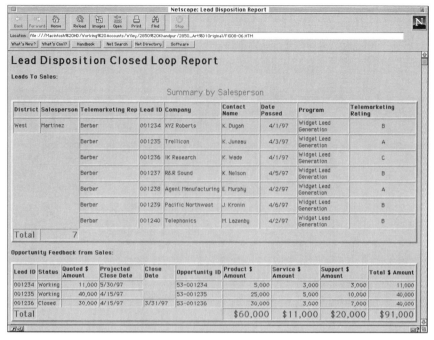

FIGURE 8.6 Lead disposition closed loop report.

Sales Reports

You will find that the SFA data will help you to understand your performance metrics and to size your organization appropriately:

- Increase sales force
- Downsize revenue expectations
- Client analysis—understand distribution of revenue

Opportunity Report by Salesperson

This weekly report gives sales management a snapshot of active opportunities, whether in the forecast, upside, or pipeline. This data gives you an early barometer of what the forecast is going to look like.

The report in Figure 8.7 is summarized to give you regional opportunity revenue numbers, as well as by salesperson within

Opportunity Report by Salesperson

w/e 3/14/97 Summary by Salesperson

Sales Region	Salesperson	Company	Probability to Close	Projected Close	Opp Net Revenue	Products	Reseller
East	Wilkins	Technologic	10%	3/31/97	5,000	5 Widget	C&C Distributors
				Rep Subtotal	*5,000*		
	Smith	Fabricon	50%	3/31/97	4,000	4 Widget	C&C Distributors
		Eastern Technology	30%	3/31/97	6,000	6 Widget	Industrial Consolidators
				Rep Subtotal	*10,000*		
				Region Subtotal	**$15,000**		
Central	Higgins	Farmers Financial	30%	4/15/97	4,000	4 Widget	D&D Midwest
				Rep Subtotal	*4,000*		
				Region Subtotal	**$4,000**		
West	Peabody	TNJ Roberts	60%	3/31/97	7,000	7 Widget	Western Pacific
		Kelco	20%	4/1/97	10,000	10 Widget	Lighthouse Manufacturing
				Rep Subtotal	*17,000*		
	Miller	Calico	20%	4/15/97	2,000	2 Widget	Lighthouse Manufacturing
		Zilcon	40%	4/18/97	13,000	13 Widget	Northwest Monitors
				Rep Subtotal	*15,000*		
				Region Subtotal	**$32,000**		
Report Total					**$51,000**		

FIGURE 8.7   Opportunity report by salesperson.

each region. When running this report, you could have the report prompt you for and sort by the following selection criteria in filtering the information collected:

- Week ending date
- Salesperson name
- Region
- Sort by forecast, upside, and pipeline
- Sort by sales stage

While this sample report shows indirect sales via a reseller channel, another variation on this report would omit the reseller data to produce a direct sales opportunity report.

Action Item Summary Report

This report tells sales managers how salespeople are performing in managing their workload by measuring the number of action items outstanding against the total number of action items in an in box. This report can be used not only to determine perfor-

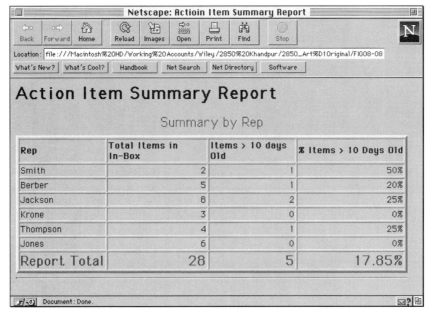

FIGURE 8.8 Action item summary report.

mance across all salespeople in a region, but also as a means to gauge the lead distribution process.

Figure 8.8 shows the in-box count of all commitments made by a salesperson, along with the number of commitments that are past due. When run on a weekly basis, the sales manager can easily get a sense for which salespeople are not likely to be following through with the prospects in a timely manner, which is an indication of what their financial performance is likely to be.

Additional selection criteria can be used for filtering the data by:

- Date range
- Specific salesperson name

Regional Lead Summary Report

Figure 8.9 shows a summary of what qualified leads have been passed on to sales, sorted by region. As a sales manager, the pur-

Regional Lead Rating Summary Report

Summary by Region

Region	District	A	% A's	B	% B's	C	% C's	X	% X's	I	% I's	Total Leads	% Total Leads
East	New York	2	20%	3	30%	3	30%	1	10%	1	10%	10	22.22%
	Mass.	0	0%	1	2%	2	40%	1	20%	1	10%	5	11.11%
	Vermont	0	0%	1	100%	0	0%	0	0%	0	0%	1	2.22%
	East Subtotal	2	4.44%	5	11.11%	5	11.11%	2	4.44%	2	4.44%	16	35.55%
West	California	5	31.25%	4	25%	2	12.5%	1	6.25%	4	25%	16	35.55%
	Washington	1	25%	1	25%	0	0%	0	0%	2	50%	3	6.66%
	Oregon	3	30%	4	40%	1	10%	0	0%	1	10%	10	22.22%
	West Subtotal	9	20%	9	20%	3	6.66%	1	2.22%	7	15.55%	29	64.44%
Report Total		11	24.4%	14	31.1%	8	17.8%	3	6.7%	9	20%	45	100%

FIGURE 8.9 Regional lead summary report.

pose of this report is twofold. First, this information tells you the quality of leads passed to each region, which can be used as a prediction on the potential forecast of the group. Second, you also get the percentage of all A leads that a particular district and region have been assigned in comparison to the other groups. If a region or territory was getting a lot of leads, there may be more potential there than they can handle. In this case, the sales organization may decide to split the territory in two.

This report is sorted by region then by district, and is typically distributed once a month to each regional manager or VP.

Salesperson Lead Summary Report

The report in Figure 8.10 is similar to the preceding regional lead summary report. Providing one more level of granularity, this report drills down the information from the report in Figure 8.9 to show the quality of leads distributed to each salesperson, as a percentage of the total leads passed on to sales. This report is typically distributed once a month to each district.

Salesperson Lead Rating Summary Report

Summary by Region, Salesperson

Region	District	Salesperson	A	% A's	B	% B's	C	% C's	X	% X's	I	% I's	Total Leads	% Total Leads
West	N. California	Smith	2	20%	3	30%	3	30%	1	10%	1	10%	10	15.9%
	S. California	Berber	0	0%	1	20%	2	40%	1	20%	1	20%	5	7.9%
	Oregon	Jackson	0	0%	1	100%	0	0%	0	0%	0	0%	1	1.6%
	Washington	Krone	5	31.3%	4	25%	2	12.5%	1	6.3%	4	25%	16	25.4%
	Idaho	Thompson	1	25%	1	25%	0	0%	0	0%	2	50%	3	4.8%
	Arizona	Jones	3	30%	4	40%	1	10%	0	0%	1	10%	10	15.9%
West Subtotal			**11**	**17.5%**	**14**	**22.2%**	**8**	**12.7%**	**3**	**4.8%**	**9**	**14.3%**	**45**	**71.4%**
East	New York	Richardson	1	25%	1	25%	0	0%	0	0%	2	50%	3	4.8%
	New Hampshire	Myers	3	30%	4	40%	1	10%	0	0%	1	10%	10	15.9%
	Mass.	Franklin	0	0%	1	20%	2	40%	1	20%	1	20%	5	7.9%
East Subtotal			**4**	**6.3%**	**6**	**9.5%**	**3**	**4.8%**	**1**	**1.6%**	**4**	**6.3%**	**18**	**28.6%**
Report Total			15	23.8%	20	31.7%	11	17.5%	4	6.3%	13	20.6%	63	100%

FIGURE 8.10 Salesperson lead summary report.

Quota Performance Report

Quota performance is an easy measurement of the salesperson's successes against quarterly quota targets. By comparing actuals to target, both the salesperson and the district or regional manager can see how far off they may be in meeting their quarterly revenue goals.

Once run, you can post the report in Figure 8.11 on your intranet, making it available to the entire sales organization.

Outstanding Quote Summary Report

A sales manager wants to know what the salespeople are producing, and one of the measurements of interest is how many quotes have gone out this month for each salesperson.

More importantly, the report in Figure 8.12 tells you if the pipeline is being loaded appropriately. If there are not enough quotes being generated, then the sales organization is not going to meet its revenue objectives. This is a direct indicator of not enough qualified leads being generated by marketing.

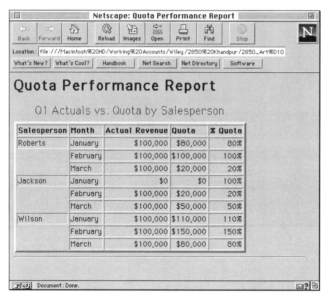

FIGURE 8.11 Quota performance report.

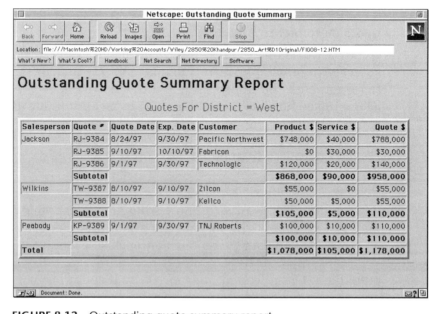

FIGURE 8.12 Outstanding quote summary report.

In addition to the actual quotes being produced, there are several additional barometer measurements that can be read from this report:

- By looking at the product and services dollar amounts, you better understand the mix of products that are being included on quotes.
- You can see which products are being quoted the most, so marketing can put more emphasis on these product lines.

IDENTIFYING WEB PAGE CONTENT

Web page content originates from various parts of your organization. Identifying what is appropriate to publish on your Web site is not a small task, not to mention the organization and currency discussed in the next section. It is critical to ensure that the content is professional, polished, and not full of memory-intensive graphics.

We often see Web sites that have been thrown together in an effort to get a Web *presence* by a company. These are often referred to as electronic graffiti boards, with information that is not related and is not comprehensive. Since the Web site should mirror your corporate identity, you want to be sure that first time visitors are left with a lasting impression—the right one.

Companies should take advantage of Web technology to promote not only their products and services, but also their corporate images. Web content management is an entire process in itself, which should be treated as formally as any other information process you have in place. The sources of material for both your intranet and Internet sites typically come from one of the following areas:

- Marketing
- Customer
- Sales
- Corporate

Marketing

We discussed using the Web as a central repository earlier in this book. All marketing encyclopedia and information can be put on your intranet for ease of access and currency of information. Depending on your product, and if you publish your price list, you can use the Web to produce an online, interactive catalog on the Internet.

Customer

We have seen the many advantages of using the intranet to track all aspects of a customer environment, from the initial lead entry form to the sales contracts and support agreements. Making this information available to your entire sales and support organizations eliminates the bottlenecks we have found with most organizations. The lack of a central customer repository is by far the most frequent, rampant problem with many of our customers looking to automate their sales, marketing, and support functions. In fact, the more customer databases a company has, the bigger the bottlenecks to their productivity.

A natural byproduct of streamlining the customer information flow is the increase in productivity from all areas of the enterprise, including the sales organization. Eliminating their barriers to productivity causes increased sales and customer satisfaction.

Sales

Sales needs critical, current information when preparing for a site visit, or preparing a quote. All appropriate forms should be kept current and uploaded to your intranet for access by the sales organization. This is even more important when considering your remote field sales offices and distribution channels.

Corporate

The corporate identity information, such as brochures, company contact and background information, white papers, customer testimonials, and press releases, help to establish an image on the Internet without expensive color printing costs. This is the singlemost efficient means of electronic publishing that a company can leverage by using the Web as an identity tool.

KEEPING CONTENT CURRENT

One of the most important points stressed in our Web-content workshops is to make sure the Web content is kept up-to-date. No matter what area of the enterprise is presented on your Web page, always make sure the information is current and accurate. This usually requires defining a Web publishing process, which at a minimum should include the following steps:

1. Collect Web content from internal sources (marketing, sales).
2. Format and sanitize the content.
3. Develop easy navigation path to the Web information.
4. Publish the content on your Web page.
5. Evaluate feedback from your Web site visitors.
6. Start at Step 1 and repeat the cycle.

The publishing process should be a continuous event, not a one-time shot at putting information on your Web site. You need to solicit ongoing content from your internal corporate resources in order to keep the Web page current. Remember, one of the goals of the Web page is to keep people visiting your Web site on a regular basis. If the information is stagnant, and several visits yield no new information, people will not continue to visit the site. These repeat visits can be as important as generating new traffic on your site.

SUMMARY

This chapter covered the importance of knowledge and information in managing the overall sales process, and highlighted examples of the most commonly requested reports by our clients.

Regardless of the SFA system you have in place, third-party tools are always available to tap into the sales information source. Don't forget that getting the information out of your SFA system is just as important as the data going into your system.

Planning and Implementation

Never promise more than you can perform.

Publilius Syrus, Maxim 528, *First century* B.C.

It is a bad plan that admits of no modification.

Publilius Syrus, Maxim 469, *First century* B.C.

9

Planning for Sales Force Automation

The last few chapters discussed the different sales processes, and gave some examples of how you can use Web technologies to automate those processes. We went over the different functions that are performed during the sales cycle, as well as how you can use the data you collect to manage your customer relationships. But how do you actually make all this happen? What does it take? What's involved in implementing a Sales Force Automation solution?

Actually implementing and deploying anything but the most trivial Sales Force Automation solution requires a considerable amount of planning. After all, you may be spending anywhere between $10,000 and $25,000 per user in direct startup costs, and over $5000 per user per year in direct operating costs. For a medium-size organization of 100 users, this could mean approximately $2 million to get started and $500,00 per year to keep it going; for a large organization of 500 users, you could be looking at spending over $10 million just to get your sales force up and running—and this does not include estimates of opportunity costs!

By some estimates, between half and three-quarters of all SFA implementations are deemed unsuccessful by the companies that undertake them; we believe that the major contributor to that low success rate is a lack of planning. Good planning before undertaking any technology implementation can save your organization a considerable amount of time and money, and can result in a sales automation solution that truly improves the effectiveness of your sales force. This is not an unusual concept, and in fact is promoted by most vendors and consultants. For example, in Andersen Consulting's Sales Force Effectiveness practice, Sales Force Automation is considered to be the technology deployment component of an overall sales force effectiveness effort; three other components (strategy, processes, and people) typically precede technology deployment. In the rush to deploy *neat* technology, many companies skip what we think is the most essential part of Sales Force Automation.

Planning for a Sales Force Automation project involves several steps:

1. Make the business case for the Sales Force Automation solution.
2. Establish the project team that will implement the solution.
3. Design the sales business processes that will be implemented.
4. Specify the functional requirements that the solution must meet.
5. Specify the technology infrastructure that the solution will use.
6. Make the buy-versus-build decision.
7. Develop the deployment plan.
8. Define the training plan.
9. Identify the internal support requirements.
10. Define the post-rollout requirements.

These steps are shown in Figure 9.1. This chapter will cover each of these steps in some detail.

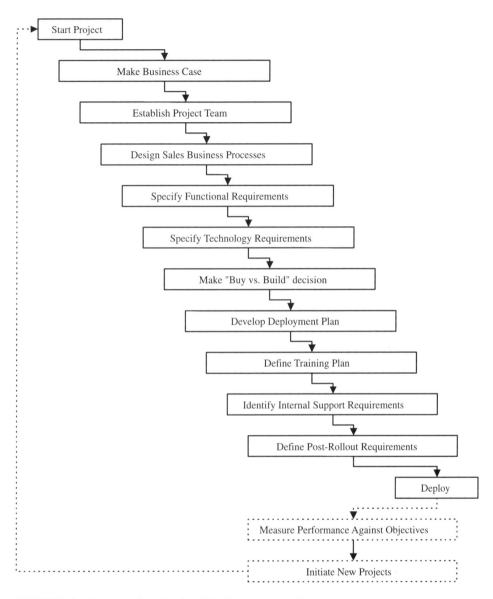

FIGURE 9.1 Steps in planning for Sales Force Automation.

MAKE THE BUSINESS CASE

This may sound obvious, but the first step in planning for Sales Force Automation is to make the business case for automation. Surprisingly, many implementation efforts do not have a business case (let alone one that is well thought out), nor do they have clear objectives for the effort; not so surprisingly, many of these implementations fail for reasons ranging from useless functionality to *scope creep*. These reasons have a common root: a lack of focus.

To implement a successful Sales Force Automation solution you and everyone else in your organization must have a clear and shared understanding of the purpose of the solution, the business problem(s) that will be solved, and the measures of success of the solution once it is implemented. In other words, all interested and affected parties must understand the value that the automation solution brings to the organization and to them. After all, how can you have a solution if you can't articulate the problem the solution solves; and how can you verify the solution if you don't know in advance what you expect the answer to be?

Clear Objectives

The business case for your automation solution must have its foundations in your sales strategy, processes, and people (see Figure 9.2). Your sales strategy will dictate your sales processes; the processes in turn must be used by your people; the people who use the processes will need tools to make the processes work. Any technology used in automation can be used to support only what your salespeople do, and how to make them more effective and efficient in their jobs. For example, if your sales strategy dictates a sales model heavily oriented toward indirect channels, then the objectives of your sales automation project must reflect that and guide the project in the direction of improving the effectiveness and efficiency of sales to your indirect channels. If your sales strategy envisions a future in which most selling is done interactively, then your sales automation project must have an objective to support interactive selling systems.

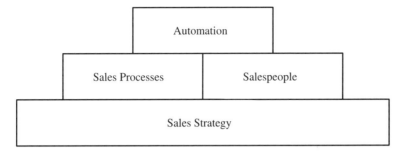

FIGURE 9.2   Foundations of the business case.

It is also important that your sales force, indeed your entire organization, understands and supports the business case of the sales automation effort. It is people in your organization that will be using the tools that result from the Sales Force Automation project. If the people do not or cannot understand and support the business case for the project, then the project is doomed to failure. The tools will be seen as a burden that takes them away from their real job of selling. There is bound to be some initial skepticism about Sales Force Automation, especially as many salespeople feel that selling is an art and technology cannot help. In fact, the purpose of automation is to assist salespeople in their daily activities. If the salespeople are involved in the development of the business case, and can understand how sales automation will help them improve their performance on the job, then there is a greater likelihood of success. An important objective of any sales automation effort then is to ensure that the tools are useful and easy enough to become an essential part of a salesperson's life; that salesperson would not think of doing the job without using the tools. To quote Keith Carlson of Andersen Consulting: "Selling is both an art and a process. The best results come from using technology to automate reengineered processes to complement the art."

As a part of defining the objectives, you should also consider defining so-called *nonobjectives,* or statements of what your project will not do. These can be very helpful in preventing scope creep, the inclination to throw in additional objectives for the project after the project has commenced. Scope creep is to be resisted very strongly, because once you start adding more objectives to your project you run the risk of never achieving any of the original objectives. Another risk associated with scope creep is that changes made to the original design to accommodate new objectives can result in compromise solutions that do not fully meet either the original objectives or the new ones.

Understand the Value

Not only must you be very clear about why you want to automate your sales functions, you must be clear about which functions you will automate, and the value you expect to realize as a result of automating those functions. Chapter 1 gave the three major reasons to justify investments in Sales Force Automation:

1. Increased sales effectiveness
2. Improved sales efficiency
3. Higher customer satisfaction

When developing your business case for automation, you must evaluate each function and assess the impact automation will have on sales effectiveness, sales efficiency, and customer satisfaction. The implementation of some automation tools—for example, tools that improve the lead qualification process—has the greatest impact on sales effectiveness. Other tools, such as automated proposal generators, have their greatest impact on sales efficiency. Yet others, such as integrated customer information management systems, have the most impact on customer satisfaction.

Your sales automation projects should always have an objective of higher customer satisfaction, because that can significantly increase your long-term profitability. Whether your other main objective is increased sales effectiveness, improved sales efficiency, or both will depend on where your organization is currently in its operations (see Figure 9.3).

You must conduct a realistic assessment of the performance of your organization, and determine in which quadrant it falls. Ideally you want to be in the top right quadrant: both effective

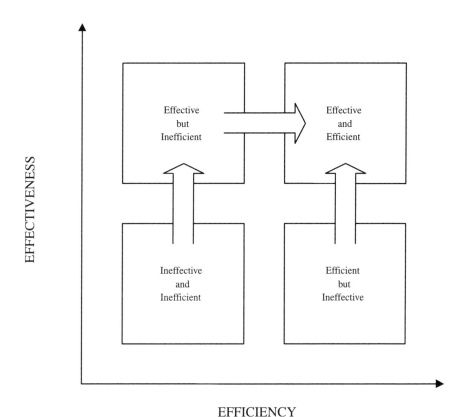

FIGURE 9.3 Efficiency versus effectiveness matrix.

and efficient. If your organization is already there, then you must ask yourself what value you would derive from any automation effort. Certainly the implementation of some tools could improve both the effectiveness and the efficiency of your organization, but the marginal value you expect to realize may not justify the costs involved with the automation effort.

If your organization is already quite efficient in its operations (lower right quadrant), then you can realize significant benefits by implementing automation tools that will improve its effectiveness. For example, you may find you are in a situation in which your sales force is very quick to close a sale with a good lead, but the number of good leads that they get are very limited. In other words, your salespeople spend a lot of time chasing down inappropriate leads. Your sales automation objective then would be to improve the effectiveness of your salespeople by giving them better qualified leads.

If, on the other hand, your sales organization is effective but not very efficient (upper left quadrant), you must implement tools that improve the efficiency of your salespeople. For example, you may find that your salespeople have a high close ratio, but that they spend a significant amount of time on paperwork and other administrative chores so that the time to close a sale is quite high. In this situation you can realize gains in sales efficiency by implementing tools that reduce the time to close a sale, such as an opportunity management system that automates workflow and escalates issues that are not addressed in a timely manner.

If the performance of your organization indicates that both effectiveness and efficiency could be better (lower left quadrant), you must implement automation that primarily improves the sales effectiveness of your organization, and secondarily improves the efficiency of your operations. Clearly, you must get better at generating revenues before you can start to reduce the costs of generating revenues.

Measures of Success

At this point you should also state how you will measure the success of your Sales Force Automation project. Too many projects are executed without a clear articulation of the measures of success. When the automation is finally in place, there is no way to know if in fact the objectives of the project were met and the investment in the technology was worth the cost of implementing it.

Measures of success obviously must be tied to the objectives of the project. For example, if the objective of the automation is to increase sales effectiveness by improving the close ratio, then you must state the improvement you expect in the close ratio (e.g., the goal of this project is to improve the close ratio by X percent every year after implementation). Similarly, if the objective is to implement automation that will reduce the average days to close, then that must be stated in the objectives: When implemented this project will reduce the average days to close a sale by two days/sale every year. If the objective is to improve customer satisfaction, then you must indicate how you will know if you have met the objective: The sales configuration system will result in 100 percent accurate orders being configured 100 percent of the time.

Some objectives of the project are not directly tied to the impact of the automation itself, but should still be stated and performance measured against that objective. For example, an objective of the project could be to deploy the Marketing Encyclopedia System to 90 percent of the sales force within nine months of project initiation.

Any objective you state for the project must be accompanied by a specific statement of the desired goal, and indicate how performance will be measured. In all the preceding examples, it is clear that the objective is measurable, and the exact measure that will be used to assess performance is clear to you and your organization. Vague statements (e.g., this project will empower the sales force) are all too common, and in our experience make it easy to declare victory, when in fact there has been no improvement in actual sales effectiveness, sales efficiency, or customer satisfaction.

ESTABLISH PROJECT TEAM

Once the objectives of the Sales Force Automation project are set, you must set up a project team that will bring about the automation. In some companies a project team is set up before the objectives are set; in fact the project team itself sets the objectives for the project. We prefer an approach in which the high-level objectives for the project are set by executive management, and detailed objectives that support the high-level objectives are set by members of the project team.

A project team must have executive sponsorship. If the automation project does not have executive sponsorship, the project will fail. Not only must executive management state the high-level objectives before the project commences, but they also must be involved in periodic status reviews during the project—and be available and willing to resolve key organizational and budget issues as they arise.

Project Manager

The project team itself should have a full-time project manager. This individual reports to executive management, and is responsible for the day-to-day management of the sales automation project. The ideal candidate for this position will be someone who has credibility with both executive management and the sales force, and has sufficient technical background to understand the technologies available for Sales Force Automation. It is critical that this individual have the support of executive management in making binding decisions. The project manager must:

- Create and maintain the project plan
- Manage the activities of team members and task teams
- Provide periodic status updates to executive management
- Escalate organizational and budget issues to executive management
- Make decisions on process and technology
- Work within the project budget

Project Team

Members of the project team should represent a cross section of the company functions that will be affected by the sales automation project under consideration (see Figure 9.4).

The key functions that absolutely must be represented on the project team, and make up the core team, are:

- Sales (salespeople, sales managers, sales administration, and operations staff)
- Marketing (telemarketing, marketing managers)
- Information technology (business analysts, operations staff, IS managers)

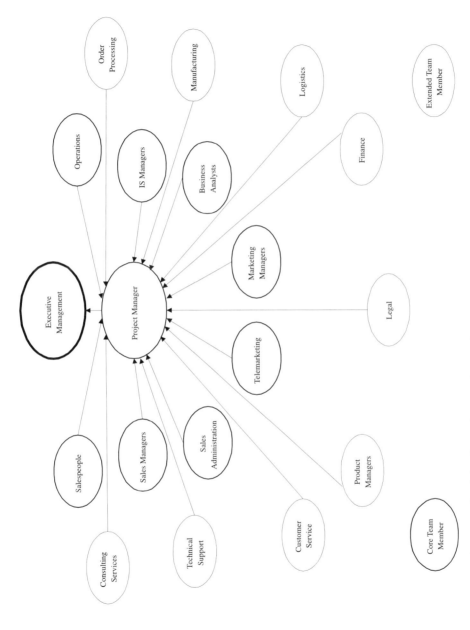

FIGURE 9.4 Project team for Sales Force Automation projects.

Other operating functions are also represented on the project team as and when the need arises. Project team members represent their individual organizations. They must be strong advocates for the interests of the organizations they represent, yet be able to compromise in the business interests of the company at large. Clearly they must have the support of the organizations they represent, and have the authority to make decisions that are binding on their respective organizations. A project team member who cannot make binding decisions, or one whose decisions are subsequently overturned by organizational management, will not be an effective member of the team. The responsibilities of a project team member include:

- Active participation in areas that affect the organization
- Provide assistance in area of expertise
- Availability to work on task teams as needed
- Authority to make decisions on behalf of organization
- Frequent status updates to organizational management
- Promote the project to constituents

It is important that the organization gives project team members the freedom and authority to serve on the project team. Team members will be very involved in the project, and cannot take on project responsibilities as an addition to their normal workload. In fact, in a large-scale project the team members may well be expected to serve on the team full time at key periods during the project.

A typical project team will have between eight and ten core team members, and an extended team of up to up to 20 or even 30 members. Core team members will be involved in every phase of the project; extended team members are brought in for their special expertise during specific phases, and to participate in task groups that report to the core team. For example, the core team may create one task group to design the sales business processes, and another task group to define the technology infrastructure. Some core team members may be in both task groups; and each task group may have additional experts, such as business analysts and networking experts.

DESIGN SALES BUSINESS PROCESSES

One of the first tasks for the sales automation project team is to design the sales business processes that will be implemented in the automation project. What is a business process? Definitions vary, and the phrase has different meanings to different people. We use *business process* as described in the following excerpt from *Delivering World-Class Technical Support* by Navtej (Kay) Khandpur and Lori Laub (published by John Wiley & Sons, Inc., 1997):

> A business process is the execution of a series of activities that together produce a product or service required by an organization to fulfill its goals. In a well-designed process each activity builds on work done in preceding activities, and contributes to the overall product or service being produced. Implicit in this definition of a business process is the assumption that the activities performed and the circumstances under which each activity is performed are consistent and repeatable. In other words, the same things are done in the same way under the same circumstances.

The goal of the sales organization is revenues, and the product of the sales organization is closed sales that result in revenues. The primary business process in the sales organization is therefore the execution of activities that together result in a closed sale. Thus all the activities performed by a salesperson in actually selling to a customer make up part of the sales business processes. Activities performed by others in the sales organization, or in other parts of the company, may or may not be part of the primary business process of the sales organization. For example, leads generation is an important activity, as is leads qualification. However, the two activities do not directly result in closed sales, and so would contribute to a secondary sales business process. On the other hand, activities involved in managing an opportunity are directly related to the primary sales business process. In this book, we consider the activities described in Chapters 5 and 6 as the primary sales business process; the activities described in Chapters 4, 7, and 8 are in support of the primary sales business process.

You must be able to describe the business processes that will be implemented by the automation effort. In some cases all this will take is documentation of the way you currently do business. In other cases, you may want to redesign some areas and activities, and then document the new processes. In yet other cases, you may want to redesign all the activities and change the way you sell. Implementing technology to automate sales processes presents an excellent opportunity to examine the way you do business. Actual process design and documentation is beyond the scope of this book; however, your team should first examine the activities and processes involved in making a sale, and then design sales processes with the assistance of the people who will actually execute those processes. Keep the following questions in mind when examining your sales business processes:

- What are the activities performed in the sales organization?
- How does the activity contribute to the operating goals of the sales organization?
- What are the inputs to each activity?
- What are the outputs of each activity?
- What steps does it take to perform each activity?
- Is each activity performed consistently?
- Is each activity necessary?
- Are the right people performing each activity?
- How long does it take to perform each activity?

Once you have an inventory of activities, and can answer the preceding questions, you are ready to design your new sales business processes. When designing new processes, keep the following guidelines in mind:

- Perform only necessary activities
- Eliminate unnecessary activities and steps
- Reduce the time it takes to perform an activity
- Eliminate the need to check and rework activities earlier in the process

At the end of this exercise, your team will have a clear picture of the sales business processes that will use the technology implemented by your project. You will be able to answer the question: How will salespeople sell? Furthermore, if during the design exercise you invited (and got) the active participation of salespeople and other personnel who will actually have to execute these processes, you will have a much easier time getting your automation project adopted by the sales organization. Affected personnel will feel a sense of ownership in the new processes, and when it comes time to train your personnel, the training exercise will be easier because many of them will already be aware of the changes.

We cannot overemphasize the importance of this sales business process design step. Automating poor and inefficient processes will result in poor and inefficient automation. Keith Carlson of Andersen Consulting says, "Buying technology before working through the sales strategy and processes is like buying building materials for a new house before hiring an architect and a builder." We concur.

SPECIFY FUNCTIONAL REQUIREMENTS

The fourth step in planning for Sales Force Automation is to develop the functional requirements for the Sales Force Automation effort. This step involves taking the business processes developed in the previous step and defining the functions that need to be performed by the automation tools. For example, the leads qualification process may call for leads to be sent on to the appropriate salesperson. The functional requirement for the automation tool may be stated as *the ability to assign qualified leads to salespeople based on routing criteria set by the system administrator.* The purpose of having functional requirements is to give whoever implements the system a clear picture of what the tools must be capable of doing.

Developing detailed functional requirements is typically done by business analysts and information technology specialists, and is beyond the scope of this book. You would typically create a task

TABLE 9.1 Example of Functional Requirements for SFA

Item	Functionality	Importance
3.2	Ability to enter lead information	High
3.3	Ability to rate leads	High
3.4	Ability to log interactions with leads	High
3.5	Ability to convert leads into prospects	Medium
3.6	Ability to track collateral sent to a lead	Medium
3.7	Ability to assign qualified leads to salespeople based on routing criteria set by system administrator	High
3.8	Ability to identify leads from existing customer base	Medium
3.9	Notification system to alert salespeople that leads have been assigned for follow-up	Low
3.10	Ability to identify leads by name, telephone number, company, SIC, sales territory, or salesperson	Medium
3.11	Ability to load leads from external leads databases	High

team to produce the functional requirements document. An excerpt of a functional requirements document is shown in Table 9.1.

An essential part of the functional requirements should be a list of reports that will be used by salespeople and sales managers to manage sales operations. Specifying the reports will give the implementers some idea of how to lay out the data model for your automation efforts.

SPECIFY TECHNOLOGY REQUIREMENTS

In all likelihood your company already has a significant investment in information technology, and the Information Technology organization has specified certain corporate standards for technology acquisitions. In this step you must capture those requirements so that if you were to go out and purchase a solution prospective, vendors would have an idea of what kinds of technology you expect to use. An example of technology requirements are shown in the excerpt in Table 9.2.

TABLE 9.2 Example of Technology Requirements for SFA

Item	Technology	Importance
4.1	*Server Support:* HP UX	High
4.2	*Client Support:* Windows 3.11 Windows 95 Windows NT UNIX	High
4.3	*RDMS Support:* Oracle v7 Microsoft SQL Server	High
4.4	*Browser Support:* Netscape Navigator	High

Technology requirements would typically be specified by information technology staff.

MAKING THE BUY VERSUS BUILD DECISION

Once functional and technology requirements have been defined, you must make a buy versus build decision. In other words you must decide if it makes more sense for you to buy Sales Force Automation tools that will meet the requirements you have stated, or if you should build the tools using in-house expertise. As a practical matter the buy versus build decision is hardly ever this binary: You will always end up buying a part of the solution even if you intend to build, and you will almost always have to build some customization even if you buy. The question is finding the right balance between how much functionality you buy off the shelf, and how much functionality you build in-house.

The advantages of buying technology solutions and adapting them for use in-house are:

- The solution is commercially available, and so tried and tested in production environments. This means that not only can you purchase the solution and start adapting it right away, but there also is expertise available in the marketplace to help you customize the solution to meet your needs.

▪ A significant amount of effort has gone into developing the solution and its data model. The hardest part of any major application development effort is the design and development of the underlying data models. Vendors of commercially available solutions have invested significant amounts of intellectual capital into their products, and you can leverage this investment.

▪ Vendors are continuously adding new functionality to their products; this will be difficult to do if the solution is built in-house.

▪ The solution exists as a product, which means that user manuals, documentation, and training are available and will not need to be developed in-house.

On the other hand, developing a solution in-house also has some benefits:

▪ The new solution can use legacy applications and the in-house expertise that exists on these applications.

▪ You can make your solution exactly meet all the requirements you have stated, and make none of the compromises that may be necessary if you try to adapt an existing solution.

▪ You can save the time it would take to find a commercially available solution.

For roughly comparable functionality, the costs of building will exceed the costs of buying and customizing. Our experience, and that of companies we interviewed, is that only about 15 percent of first-year costs for a purchased solution are actually software costs, and another 25 percent to 35 percent are implementation costs, giving a total software implementation cost of between 40 percent and 50 percent of first-year costs. Given that some of the implementation costs are related to project management, which will also be incurred if the solution is built in-house, the costs of purchasing a solution should be less than those of building.

With the proliferation of vendors and multiple solutions available for the most common Sales Force Automation problems, we believe it usually makes more sense to buy than it does to build. In rare circumstances it may be more economical to build than purchase. This situation may arise when the specific requirements of your project would require a significant amount of customization to any purchased solution; the costs of the purchased solution and the efforts required to customize it could well exceed the costs of designing and implementing the solution in-house.

PREPARE DEVELOPMENT PLAN

After making your functional, technology, and buy-versus-build decisions, you are now ready to prepare your development plan. This plan will outline how the solution will be built and the order in which functionality will be deployed.

The functional and technology requirements specify what needs to be done, and the platforms on technologies on which the functions will be deployed. Actual sequencing of the functionality development and deployment must be specified in the development plan based upon the project objectives and the results of the sales business process design. Figure 9.5 shows how a development plan can be developed.

The first step in preparing a development plan is to define the scope of work. Based on the functional and technology requirements, and the results of the build-versus-buy decision, your team will need to define the scope of work of the development effort for the entire project. The scope of work specifies the end product of the development effort. It will form the basis of your development plan.

The next step is to define what it will take to start up the development effort. Based on the scope of work and whether you are building or buying the solution, you must estimate what you need to do to get started. For example, you must estimate both

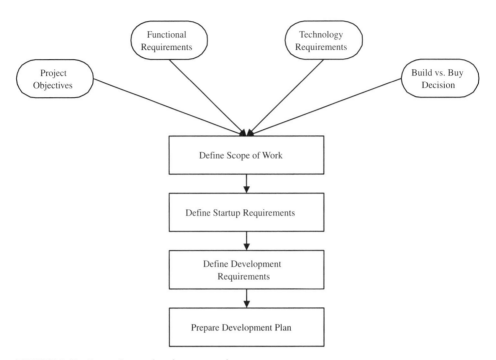

FIGURE 9.5 Preparing a development plan.

the personnel and technical resources required to initiate the development. If some of the platform technology and expertise already exists in your organization, you may be able to start development in a relatively short time frame. If, on the other hand, you intend to implement a purchased solution on new technology platforms, you will need to ramp up on both the technology and the solution before you can develop your solution.

After defining the startup requirements, you must identify the specific development requirements. These include all the technical details of the solution itself, the requirements of the underlying model, the changes that will be necessary to the purchased solution (if applicable), and the look and layout of the client interfaces.

The last step in preparing the development plan is to identify the dependencies in the development requirements, and to create a development schedule. As you go through the development requirements, you will see that certain requirements must be implemented to make others possible. For example, the data model must be completed before reports can be designed. The development schedule that is prepared must take into account the dependencies of the development requirements, and also the requirements imposed by the project objectives. For example, your overall project may call for a fully integrated enterprise Sales Force Automation system, but may phase the deployment of the different functions out over 12 to 15 months. The first function to be deployed may be a contact manager, the next an opportunity management system, and so on. In all likelihood, however, your development requirements will call for the data model to be fully completed for all the functions in the system even before you can deploy the contact manager.

At the end of this phase, you will have a development schedule that shows you when the functionality will be available to deploy.

DEVELOP DEPLOYMENT PLAN

The next step is to develop your deployment plan. This means that you have to lay out how the sales automation solution is going to be implemented in the sales organization. How you intend to deploy will determine the resource impact on the organization. For example, if you intend to deploy to your entire sales force all at once, you will have to prepare your entire sales force to handle the deployment all at one time.

Clearly there are many approaches to deployment. One approach, the *all-at-once* approach, was mentioned earlier. The approach we prefer is an incremental one, with increasing functionality introduced to an increasing user community over a period of time. In this approach, a minimum set of functionality is first introduced to a small pilot group of users. The users assimilate this new technology and get used to employing it in the execution of their jobs. The feedback from the pilot group is used to change and improve the initial functionality; this functionality is in turn deployed to the initial group, and also to more groups of users over time. Once functionality has been deployed to a few groups, the next set of functionality is deployed to the same (or sometimes another) pilot group; the process is repeated until all the functionality is deployed to all the users. This approach is shown in Figure 9.6.

As an example, your project may call for the implementation of an opportunity management system, a proposal generator, and a product configurator. The incremental approach may call for the opportunity management system to be implemented first, and deployed to a few salespeople in different territories in your organization. Those salespeople will use the system for a few weeks, and their usage will be closely monitored by your project team and the development team. Bugs in the applications are fixed as soon as they are reported, and minor changes made to the system as requested by the salespeople. Once the salespeople report they are comfortable with the system, and can see the value in using it, you can deploy the system to other users.

Your pilot group, which is now comfortable with using the technology in the day-to-day execution of their jobs, is now ready to include the proposal generator in their automation toolbox. You would follow the same process with the proposal generator, and then with the product configurator.

The advantage of this approach is that you enhance your chances of a successful deployment:

- Users have ample time to get familiar with the technology
- Pilot group feedback improves the quality of the product
- The development group is able to focus on a little functionality at a time
- Word gets around about the successes of the pilot group
- You keep up with the latest technology

The last point above is especially important when implementing a Web-based SFA solution. Technological change in Internet technologies has been so rapid that a new term, *Internet year*, has been coined to express how quickly things can change. By consensus there are four Internet years to one calendar year, implying that as much happens in Internet technologies in three

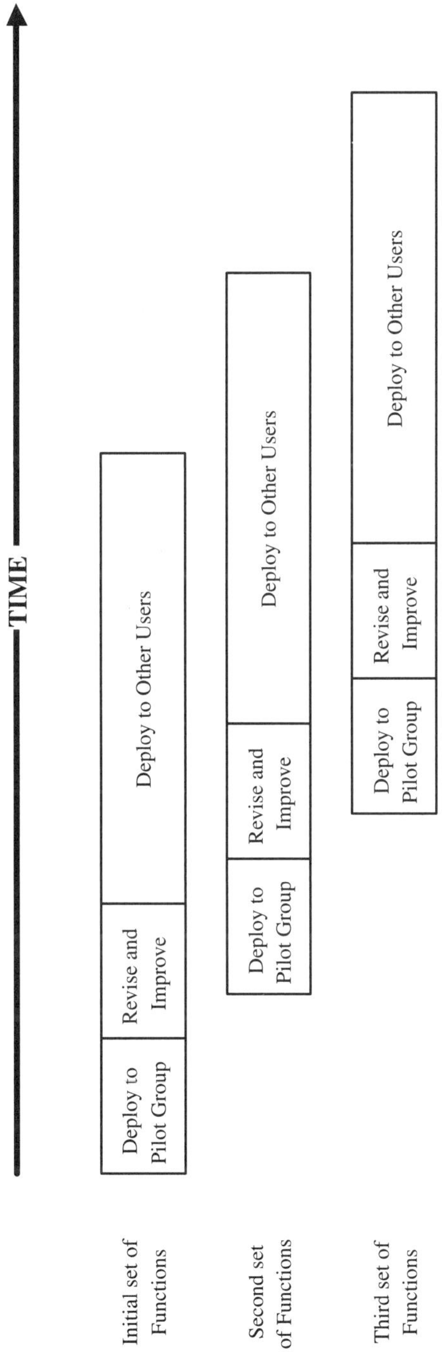

FIGURE 9.6 Incremental deployment.

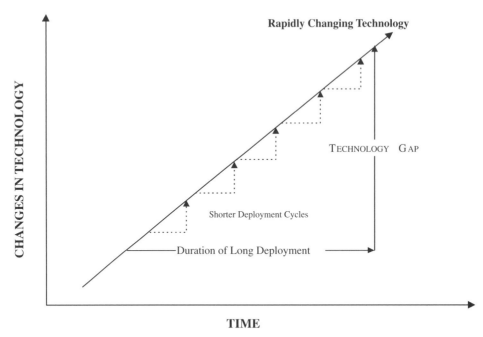

FIGURE 9.7 Technological currency with incremental deployment.

months as happens in other technologies in one year. The effect of the rapid technological change is that a project that uses Internet technologies and takes more than nine months to deploy runs the risk of being considerably out of date by the time it is available to your sales force. A better approach is to deploy in small increments of functionality, as described earlier, and use the latest available technology to release new functionality, as well as update the functionality that has already been released. This way the sales force can derive the benefits of the latest technologies, and minimize the technology gap (see Figure 9.7).

DEFINE TRAINING PLAN

One of the critical success factors of any Sales Force Automation project is the training delivered to the user community at large. When introducing new ways of doing work, and new technologies to a large group of users, you face a major challenge in ensuring that the users can use the technology; if they cannot they will not, and your project will fail.

You must prepare a training plan that provides training on not only how to do the job (process training), but also how to use the tools that are available to do the job (technology training). Clearly the training must be linked to the objectives of the Sales Force Automation project, and users must see during the training how changes in process and tools will make them more successful in the execution of their jobs.

The steps needed to deploy effective training are shown in Figure 9.8.

The training schedule should be closely linked to the preceding deployment schedule. People usually tend to retain the most when they apply what they learn as soon as possible after learning it. If you can time your training delivery so that it arrives just before, or ideally in conjunction with, the technology,

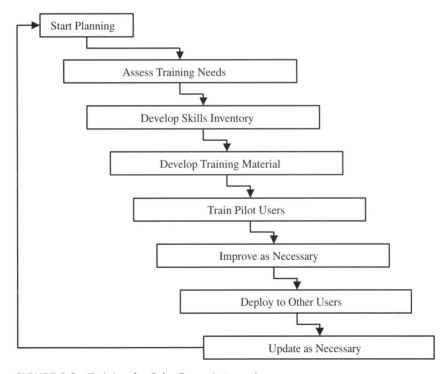

FIGURE 9.8 Training for Sales Force Automation.

the salespeople can apply the training exercises to actual sales on which they are working, and so learn both the tools and the way to use them in their day-to-day jobs.

Training must first be deployed to the pilot user group, and then improved based on their feedback before being delivered to the rest of the user community. Training can be delivered in a number of different ways, such as in a classroom, via user manuals, by interactive video, through self-paced, multimedia computer-based training (CBT), via online help embedded in the tool, and through third parties.

IDENTIFY INTERNAL SUPPORT REQUIREMENTS

Also critical is the definition of internal support requirements. Remember, you may be spending upwards of $5000 per user per year to support all the automation tools and platforms. Your Sales Force Automation tools fill an important business need, so when a salesperson cannot use the tools, revenue may be at risk. To ensure that users can utilize the sales automation tools to the maximum extent possible, you must set up an internal support function.

The internal support function, sometimes called an *internal help desk,* guides and assists users of the sales automation tools in both the usage of the tools, and the application of the tools to doing the job. Support should be provided by the internal support function for:

- All sales automation tools
- Platform hardware and operating system
- Browser software
- Synchronization software
- Communications software
- E-mail software
- Reporting tools

A common strategy these days is to outsource the internal support function to companies that specialize in supporting sales automation technologies.

DEFINE POST-ROLLOUT REQUIREMENTS

The project is not over even after all the functionality has been deployed. At this point you must manage the fallout from the deployment, as you know that everything will not go as expected. Changes and compromises made during the project must be reexamined and reevaluated, and corrections made as necessary.

You must also now start measuring performance, as this was an essential part of the business case. If performance measures indicate a successful deployment, you have cause to celebrate. If not, you must conduct an audit and review, and determine what corrective action is necessary.

Ongoing requirements must also be stated at this time. For example, how are new salespeople to be trained on the tools and technologies? How is new functionality to be identified and implemented? Who is responsible for the ongoing success of your new Sales Force Automation system? Before declaring success, you must identify who will manage the sales automation tools going forward, and conduct a formal hand-off to that person.

SUMMARY

This chapter discussed the importance of planning for Sales Force Automation, and covered all the steps in the planning cycle.

The next chapter will cover the steps you need to take in selecting a Sales Force Automation solution.

10

Selecting Sales Force Automation Tools

The previous chapter talked about the things that must be done to implement Sales Force Automation. As you saw, it can be a very involved process, and requires a lot of planning, thinking, and coordination of activities of many people. This is as it should be, for the implementation of SFA tools has the potential to significantly affect your company's revenues, and can cost a lot of money if it is not thought through completely or managed well.

One of the steps discussed earlier was making the build-versus-buy decision. In other words, should you build your Sales Force Automation tools from scratch, purchase a custom-built tool for your specific needs, or purchase a commercially available SFA tool and customize it for your organization? We concluded that you would in all likelihood purchase at least some technology from one or more vendors, and then customize that technology to meet your needs.

This chapter will discuss how you select the Sales Force Automation tools and technologies you will implement, and the vendors with which you will do business. We first describe the process by which the decision is made, then go over the elements of the information you should ask your prospective vendors to provide to help you make that decision. In this situation you are the customer, and different companies will be vying for your business. The way in which the vendor companies handle your potential business will give you some insight into the way each vendor uses Sales Force Automation, and specifically each vendor's products.

EVALUATION AND SELECTION PROCESS

If you have followed the planning process described in the previous chapter, then selecting Sales Force Automation tools and vendors should be relatively straightforward, though possibly time-consuming. Many large companies have corporate purchasing guidelines, and if your organization is subject to those standards, you must comply with them. Even so, the generic evaluation and selection process shown in Figure 10.1 applies to almost all large technology purchase situations. Readers who work in sales organizations will recognize that this is how most of their customers make purchases.

The basic steps in the process are: First define the goal of the evaluation and selection process; identify the team that will work on the process; prepare a Request for Proposal; identify the evaluation criteria; identify potential vendors; solicit responses, then review written submissions; apply the evaluation criteria to make a shortlist of vendors; get detailed demonstrations and even some application prototypes for review from the vendors on the shortlist; check the references of the vendors; and finally make a selection.

Define Goal

The first step in any evaluation and selection process is to be very clear about the purpose of the evaluation and selection exercise, and the constraints that will apply to the exercise. The person who is ultimately responsible for this task must know how the success of the task will be measured, and be able to articulate it to others who will work on the process.

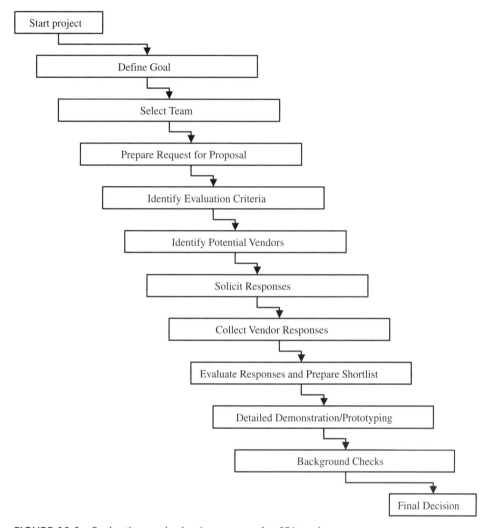

FIGURE 10.1 Evaluation and selection process for SFA tools.

The goal of the evaluation and selection exercise will be different in each company; in fact it may be different within one sales organization if there are multiple purchases to be made. Some examples of goal statements for the evaluation and selection exercise are:

- Recommend a Sales Force Automation tool that can be used to meet 80 percent of the specific functional requirements identified earlier.
- Select and purchase a tool that implements a majority of the required functionality out of the box.
- Within four weeks identify the three leading tools for the Sales Force Automation project.
- Specify the leading tool that meets the functional requirements, subject to a purchase budget constraint of $500,000.
- Select Sales Force Automation tools that can be integrated, implemented, and deployed to 100 percent of the sales force within nine months of purchase.

The specific goal of the evaluation and selection exercise will guide the entire process.

Select Team

As mentioned earlier, the purchase of Sales Force Automation tools can be a significant expenditure, and will impact the operations and even future success of your company. Many minds are usually better than one in such a selection exercise, so we recommend that you set up a team of individuals that will assist you in evaluating tools and selecting the one(s) that suit your needs. We recommend the team be large enough to bring in enough expertise, but not so large as to become unnecessarily cumbersome and bureaucratic. In our experience teams of between five and eight members are the most effective; any fewer and there may not be enough expertise and representation on the team; any more and the communications between team members become time-consuming and it becomes difficult to finalize a decision.

At a minimum the collective experience of the evaluation and selection team should include:

- Actual sales techniques and methodologies in all channels used in the company
- Sales operations and administration
- Sales management experience in the company
- Marketing programs (including leads and promotions)

- Technology assessment experience
- Technology deployment and operations experience
- Financial analysis experience

If the scope of the tools being evaluated is broader than just sales automation, the team should have some (perhaps part-time) assistance in the appropriate areas, such as:

- Customer support
- Manufacturing
- Legal services

Once the team has been established, its first task is to prepare the Request for Proposal.

Prepare Request for Proposal

The Request for Proposal (RFP) is a document that states what you intend to do with your Sales Force Automation tool, and what you are looking for. Its purpose is to give all interested vendors the same information about your requirements, and to provide a list of questions that each vendor needs to answer so that you can compare vendor responses as part of your evaluation process. A secondary purpose of the RFP is to help you document what you want, and is a good way to ensure you receive comprehensive information on which to base your decision.

By ensuring a level playing field you are more likely to receive competitive bids, as vendors know they have all the information available to all other vendors. In the event you receive questions about the RFP from any vendor, you should answer the questions and distribute both the questions and the answers to all vendors who have indicated an interest in your RFP. You would, of course, not identify the vendor that originated the questions. Depending on how good a job you have done with the RFP, you may receive few or many questions. The volume of questions you receive will determine how frequently you send out answers: With a few questions you may collect all questions and answer them once a week; with many questions you may have to do this on a daily basis.

Later in this chapter we list many questions you may ask in an RFP, and describe the purpose of each question and what to look for in the response.

Identify Evaluation Criteria

After the Request for Proposal is completed (and before it is sent out to vendors for a response) your team must decide how to evaluate all responses to the RFP. It is important to do this before responses are reviewed to make the evaluation and selection as objective as possible. Purchases of Sales Force Automation tools often involve significant investments, and therefore all aspects of the evaluation and selection should stand up to rigorous scrutiny from both company management and external auditors (especially for publicly traded companies).

A common way to decide evaluation criteria is to create a list that matches the questions in the RFP, and then indicate on that list the desired response. The desired response is often prioritized so that RFP items that are critical to the success of the project receive a higher score than RFP items that may be not so critical, or items that can be worked around. For example, if it is critical that the client-side is Web-based, then that item should receive the highest priority. On the other hand, if your company does not have a database server standard, then the item requesting a list of database servers supported by the vendor may be assigned a low priority. A priority scheme may be quite complex, with many levels of priority; or it may be simple, with just a few levels. A very common three-level scheme is as follows:

- Critical, or priority = A (Got to have)
- Medium, or priority = B (Nice to have)
- Low, or priority = C (Helps to have)

You should be disciplined about setting priorities; it is all too easy to say that everything is critical and nothing is of low priority. In reality there are certain things that are absolutely essential to the success of your automation efforts, and others that my be important but can be worked around if the vendor does not provide that feature. It is important that your team reach a consensus on the priority scheme you will use in the evaluation, and also the assignment of priorities to items in the RFP.

Some companies also develop evaluation guidelines at this time. While some items may be clear-cut, others are not. It is easy to find out whether a vendor provides a particular feature in the products, or if the vendor has been in business for a certain number of years. It becomes more difficult to measure subjective things like ease of use or ease of customization. If your RFP is such that it requires your team to make many subjective decisions, you may want to consider developing evaluation guidelines at this time so that your team is clear on how to evaluate these items. To make this process easier many companies specify numerical ratings that should be used when assessing an item, and they describe the circumstances under which each rating is appropriate.

Identify Potential Vendors

In all likelihood you have been to conferences and subscribe to trade journals, so you have a fairly good idea of the vendors that may have products that meet your needs. You may even have hired a consultant to assist you with the sales strategy and process definition, and this consultant may be associated with a product vendor, or be able to provide a list of appropriate vendors. In some situations, for example, if the technology is very new to you (unlikely after reading this book), you may ask some vendors to come in and give product overviews and demonstrations. This gives you some idea of what is possible with the vendor's technology, and may help you update (or even prepare) your RFP.

In any case we recommend you conduct a quick search on the Internet to find a complete list of Sales Force Automation vendors, and then create a list of potential vendors from that. One place to start is the Sales Automation Association (www.saaintl.org). There are many vendors with sites on the World Wide Web that can give you further information. One technique we used when researching material for this book was to enter the phrase *Sales Force Automation* into search engines such as Yahoo (www.yahoo.com) and Alta Vista (altavista.digital.com). Another way is to look at the programs of major conferences (e.g., the DCI Sales Automation Conference, www.dciexpo.com) and look at the company affiliations of speakers whose talks are of interest. We suspect you will get many more hits than you expect or even thought possible. Appendix B has a representative list of some SFA vendors.

It is important to go through this step to make sure you have included new vendors with the latest technology, who may not have caught your attention prior to now. You want to make sure that your company has access to the widest possible range of Sales Force Automation solutions, and find the solution that best meets your needs. At the same time, you do not want to waste time and money contacting vendors who clearly cannot meet your business needs.

As a part of identifying the vendors that may have an appropriate solution for your automation efforts, you should also ask for marketing data that describes the vendor's products, and how they have been used by other companies. You can use this material then to narrow down your list of potential vendors to those whose product descriptions show that they have a reasonably good chance of meeting your needs.

Solicit Responses

Once you have identified your potential vendors, you should contact each vendor and get the name of a salesperson that has responsibility for your account. Give vendors enough summary information about your project so that they can identify the appropriate sales territory for you, and assign a salesperson. When this salesperson contacts you, send a copy of your RFP to that salesperson. It is important to tell the salesperson when you expect a response to the RFP, and when you will be making a purchase decision.

In all but the most trivial exercises, and even then, you should ask vendors to keep the RFP confidential. You may even ask them to sign a *nondisclosure agreement* prior to sending them an RFP. A nondisclosure agreement legally binds the signatory to respect the confidentiality of the documents listed in the agreement. The reason for having such an agreement is obvious: The RFP will contain information about your company that may be very useful to your competition, and you don't want it falling into the wrong hands. In our experience vendors expect to sign such an agreement, and respect the confidential nature of the information in your RFP.

Vendor Responses

You should also ask each vendor to indicate shortly after receiving the RFP whether that vendor is planning on bidding for your business. It is possible that after reviewing the RFP, the vendor may decide that this sale would not be a good fit and may not want to invest the time to put together a proposal.

In all likelihood the salespeople of the vendors that will be bidding on your business will be contacting you as they are working on the response; as described earlier you should document your interactions with the salespeople, and disseminate questions and answers to all those vendors who are still planning a response. Some vendors may even ask for face-to-face meetings and an opportunity to give product demonstrations. As stated earlier, dealing with salespeople of vendors of Sales Force Automation tools is a unique opportunity to observe how the salespeople are using their own technology. It is not a good sign if the salespeople cannot keep track of commitments (if the vendor makes opportunity management systems), are unable to customize their presentations (if the vendor sells marketing encyclopedia systems), or have trouble using laptop computers (if the vendor touts the capabilities of its mobile sales force offerings).

At the end of this phase you will have responses from all vendors that are interested in your business, and you are ready to narrow down the candidates.

Prepare Shortlist

In this phase you would apply the evaluation criteria you developed earlier to the responses of the vendors. Have your entire team individually go through each vendor's response, assess the vendor's response, and assign a rating. When this is complete, you would all get together as a team to discuss and debate your individual ratings, and come up with a consensus rating for each item. Another approach is to take the assigned numerical ratings of each item, and then calculate the average rating. We prefer the consensus approach because we believe that the debate between team members who have different ratings for the same item can be very fruitful and highlight issues that the rest of the team had not considered. Furthermore a consensus approach leads to a decision that will be supported by the whole team.

After a rating is assigned for each item in a vendor's response, you must come up with an overall rating for the vendor's response. One way of doing this is to calculate a weighted average of all the ratings using the priorities you established earlier for each item. The advantage of this method is that it takes into account both the importance of an item to your organization, as well as the assessment by your team of the vendor in this area. A disadvantage of this approach is that it gives equal weight to all items that fall into any one category, which may not always be the case.

After rating all responses, you are in a position to create a shortlist of vendors that are worth investigating further. The shortlist should have at least two vendors, but no more than four. At this time you would inform the vendors that are selected for the shortlist, and notify those that are not. The vendors that are selected for the shortlist will now enter into a more detailed phase of the selection process.

Detailed Demonstration/Prototyping

Vendors that make it onto the shortlist should be asked to provide a detailed demonstration that specifically addresses the functional requirements listed in your RFP. If this is a large enough sale the vendor may be asked to create a prototype application that demonstrates the key functionality you need. The purpose of this phase is to verify that each vendor's products can in fact be used to implement your Sales Force Automation solution; this is also called the *proof of concept*. This is particularly important when you have some special requirements that are not addressed by the vendor's products. For example, you may have a requirement that the vendor's products integrate with your legacy applications; or you may require that the proposed solution be able to assign customer numbers in a way that is required by your corporate applications. However, if your requirements are relatively straightforward and will not require many changes, you may not need a proof of concept.

In this phase your team will work closely with each vendor, and assist them with design decisions. This is a good time for your team to assess the technical and implementation skills of each vendor on the shortlist. The willingness and ability of the vendor to create detailed demonstrations and prototypes is an indicator of the quality of support you may expect from the vendor after the sale is made.

Background Checks

While the vendors are preparing the detailed demonstrations and prototypes, your team should also follow up on the references provided by each vendor, as well as independently verify claims made by the vendors.

Each vendor will provide customer references that you can call upon to get some feedback about the vendor. It may be obvious, but it bears mentioning that many customer references reflect the vendor's successes, not necessarily the customers that had issues with the vendor that were not resolved to the customer's satisfaction. When speaking to references, ask for both the good and the bad aspects of doing business with the vendor. Try to get a sense of whether the vendor was accurate in time and budget estimates for deployment, and if the vendor was available after the sale to assist with the implementation. Ask if you can speak to other people at the vendor's referenced customers, as well as visit the customer's site to see the products in operation.

Another approach is to purchase market surveys done periodically by many market research companies (for example, the Gartner Group, www.gartnergroup.com; the Aberdeen Group, www.aberdeengroup.com; the Meta Group, www.metagroup.com; Prognostics, www.prognostics.com). You may also be able to identify customers of the vendors that are not on the list of references. You may gain a lot of valuable information if you can talk to these customers.

You should also ask your financial group to check into the business viability of the vendor; you don't want to spend a lot of money on a Sales Force Automation tool only to have the vendor go out of business.

The goal in this phase is to get as much background information as possible on your prospective partner. The better informed you are, the better able you'll be to make your final decision.

Final Decision

Final decisions are hardly ever made on strictly quantitative analyses. With the marketplace being what it is these days, your team will in all likelihood identify two or three vendors that could provide the tools and services you are looking for, at roughly comparable prices. Your decision then is going to hinge on intangibles, such as how your team feels about the quality of the vendors, their commitment to postsales technical support, their ability to deliver on future products, and so on. This part of the selection process is the most troublesome precisely because there is often no clear-cut leader at the end of the evaluations. You must rely on your intuition, and that of your team members, to make the final decision.

The single vendor you choose will be the one with whom your company may conduct detailed negotiations for the purchase of products and services. The other vendors who were not chosen should be informed of your decision at this time. If negotiations with the first choice fall through, one of the other vendors may still be a good selection.

REQUEST FOR PROPOSAL

The rest of this chapter presents a fairly complete set of questions that you can use to prepare a Request for Proposal for your Sales Force Automation exercise. Not all questions will be appropriate for all applications, so include only those questions for which the answers will help you make your tool and vendor selection. The questions are on the accompanying CD-ROM in Microsoft Word 7.0 format, in the file RFP.DOC.

The RFP is normally broken up into the following parts:

- Introduction
- Vendor's Sales Force Automation Vision
- Vendor's Business Profile
- Technology Infrastructure
- Product Functionality
- Costs

Introduction

In this section you give an overview of your company, and state the scope of your Sales Force Automation efforts, why you are undertaking the automation, the benefits you hope to derive from implementing the automation, and the purpose of the RFP.

Organization Overview

Describe in a few paragraphs the company you work for, the markets it is in, and where your organization fits into the overall company. For example, are you a part of the corporate sales function, or is your organization a division of a large company? The purpose of this is to give the vendor some familiarity with your company and the markets, in case there are some market segment-specific requirements they may be asked to provide.

Scope of Sales Force Automation Efforts

Describe the scope of your SFA efforts. Specifically, summarize the functions in your organizations that will be affected by the automation (e.g., leads generation, field sales force, channels, etc.), and the approximate number of people that will be using the tools you intend to purchase now and in the future. This information is to help prospective vendors estimate how large the potential sale may be, and to decide if this is a sale in which they want to participate.

Expected Benefits of Sales Force Automation

In this section you would briefly describe the problems you wish to address by implementing Sales Force Automation, and the benefits you expect to realize as a result of the implementation. This section gives vendors an idea of what your expectations are regarding the impact of their products. Some vendors may not want to participate in the sale if they feel your expectations are unrealistic and it will be difficult to maintain you as a satisfied customer.

Purpose of This Request for Proposal

Finally in this section you should state the purpose of this RFP. Specifically, you should inform prospective vendors about what specifically you wish to purchase, for how many people, and over what time period. For example, earlier you may have stated that the automation efforts would eventually affect 1000 people in your organization; however, this RFP is to purchase limited functionality for only a small pilot group of 100 people, and the remainder of the purchase will be opened up for competitive bidding after the implementation.

Sales Force Automation Vision

In this section ask the vendor to provide an overview of the Sales Force Automation tools offered, if and how they work together, and the demonstrated benefits of this vendor's approach. The responses should indicate how well the vendor understands the market.

Please provide an overview of your product suite, and the interrelationships between your products.

This question gives you some insight into the functionality provided by the vendor's products, and how the vendor views Sales Force Automation tools (stand-alone, interconnected, or integrated). Key things to look for here are the comprehensiveness of the tools, and what functionality the vendor believes is important.

What are the benefits of this approach, and why is this approach better than others?

This question allows the vendor to give you some information on why the vendor believes the vendor's approach leads to business benefits. Again, this points to the vendor's understanding of the market, and specifically your market segment. The vendor should also be able to show why the vendor's approach is superior; other vendors will give you their opinions, so you should be able to get quite a complete analysis of the products of all vendors.

 ### What is your future vision of Sales Force Automation, and what products do you plan to introduce in the next 12 months?

The purpose of this question is twofold: The first purpose is to assess if in fact the vendor is thinking about the future of the industry and where it is headed; the second purpose is to see if the vendor is planning for changes in the marketplace. You want to be sure that the vendor is keeping up with technologies and shifts in the way of doing business. Remember, your business environment is sure to change; to be successful you will in all likelihood need to change your business processes, and may need additional functionality to support those changes. The vendor should be able to show some insight into what those changes may be, and how the vendor intends to make you successful in the future.

Business Profile

In this section you ask the vendor to give you information on business operations so that you can assess the long-term business viability of the vendor.

Longevity Indicators

The purpose of asking questions related to the longevity of a company is to get a feel for how long the company has been in business, and to assess its future success. A Sales Force Automation implementation is a significant effort, and once implemented the system will be in place for a few years. During its operating life your organization will need the help and assistance of the vendor to resolve the technical issues that will invariably come up. It is important, therefore, to assess the likelihood of the vendor's survival while the application is such an essential part of your business.

 Please indicate how many years you have been in business.

The purpose of this question is to see if the vendor is a new entrant, or one that has been around in the marketplace for some years. Responses indicating relatively new companies should be flagged for a rigorous assessment of the management team. This is not to say that new companies are not viable competitors—rather that a proposal from a new company merits special attention, as it will have less of a track record that may point to the probability of its future success.

 Please provide pro forma financial statements for the last 12 quarters.

This question is to get a feeling for the profitability of the vendor, and how much of the vendor's business your sale will represent. Being a small account for a large vendor may mean you may not be well treated; on the other hand, being a large account for a small vendor may mean that the vendor may not have the means to deliver on products and services on so large a scale. In either case, this information should be balanced by reference checks from both small and large customers of this vendor.

 What is your revenue recognition policy?

The purpose of this question is to assess whether the vendor counts revenue when the contract is signed, the product is shipped, or when you finally install and accept it. Vendors who tend to recognize revenues later in the implementation tend to provide better installation and post-sales support, since they have a vested interest in your success. The issue is not so much the actual payments or transfers of money, but rather the vendor's perception of when the sale is complete: upon shipment or installation.

Please provide short biographies of your senior management team.

One indicator of a (potentially) successful company is the quality of its management team. If a vendor's response indicates that most of the management team has worked in the Sales Force Automation area for some time, there is a greater likelihood that they understand the business and how to approach the issues in Sales Force Automation. You also want to look at the success of companies that the members of the vendor's management team have managed in the past.

Please indicate how your headcount has grown over the past 12 quarters by both function and geographic region.

The purpose of this question is to see how quickly this vendor has grown, and where that growth has gone. Growth in Research and Development and Technical Support indicate that the vendor is investing in both future products and the success of current customers. Disproportionate growth in headquarters functions indicates that the vendor may be building up an infrastructure that is inconsistent with sales. In general you want to see a balanced growth in headcount that is consistent with the vendor's growth in revenues and the installed base.

What is your sales model?

Ask the vendor to describe the sales channels used, and why the vendor uses those channels. If the vendor's sales are very dependent on indirect sales and resellers, you should investigate further the kind of support you may expect to receive, and from whom. For example, if your Sales Force Automation tool comes from a value-added reseller (VAR) that packages the vendor's products with some services and possibly some hardware, you will want to ascertain whether you will be calling the vendor or the VAR for support. If it is the former, you will assess the quality of the vendor's support operations. If the latter, you will also want to assess the quality of the VAR's support operations, as well as the vendor's relationship with the VAR.

Please describe if and how you use your own products.

The desired response to this question is for the vendor to show how all products sold by the vendor are used by the vendor's own sales force. If the vendor does not use those tools, then you may ask why tools not good enough for the vendor are appropriate for you. Ask the vendor's salesperson to walk you through how they are tracking and managing the activities related to your RFP. Ask also how often the vendor upgrades to the latest versions of the software, and how often the application is customized. Low frequency of changes in either could indicate that it is not easy to upgrade or customize the software.

Please describe your alliances and partnerships with other vendors, and if you are proposing a solution that will involve one or more of these.

Many companies offer selected tools that meet specific needs; to deliver on larger implementations that require a greater amount of functionality, some vendors have formed alliances with other product vendors and implementation partners. If the response indicates that the vendor will be using a partner for this sale, you should get additional information on the partner. For example, a vendor may have implementation alliances with a number of small consulting companies. You should evaluate the quality of these consulting companies, especially the ones that the vendor has selected to bring into this opportunity. As discussed earlier, implementing and deploying a Sales Force Automation tool requires considerable expertise and resources, and you want to be sure that the vendor's partners are capable of delivering.

Customer Indicators

The purpose of asking questions related to customers is to understand how the vendor treats customers, and what guidelines are in place for account management. The relationship each vendor has with existing customers is a good indicator of the quality of relationships with future customers, including your organization.

When was your first Sales Force Automation product put into production, and is that customer still using your products?

This question gives you information on how long the vendor has been installing Sales Force Automation tools, indicating the vendor's experience in this area. First customers tend to have good relationships with vendors, because they took a chance on the success of the vendor. If the first customer is no longer using the vendor's products, you should investigate further and see if the relationship was terminated due to a poor relationship, rather than changes in business needs.

What is the size of your installed base, in terms of both number of customers, and the number of users?

This question gives you insight into how quickly the company has grown in terms of customers, and the average number of users per customer. This is more information to compare to the revenue information provided in the previous section. If the vendor sells high-end solutions, such as enterprise tools, and can show only a few users per customer, it may indicate that the products are difficult to implement or use.

What is the average tenure of your installed base? Please break out the number of customers and the number of users by tenure in months.

What you hope to estimate from the response to this question is how long customers tend to stay with this vendor. You would expect to see a few customers of long tenure, and progressively more of shorter tenure as the vendor's sales have grown in the recent past. By using the numbers given here you would also get some idea of the average time to deploy the tools provided by this vendor; increases in the number of customers should be followed by distinct increases in the number of users after a suitable time period.

What percentage of your installed base can be used as a reference? How many customers have you lost in the past three years, and why?

The response to these questions will indicate how well the vendor manages its relationship with its customers, and whether the vendor understands why customers are lost. A high percentage of referenceable customers, especially customers of long tenure, indicates that the vendor manages the customer relationship well and will pay attention to your account. If many customers are leaving this vendor, that indicates that the original sale was not appropriate, or that the vendor cannot meet the ongoing and changing needs of its customers.

What is your customer relationship management philosophy, and what programs do you have in place to implement this philosophy?

Chapter 7 discussed the importance of customer relationship management. The responses to this question will indicate the importance this vendor places on customer relationship management. Does this vendor have specific programs in place to manage the relationship, or is account management done in an *ad hoc* manner? Does the vendor believe that to be successful its customers must also be successful? Does the vendor sponsor an international user's group?

Support Services

Sales Force Automation will have a significant impact on your business. No matter how good a job you do in implementing your automation, you will from time to time need to contact the vendor for technical support. In this section the vendors are asked about how they support customers.

Please describe your technical support offerings, with responsiveness goals, available methods of support, hours of operation, and pricing.

Key items to look for in the response include the availability of support (will the vendor be there when you need help?) and the pricing. If support prices are high, you should ask what exactly you will be getting for that money. If support prices seem low relative to the competition, you may question the quality of service you will receive, and look into the satisfaction levels of current customers.

 When does the support coverage start (upon receipt of software, after install, or after implementation)?

It is important to know when you are eligible for support coverage. Some vendors classify support prior to an implementation as billable consulting time. Each vendor has its own policy, so you should find out in advance to avoid any surprises.

 Do you have install specialists working on your support line?

Some vendors have support staff dedicated to the software install process. This type of support is given high priority since it is important to get the customer up and running as smoothly as possible. If you are working on a short time line, you may not want to wait in the standard support queue for a response to your question. This is a good indicator of how responsive the vendor is after the sale.

 What is your support call volume per support representative?

Get the vendor to supply volume metrics, so you can get an idea of how well staffed their support center is. Too high a volume will indicate inadequate staffing and hence long wait times in the queue, unless, of course, the vendor can show statistics that tell another story.

*Please describe the training programs you offer,
and how they are delivered.*

The intent of this question is to assess how much training is
available on the vendor's products, and whether training is complete and comprehensive. If training is delivered by the vendor,
ask how big the training facility is, and how many full-time in-
structors are on the vendor's staff. If training is delivered by the
vendor's partners, ask how those partners are identified, developed, and certified. Some vendors are now also delivering interactive training on CD-ROM or even the Web; if that is the case,
you should ask how often the course material is updated, and if
it is kept current with the latest releases of software.

*Please describe the product and user documentation
you provide, and the media on which it is available.*

As with the preceding training question, the intent of this question is to assess the quantity and quality of the vendor's documentation. You are looking for documentation that is well
written and comprehensive, and available in both paper and
electronic media. You also should ask about the vendor's documentation update processes, and if revised documentation is
available prior to release of a new version of a product.

*What amount of consulting assistance is included or
recommended in order to get the product installed?*

Some vendors offer installation as part of the software package
price. They anticipate some level of assistance required by the
customer, so they build the install cost into the price of the software. You need to know if you are expected to pay for consulting
help during an install, and if so, how much consulting time is
typically required.

*What is the business and technical experience of your
consulting organization? Please provide brief background
on each member of your consulting organization.*

You don't want to end up paying hourly consulting rates for green
employees. Find out how many projects the consultants have com-

pleted for the vendor, how long they have worked for the vendor, and how many years they have worked in the industry. It is important to work with a consultant that has practical industry experience, both from a business process and technical perspective.

 What types and amount of training are your consultants required to attend prior to working on an implementation?

You should find out how rigorous the vendor's standards are for quality in their consulting organization. The type and amount of training of the vendor's consultants is an indication of not only the quality of the staff, but also how current they are. Look for training in both products and industry practices. How often do the vendor's consultants speak at or attend industry conferences.

 Please provide us with your typical implementation project methodology.

Most vendors have a standard project methodology and a standard boilerplate project plan for a typical software implementation. Understanding the methodology will give you a good idea of how the vendor will approach the project, and the project plan will give you some insight into what you will need to do to prepare for the project.

 What is the average time to implement?

Find out the average implementation time frame to gauge how difficult it is to implement their product. A time frame of greater than three to six months could be a red flag that the product is more complex to install and maintain than it may seem from the surface.

 Please list any implementation partners you work with, and what level of certification they have achieved with your company.

It is always nice to know you have consulting options, in case the vendor does not have resources available to you in the time frame you may need, or at a price that you consider reasonable. Implementation partners will often charge less than the vendor for professional services.

What type of certification process must your implementation partners go through?

This is an indicator of the quality standards required by the vendor from their consulting partners. Look especially for training and technical expertise requirements.

Research and Development

What is your product release policy, especially with respect to bug fixes?

The intent of this question is to find out how often the vendor will release new versions of the product, and whether bug fixes will be available to you when you need them. If releases are too frequent it could indicate a product that is full of defects; on the other hand, long times between new versions could indicate that the vendor does not have the resources to fix defects. Frequent bug-fix releases and new versions could also create an administrative burden for you if you have to install new software every time there is a new release from the vendor. As mentioned earlier, you should ask the vendor what release the vendor runs in-house on their production environment. In other words, is the vendor confident enough in the latest release to bet the business on it?

What is the current release level of your product and when was it released? Please provide a history of your releases, and the demographics of the customer base on those releases.

The purpose of these questions is to check that the release schedule matches the stated policy, and if customers regularly upgrade to more current releases. If the release schedule does not match the stated policy, you should investigate why this is the case. It could be an indicator of tight resources in the Research and Development or Quality Assurance functions in the vendor's organization.

How much do you spend annually on research and development, and what is that number as a percentage of total spending?

The intent here is to find out how committed the vendor is to product futures. A low number for R&D may be an indication that the vendor does not expect to be in this business too long. Expect to see a number in the 15 to 25 percent range.

Please provide a list of upcoming releases and all new functionality planned.

This is important to know in case you have requirements that the vendor does not meet today but will have available by the time you make your purchase decision or start your implementation. If a significant amount of functionality you need is planned for a future release, you may be better off going with another vendor. The vendor will probably ask you to keep the information provided in this section confidential from competitors, an understandable request.

Please describe your quality assurance process.

Find out what standards the vendor's QA group has for product quality. A rigorous quality assurance plan indicates that the vendor pays a lot of attention to quality.

Do you have an formal beta program? If so, please describe.

You want to find out how many different audiences a new release has been tested against. Formal beta programs indicate that the vendor has allowed enough time in the development schedule to manage a beta process with select customers. It also indicates that the new release will be tested in a greater variety of environments, possibly including environments not reproducible at the vendor site.

Technology Infrastructure

The purpose of this section is to find out from the vendor the technology infrastructure necessary for the vendor's products, and to see if your environment is compatible or if it will need to be changed in some way.

Platforms Supported

 Please provide a hardware and software compatibility matrix for all platform/database/OS configurations supported by your current release.

It is important to know if your particular configuration has been tested and is supported by the vendor. It is better to find out in advance than when you are going through an install. The answer to this question may also indicate how much new platform infrastructure you might need to acquire.

 Please list the minimum hardware and software requirements for each client platform listed above.

Again you want to make sure you have the correct configuration requirements for your clients, in case you need to go through some client upgrades prior to installation. This information will also be useful in costing the deployment of the tool.

 Please list the minimum hardware and software requirements for each server type supported.

Same as with the preceding client requirements, you want to find out in advance if you need to go through a server hardware or software upgrade. You may find that you have a legacy system on your server that is not compatible with a newer piece of hardware or software required by the vendor's package, an issue you would need to resolve prior to deployment.

Network Requirements

 ### *What network protocols are supported?*

Find out if you are going to have connectivity issues with your existing network, and whether you need to purchase an alternate protocol in order to use the vendor's product.

Client/Server Architecture

 ### *What type and number of tiers do you support in your product architecture?*

You want to find out if the product has been optimized for a client/server environment. If the vendor supports more than two tiers, or *n* tiers, then you can expect an optimized application that has been streamlined for performance in a client/server environment.

 ### *Do you provide a thin client?*

Some vendors are migrating toward the thin client, typically when they have an architecture that supports more than two tiers. This will indicate that the vendor has been forward thinking in its client-development efforts and the likelihood of moving toward a Web client if not available already.

Remote Client Approach

 ### *Do you support offline reader capabilities?*

Find out how the vendor implements a remote client technology strategy. Does it enable your salesperson to view data offline, with data local on the salesperson's laptop? The ability to do this means that the salesperson will only have to be connected to download and upload data, or to conduct transactions in real time while connected.

 ### *Do your products support data synchronization?*

If your sales force is working offline, you want them to be able to not only read, but also write to the database and make edits to customer data, and then merge the edits with the master corporate database. Synchronization is a complex feature and can significantly affect the performance of sales automation tools. Ask to see independently verifiable performance information on synchronization, and be sure to check on this when following up with references.

Systems Management

 Please describe your product's database and application administrative tools in terms of functionality and whether the tools have a Graphical User Interface (GUI) front end.

You want to find out how difficult the maintenance of the product will be. Absence of GUI tools for administrative functions may indicate a clumsy administration module. Some vendors do not provide administrative tools at all, and require you to create scripts to access the database components directly. This is not a good sign, and is an indication that the vendor is not paying much attention to the actual operation and maintenance of the system once it is installed.

 Do you provide user-defined group level security?

You want to know how flexible the security features of the product are. Group-level access that can be modified by the customer provides the ability to assign users to functional groups, each with a different set of access privileges. Thus some users can perform a limited set of functions, others can perform another limited set of functions, but some privileged users can perform all functions in the system.

 Do you provide user authentication?

This is standard name/password type of security access. Each user must log in and be authenticated before using the system.

 Please describe any archiving capability you provide.

Once your system is installed and has been in production for some time, you may have a requirement to archive old records to free up database space. This should also provide a mechanism for restoring the historical data if needed.

Do you provide audit trails?

Audit trails are important in that they record user transactions with user login, transaction type, and date and time of transaction. This may also be an ISO 9000 requirement for your company.

Performance

Do you publish independent benchmark results?

You may want to know what types of performance benchmarks have been performed by any independent groups. Beware of benchmark results reported by the vendor's own testing, as these are often conducted in highly controlled environments that may not reflect actual real-life scenarios.

How many concurrent user connections will the product support?

This will indicate how scalable the application is. Some products come to their knees when hit with 50 or 100 concurrent user sessions, because of the potential for a high number of transactions and large amounts of data transfer between the clients and the server. You need to find out if the product will support your anticipated growth in users.

Please list the average and maximum number of concurrent users currently in productions.

The answer to the second part of this question is one you should be able to verify independently by asking the customers that have a large number of concurrent users.

Please list the average and largest database size in production.

As before, this is also something you can verify independently. The two preceding questions will give you another indication of how scalable the application is.

Data Capability

 Do you support multiple character sets?

 Do you support multiple date formats?

 Do you support international currencies?

The three questions will give you an indication of whether you will have difficulty rolling the application out to your international subsidiaries. If all three questions are answered Yes, then the vendor has probably applied a thorough internationalization integration into the product.

Configuration and Customization

 Do you provide a GUI client customization tool?

Find out how difficult user interface customizations will be. A GUI tool usually indicates that the customization will be somewhat easier than plain programming. Ask also to see a copy of the Client Customization User Guide to assess what level of effort is involved in the customization.

 What GUI standard is used?

This will tell you if the client is likely to be native to the platform you intend to use. You may be disappointed with the look and feel of an application that was developed on another platform, and ported over to your platform of choice.

 Do you provide HTML and Java support?

If your intention is to provide full access to the application over the Web, you want to make sure the vendor has provisions in the product to fully support and create the HTML and Java files with the customization tools.

Do you provide an online help system?

Many vendors do not supply online help, which is a great disappointment for the eventual users of the system. No one reads manuals anymore.

Is online help customizable?

You want to be able to edit the online help to incorporate your business process as well as new fields you may have added to any screens. You don't want the help to be limited to just the fields the vendor provided out of the box.

Do you provide a GUI data model customization tool?

Find out how difficult database customizations will be. A GUI tool usually indicates that the customization will be somewhat less difficult. You generally want to minimize customizations to the vendor's data model, but in some cases you must do so.

What do you provide in the way of data conversion tools (to convert legacy data)?

Find out if you will be able to easily import your legacy data. This may have a major implementation impact, because if you have to convert a lot of legacy data and there are no tools to help you, you will have to develop your own conversion tools.

How will customizations roll over to future releases?

You will in all likelihood customize the application to suit your particular needs. This kind of customization requires a considerable investment in time and labor, and you want to be sure that the customizations you implement in one release of the application can easily be rolled over to a future release. The answer to this question will tell you if the vendor has a well-thought-out upgrade strategy and process.

How long is the average upgrade process?

You want to know the impact of the upgrade process, and how long your system will be expected to be down while an upgrade is performed. This is another question you will want to ask other customers.

Application Architecture

Do you publish a data dictionary?

A well-documented application will have a formal data dictionary that describes not only all fields in all tables, but also the purpose of each field. Beware of a vendor that says you can generate a data dictionary as a report. The data dictionary generated by such a report may not be well documented, and may be very difficult to use.

Do you provide a high-level Entity Relationship (ER) diagram?

This will show you the linkages between modules, as well as the key data elements. Your IT people will want this to understand how the application works.

Do you have a documented Application Programming Interface (API)?

The API is a set of programming routines that allow you to pass data to and from the application. You will need an API if you want to integrate the application with other applications used in your company.

Product Functionality

Chapter 3 discussed the different types of tools in a Sales Force Automation system. The following items are intended to provide specific functionality you may want to see in the product you select; you can pick and choose which functionality you need. Since we have covered much of the functionality in detail in Chapter 3, the descriptions here are brief and are intended only to jog your memory.

Please provide a current product overview and future vision for functionality.

The product overview frames the presentation for the rest of the responses in this section.

Sales Models and Methodologies Supported

 Please indicate the current sales models and methodologies incorporated into the product, as well as any future planned models.

The purpose of this question is to see how comprehensive the product is in the sales models and methodologies it implements. If your sales model is not supported, or if the specific selling methodology used in your sales organization is not implemented in the product, then the product is probably not for you.

Approach to Team Selling

 Does your product support skills identification? How?

 Does your product support resource scheduling? How?

 Does your product support territory management? How?

The intent of these questions is to find out if the product has features that support team selling, and how those features are implemented.

Leads Management

 Does your product support a mass mailing function?

If your normal business practice is to generate or otherwise manage leads through mass mailings, the product you purchase should support this function.

Forecasting

Describe the forecasting model methodology used in your product.

As discussed in Chapter 6, there are many ways in which a forecast can be prepared. The intent of this question is to see how the product implements forecasting, and if your forecasting methodology can be used with this product.

What type of roll-up capability (organization versus individual versus product) do you provide?

Forecasts need to be rolled up in a number of different ways. The product should support a number of automatic roll-up schemes, and allow you to specify special roll-up schemes if needed.

Marketing Encyclopedia

Do you provide a marketing encyclopedia that provides access to different document types?

Be sure that the marketing encyclopedia can support different types of documents, such as word-processing files, presentations, images, audio files, video clips, and so on. Otherwise you will need to convert all documents to a standard format, and perhaps not be able to use all the documents you need to use.

Does the marketing encyclopedia support access controls?

A marketing encyclopedia is far more useful when it can be used as a central document repository, and access to documents is controlled and limited to authorized users, much as a library may have different access and lending privileges.

How much of the marketing encyclopedia can be made available over the Internet?

Can the marketing encyclopedia incorporate content on the Internet?

What kind of publishing process, if any, does the marketing encyclopedia enforce?

The answers to the preceding questions will give you some insight into how far along the vendor is in thinking about Web-enabling the marketing encyclopedia, and in making it possible to manage the content in the encyclopedia.

Sales Configurator

 How does the sales configurator work?

The purpose of this question is to find out how the sales configurator provided by the vendor works: what it takes as input, how it processes the input by applying dependencies and constraints, and how it presents the results.

 Does the sales configurator provide a means to translate customer requirements into product selections?

The more of this type of translation a user can do, the less the user will need to understand all the features and benefits of all the offerings you sell. A highly sophisticated configurator will allow you to set up an Interactive Selling System (ISS).

 How does the configurator maintain product information, dependencies, and constraints?

Maintaining a configurator can be a very time-consuming exercise if the product does not provide an easy-to-use tool to maintain all the information needed to drive the configuration.

 Does the configurator have interfaces to manufacturing and logistics applications?

Permissible product configurations are often specified in manufacturing systems, so one way to reduce the maintenance overhead is to use data from your company's manufacturing system in the product configurator. Similarly, product availability information can be imported from your company's logistics application.

Can the output from the configurator be sent to a quotation system?

Once a sale is configured, the quotation system is used to price the configuration. The configurator should support an easy transfer of data from the configurator to the quotation system.

Can the configurator be run on a salesperson's laptop computer, or does it require a connection to a server?

If your field sales force spends a lot of time on the road, you should make sure that they can configure a sale without having to access the sales automation tool remotely. The salesperson should be able to configure a sale in the presence of a prospect.

Quotation Management

How does the quotation system work?

The reason for asking this question is self-evident: You want to understand how the vendor has implemented the quotation system.

Do you provide multiple price lists? How is this implemented in the application?

Your organization may work off multiple price lists, such as one for government sales, another for educational sales, and so on. The quotation system should be able to recognize the type of list that needs to be used, and apply prices from that list.

Do you provide for automatic discounting?

Certain fields in the description of a prospect may indicate that a special discount is to be applied, such as a discount for add-on products or upgrades. The quotation system should recognize those fields and apply the appropriate discount.

Do you provide automatic links to the forecasting module?

As an opportunity moves closer to the close of the sale, the quotation system must interface with the forecasting module to ensure that the latest information is included in the forecast.

 Can the quotation system apply discounts negotiated in previous contracts?

Some customers may negotiate a volume or enterprisewide discount in their first purchase from your company. Subsequent purchases, even if they are new sales, may require the application of the discount. This is a feature that should be supported by the quotation system.

 How closely is the quotation system linked to the sales configurator?

The items in a quotation system are provided by the sales configurator. It would defeat the purpose of automation if the quotation system had to be fed manually. A good quotation system should be tightly integrated with the sales configuration tool, and be able to apply pricing to all items passed on from the configurator.

 Can the quotation system export data to the proposal-generation tool?

A quote that is prepared by the quotation system will need to be used in a proposal, which may require that the entire quote be packaged and sent to a proposal-generation system.

 Can the quotation system export data to an order-processing application?

Once the sale is closed, an order must be placed in your company's order processing system. The quotation system should be able to pass along the quote to an order-processing system so that there is no need to reenter data.

Telemarketing and Telesales

 What type of computer telephony integration support do you have?

If your sales organization expects to receive leads over the telephone, or you have a large telesales operation, you want to know if the vendor has an interface between the application and commercially available automatic call distributors (ACDs). This allows a call to be synchronized with the data displayed on a user's computer screen.

 Do you provide integration with commercially available telephone lists?

If you use telephone lists available from outside sources, the product should be able to integrate and use those lists.

Personal Productivity Integration

Have the vendor check all of the following links or functionality that apply:

 Calendar (and level of integration)

 Time accounting

 Word processors

 Spreadsheets

 Expense report programs

 E-mail

 Fax

Contact manager

If there are particular personal productivity tools that your sales force is used to, then list them and ask if the vendor's application supports those tools.

Workflow Engine

A good workflow engine is essential to a successful deployment of a sales automation system. The following questions are intended to assess how the vendor's products manage workflow.

 How does the product handle task assignment?

You will want a way to specify tasks and assign them to individuals known to the sales automation system. For example, a salesperson may create and assign a task to a sales engineer to prepare a technical demonstration.

 How are commitments tracked in your product?

Many commitments are made during the course of a sale, and each commitment must be tracked to ensure that nothing falls through the cracks. A workflow engine should provide a good commitment tracking mechanism.

 How are task hand-offs made between individuals/organizations?

Tasks are sometimes handed off between individuals and organizations, and the workflow engine should enable task hand-off and manage and track these hand-offs. For example, a sales engineer may prepare a technical demonstration, then hand off the task to another sales engineer for review.

 Describe your notification and escalation system.

The workflow engine should provide a means to notify users when certain events occur. The escalation system is used to trigger notifications and cause tasks to be assigned to individuals when criteria specified in business rules are met. You want to see a notification and escalation system that has a sophisticated system of business rules, and many ways to notify individuals.

Describe how a user can log notes, and specify where notes can be logged.

Knowing the current status of events, and keeping up-to-date records on all activities is essential to good opportunity management. The sales workflow engine should provide a means for users to log notes on all tasks.

Does your system keep audit trails?

An audit trail provides a historical record of what happened to a task over a period of time, such as who was assigned to the task, what that person did, the changes in the status of the task, and so on. An audit trail also provides an excellent resource during postmortems, and for information to be used in sales process improvement.

Reporting/Searching Capability

The following functionality will give you an indication of how flexible the query and reporting availability is.

Describe the query methods your product supports.

Describe the search fields that can be used in a query.

Is there a GUI ad hoc query tool?

Please describe all standard reports already in your product.

Get a list of all standard reports provided by the vendor.

Reporting tools

Find out if the reporting tool supported by the vendor is a common third-party tool, or a proprietary tool. In our experience third-party tools are preferable, because you can select the tool that your people are most comfortable using.

Customer Management

 How does your product support linkages to other applications?

As mentioned earlier, the product should provide an API that can be used to link the application to other applications. In addition, the vendor may already have standard interfaces to many other commercially available corporate applications.

Costs

Have the vendor list costs for each of the following:

 License costs—per seat versus per concurrent user

 Training

 Implementation consulting (including minimum and incremental charges)

 Other consulting (including minimum and incremental charges)

 Programming/customization

 Project management

 Support

Telecommunications costs

 Additional third-party software

 Additional hardware

 Life-cycle costs

The purpose of this cost information is to help you make an economic model of the purchase.

SUMMARY

This chapter covered the selection process you would use to find a vendor for your technology needs. The process may appear to be long and involved, but considering the amount of money and resources you will be investing in Sales Force Automation, the process is well worth following.

Survey of Sales Force Automation Technologies

By a small sample we may judge of the whole piece.

Miguel de Cervantes in Don Quixote de la Mancha, *1605–1615*

Content Management for a Web-Based Marketing Encyclopedia— Interwoven TeamSite

11

Chapter 3 discussed Marketing Encyclopedia Systems (MES), and showed why they are an important Sales Force Automation tool. Using Web technologies to implement (or supplement) a marketing encyclopedia has great promise for Sales Force Automation because of its high leverage. In fact, a Marketing Encyclopedia System can be implemented on the Web with relatively little effort, and independently of other types of Sales Force Automation. Benefits can be realized in a short time frame, as accurate and up-to-date information is made available to the sales force. But setting up the Web-based MES is the easy part; the more challenging and time-consuming part is to maintain the quality and accuracy of the site as it is updated repeatedly, especially with contributions from multiple sources.

IMPLEMENTING A MARKETING ENCYCLOPEDIA SYSTEM

To implement a marketing encyclopedia on the Web, after deciding what you want to put into the encyclopedia you must create the content, organize it, publish it, and then distribute the content to the appropriate audiences. We like to think of a marketing encyclopedia as a high-quality publication that has constantly changing content supplied by multiple authors, yet must be published with a very short lead time. A simple process for publishing content on a Web-based marketing encyclopedia is shown in Figure 11.1.

There are many different sources for the content in a marketing encyclopedia, and usually there will be many different authors for much of the content. For example, content for the encyclopedia may be created by product managers (product specifications), marketing managers (promotions), industry analysts (competitive analyses), marketing communications specialists (presentation material), and so on. To publish content, each of these authors could put material directly on the Web site for access by all users. While this has the advantage of being immediate (i.e., the content will be immediately available to anyone who can access the Web site), you run a major risk with this approach: Your marketing encyclopedia can become very chaotic as the number of contributors and the volume of published information grows.

For instance, there would be no means of ensuring that the

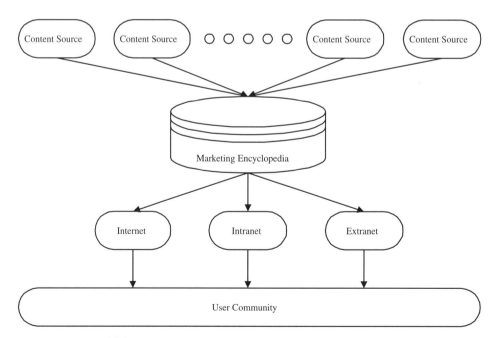

FIGURE 11.1   Publishing process for a marketing encyclopedia.

content meets corporate standards, and if the content is positioned in the correct place on the site. If the content doesn't meet corporate standards, each page would potentially have a different look and feel from the others; this in turn could be frustrating to the sales force, who would not know in which format they may see a brochure, competitive analysis, or presentation. Second, if authors of the content can place their material directly on the Web site, it may be very difficult for the sales force to find.

In the worst case, sections of the site could be blacked out and wrong information could be unintentionally published. Consider a simple example: A typical product page might contain a photographic image, product description, link to a detailed list of specifications, price list, and mail link to a salesperson. Each of these components might be developed by different authors, stored in different directories, and brought together to create the page. As the site is expanded and updated, changes are made to pages and their components. Unless the Web team has a production control system, it is very easy for errors to be introduced and published unnoticed, giving Web site visitors incorrect prices, specifications, images, and sales contact information.

PRODUCTION PROCESS

The way around these issues is to establish standards, and a process to ensure compliance with the standards. One approach is to have content managers responsible for both the material itself and its style and layout. This is analogous to having editors in a magazine: a set of assistant editors, each responsible for a certain section of the magazine, and an overall editor that sets the standards for the magazine as a whole. The editors would approve material contributed by authors, and submit it to the production staff (the Webmaster) for publication. Just as in a magazine, the production staff ensure that the material is placed in the correct place, available to the appropriate audiences, and easy to find. This approach is shown in Figure 11.2.

Although the approach is conceptually simple, good implementation of any nontrivial marketing encyclopedia presents many challenges. As Internet Web sites and corporate intranets grow, and as the content in a marketing encyclopedia is devel-

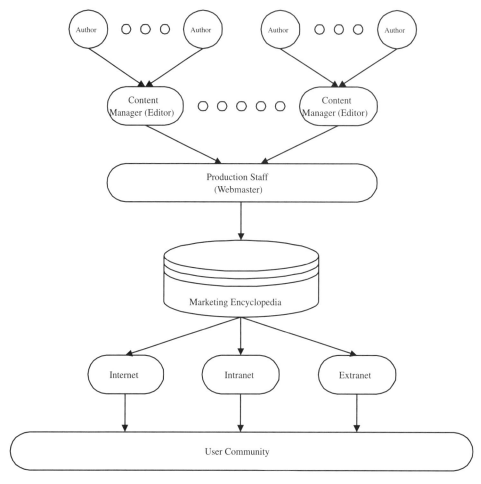

FIGURE 11.2 Producing a marketing encyclopedia.

oped by diverse teams, Web-based marketing encyclopedias will encounter the looming problems of complex Web site content management, including:

- Disparate and distributed teams working in parallel processes
- Very large amounts of interrelated information
- Large numbers of contributors, many of whom are not Web professionals

- Very frequent content updating
- An ever increasing array of authoring and back-end tools
- Lack of version control for accurate content management
- Need for automation of site management tasks
- Demand for multiple site configurations for different audiences

The critical issue for a Marketing Encyclopedia System is not the technology or simply managing a much larger base of data, but the production process: coordinating and publishing content from a much broader team of contributors. To solve this problem, a growing number of high-end Web sites are now employing production control systems to manage Web site assets and facilitate Web team workflow. Because these systems are designed specifically for the problems of complex content management in high-end Web sites, they can be a significant help in the creation and maintenance of a marketing encyclopedia.

A Web site production control system is not a tool for content development (the actual creation of Web site elements), site development (the site-level infrastructure), or site deployment (the site-level runtime environment); nor is it just a development environment. Rather than duplicating the work of these tools, it serves as the foundation for the Web site development process, providing the framework in which all contributors use their tools and share their work. In a Web-based marketing encyclopedia, the production control system establishes a process in which:

- Authors develop and edit content, concurrently and with a minimum of conflict.
- Editors manage the content from teams of authors.
- The Webmaster organizes and coordinates the assembly of content.
- All files are tracked and archived so that information is never lost and can be recalled instantly.

One commercially available production control system that supports the preceding production process is TeamSite, from a company called Interwoven.

INTERWOVEN'S TEAMSITE PRODUCTION CONTROL SYSTEM

TeamSite is a high-end solution in use at Fortune 1000 companies, which facilitates the Web site production process by providing:

- Support for multiple authors working in parallel
- Individual author work areas for collaborative development without conflict
- Means to see content being developed in the context of the entire site
- Editor control over content approval
- Webmaster control over content publication
- Ways of assigning versions to all types of content, and even the whole Web site
- The ability to roll back any site component, or the entire site to a previous version

The way TeamSite fits with content development, site development, and site deployment tools is shown in Figure 11.3.

TeamSite is in use at a leading technology company, where Catherine Hampton is Webmaster. Encouraging product specialists to develop Web content was no problem—almost every marketing manager at her firm is learning to use at least one Web authoring tool. The problem she observed was that there

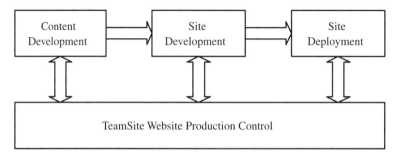

FIGURE 11.3   The TeamSite production control system.

was no framework for integrating content, so she had to play autocrat and personally oversee the publication of all Web content, effectively becoming a bottleneck. Because routine bug fixing consumed as much as 25 percent of her time, she couldn't involve a large number of people in content development without hiring special staff just to police the Web site and check for content errors.

TeamSite overcomes this problem by providing content contributors safe workareas in which they create and edit content. Contributors can check their work for errors, so when they offer it to the Webmaster for publishing, it requires much less bug fixing. The result of this is that a much greater number of product specialists can publish a much larger volume of information on the company intranet and Internet Web site, without increasing the Webmaster's workload.

Additionally, TeamSite provides the Webmaster the ability to roll back a section of the site or even the entire site to any previous version at anytime. If a mistake is published, the Webmaster can roll the site back to the previous version instantly. This gives the Webmaster greater confidence in the integrity of the site's content, even with a much larger base of contributors and a huge increase in the number of files published.

Ms. Hampton observes that prior to the adoption of TeamSite, the strategic vision for the firm's Web site was tempered by considerations of practicality. Although senior managers wanted product managers to develop and publish HTML versions of their specification sheets, white papers, and customer case studies for distribution via the Web, the enormous volume of Web content would still have to be managed by the same limited team of Webmasters. In particular, it was difficult to make a long-term commitment to a Web-based marketing encyclopedia, given the uncertainty of how content would be updated.

TeamSite brought Ms. Hampton a new paradigm for Web content development, integration, quality assurance, publication, and updating, in which product specialists are empowered to develop and integrate Web content to a much greater degree, and the Web site staff still enjoy control over what appears on the corporate Web site. The result is the genesis of a completely Web-based, information-rich marketing encyclopedia.

ADDITIONAL INFORMATION

Interwoven, Inc. has its corporate headquarters at 885 North San Antonio Road, Los Altos, CA 94022; Fax: (415) 917-3603. Readers can find more information on Interwoven's products at Interwoven's Web site, www.interwoven.com; or can contact Interwoven at (415) 917-3600. Some additional information on Interwoven products is also included on the accompanying CD-ROM. The Interwoven name and logo, TeamSite name and logo, and Website Production Control are all trademarks of Interwoven, Inc.

The authors would like to acknowledge the assistance of Rich Petersen, of Interwoven, Inc., in the preparation of this chapter.

Better Effectiveness through Better Information— FirstFloor Smart Delivery

Chapter 11 discussed the importance of the production process for a Marketing Encyclopedia System, and showed Interwoven's TeamSite Production Control System as an example of a solution to issues surrounding the production process. But getting the content onto the Web site is only part of the marketing encyclopedia publishing process; you still have to organize the content and deliver it to your sales force. Not only must the content be relevant, timely, and available, but it should also be easy to find and easy to access. If it isn't, you won't have any users; and having a marketing encyclopedia without any users is the same as having no encyclopedia at all.

Whether your sales force is analyzing the competition or reviewing pricing, it is critical that they have access to the right information at the right time. That information can be as simple as the current price list, or as complex as a competitive report compiled from multiple sources. Just as important as having access to the information they need is making sure it is available to them when they need it, whether they are in the office or on the road, organized the way they need to use it, and integrated into their other sales automation tools in a way that makes it easy and effective to use.

Getting Information to the Sales Force

Much of the critical information needed by salespeople is stored in various kinds of documents. The most obvious documents are the files on your employees' desktops and your servers. These can be as simple as text instructions on how to use applications, or as complex as compound documents built from spreadsheets and word processing files. The advantage of using Web technologies for a marketing encyclopedia is that all kinds of documents can be distributed over the Web.

Simple marketing encyclopedia applications include distributing the appropriate slide presentations to specific sales teams or making sure that price lists are only available to the customers who can buy from them. More complex applications can automatically distribute all the pertinent documents and Web pages to a salesperson prior to the sales call, or automatically alert the sales force to the introduction of competitive products that may affect one of their prospects—along with all the necessary press releases and competitive briefings to help them make an intelligent response.

The advent of the Internet and corporate or private intranets has forced many Sales Force Automation vendors to come up with a plan to incorporate Web functionality in all their products, and especially for the marketing encyclopedia. The overall requirement is Web-enabling existing sales force automation products; specific requirements for the marketing encyclopedia include:

■ Combine both Web page and documents for targeted information distribution
■ Meet the needs of mobile or *sometimes connected* sales professionals
■ Automatically organize information that allows for quick viewing and retrieval

■ Can easily be integrated into existing and future sales force automation applications

Meeting the Information Distribution Requirements

To meet these requirements in a Marketing Encyclopedia System, the system must have the following functionality:

■ Targeted document delivery
■ Offline viewers
■ Automatic indexing and summarization
■ Tight integration with the rest of the sales automation tools

Targeted Document Delivery

There are three ways to distribute information to users (see Figure 12.1). Of these three ways, the one that is of interest to us for

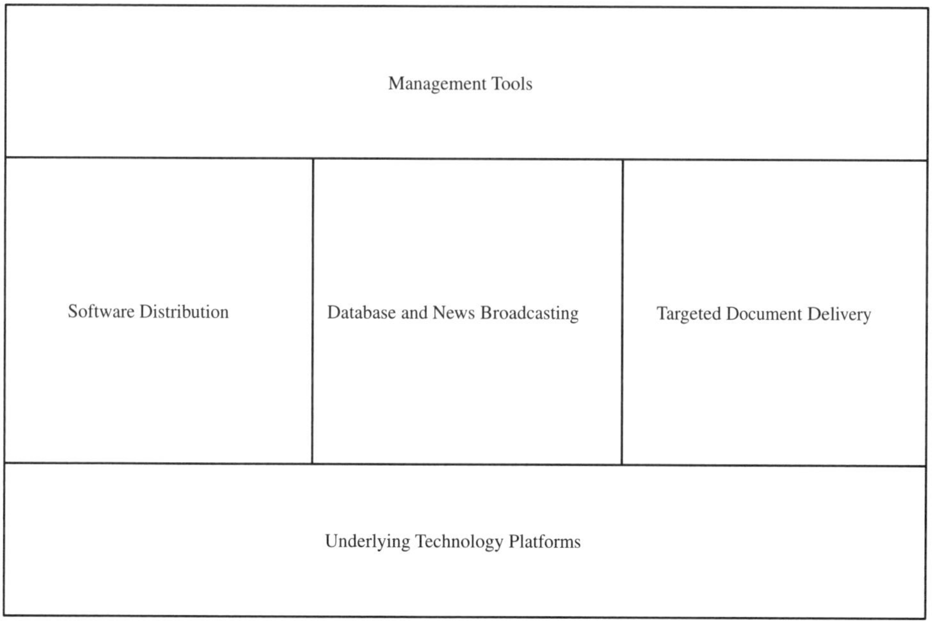

FIGURE 12.1   Types of push technologies.

use in a Marketing Encyclopedia System is Targeted Document Delivery. Since software distribution is of little interest to us, we will compare targeted document delivery products to the other main category, Database and News Broadcasting.

Targeted document delivery products allow *information architects* to gather collections of relevant Web pages and documents from the Internet, corporate intranet, and local area network; and *push* the information directly to a salesperson based upon that salesperson's profile. Unlike other push products that simply broadcast large amounts of information to large audiences, targeted document delivery products deliver relevant Web pages and documents only to users who need them, a technique known as *narrowcasting.*

Narrowcasting allows the simple construction of user groups such as departments, functions, or territories, so that each group receives the set of documents they need. This targeted approach reduces the volume of information users must wade through, improves the quality of information, and allows corporate users to get exactly the documents they need, when they need them.

Offline Viewers

Offline viewing technology allows mobile salespeople to automatically maintain corporate information on their local hard drive for review while disconnected from the content source. Users can automatically receive new networked Web pages and documents whenever they reconnect and launch the application. By allowing mobile salespeople to automatically maintain business information, including images and documents, on their local hard drive, a salesperson can always keep up-to-date with the latest information in the marketing encyclopedia.

Effective products and technologies know to look for the most recent version of a document when a client is connected so that the user always has access to the most recent and appropriate version of documents and data. This is in direct contrast to traditional delivery models, such as paper, pager, fax, and e-mail— where the user is stuck either with the document as originally sent or saddled with many new and hard-to-manage versions of the same document.

Automatic Indexing and Summarization

Raw data is of limited value, because it requires users to manually sift through large volumes of raw input to look for what they want. A good distribution system should use the most sophisticated indexing and summarization technology available to generate not only flexible, full-text indexes, but also summaries and keywords. This information can be used for traditional search, retrieval, and *personalization* based on subject areas of interest to the user.

Tight Integration

The most important piece of a marketing encyclopedia solution is the integration of Web page and document delivery features into the your existing sales force automation application. The solution must include the tools needed to tightly integrate Sales Force Automation applications with the marketing encyclopedia, resulting in a Marketing Encyclopedia System with an easy and intuitive user interface.

From the beginning, products should designed to be integrated into an existing or future Sales Force Automation application; they should be available with substantial sample code, Application Programming Interfaces (APIs), and user-interface elements that can be used to create unique interfaces. They also must have the ability to quickly and seamlessly integrate desired portions of the user interface into a Sales Force Automation application. Ideally, this API can be used for creating and managing folders, document and data items, agents, and schedules; and controlling monitoring and publishing. APIs should also available for the creation and administration of users and groups.

FIRSTFLOOR IN SALES FORCE AUTOMATION

The FirstFloor Smart Delivery product line enables you to build targeted document and Web page delivery features into your existing and future applications. FirstFloor's products support any file type, so documents in their native format, without the need to re-author, can be combined with Web pages for delivery via the

Web or your intranet—a critical requirement in today's corporate environments. By making an application developers kit (ADK) available, FirstFloor's products allow companies to create a single, cohesive solution for Sales Force Automation and business communications. FirstFloor's products are used by many Sales Force Automation vendors: Their customers include Aurum, Calico Technology, Market Power, Sales Technology, Saratoga Systems, and The Vantive Corporation.

The Smart Delivery line of products includes the FirstFloor Smart Notification Server, Smart Publisher, Smart Subscriber, and Smart Delivery ADK (see Figure 12.2).

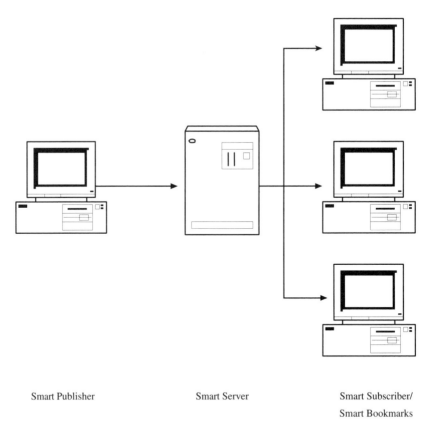

Smart Publisher   Smart Server   Smart Subscriber/
                                                           Smart Bookmarks

FIGURE 12.2 FirstFloor Smart Delivery product line.
(© First Floor, Inc. Reproduced with permission.)

Smart Publisher

The Smart Publisher streamlines the process of organizing and distributing structured information to targeted groups of users. Collections of corporate data, including Web and document-based information, can be assembled by dragging lists of URLs or links into folders. These collections are placed or *published* to the intranet server, automatically keeping all Smart Subscribers up-to-date.

Smart Notification Server

The Smart Notification Server finds, monitors, updates, indexes, and summarizes pertinent information, both from business documents and Web pages, and pushes it to target groups of users. This allows corporations to deliver the latest business information to users, reduce the volume of information they must wade through, and deliver the right information to the right people at the right time.

Smart Subscriber

The Smart Subscriber, or a developer's implementation of its features, automatically receives and is notified of updated Web pages or documents. It pulls any additional personalized information and can access information and documents anytime, anywhere, with offline viewing.

Smart Delivery ADK

The Smart Delivery Application Development Kit provides the tools needed to tightly integrate vendors' applications with Smart Delivery, which results in a complete solution with an easy and intuitive user interface. The Development Kit provides tools, documentation, and redistributable components to aid Windows 16- and 32-bit developers in this integration.

ADDITIONAL INFORMATION

FirstFloor Software has its corporate headquarters at 444 Castro Street, Suite 200, Mountain View, CA 94041; Fax: (415) 254-1193. Readers can find more information on FirstFloor's products at FirstFloor's Web site www.firstfloor.com; or can contact First-Floor at (415) 968-1101. Some additional information on First-Floor products is also included on the accompanying CD-ROM. FirstFloor, FirstFloor Smart Delivery, FirstFloor Smart Publisher, FirstFloor Smart Subscriber, and Smart Bookmarks are trademarks of First Floor, Inc.

The authors would like to acknowledge the assistance of Mark Bonacorso of FirstFloor, Inc., in the preparation of this chapter.

Requirements-Based Sales Configuration— Calico Technology

A good sales configuration tool is one of the most useful elements of a Sales Force Automation system. As shown in Chapter 3, the benefits of sales configurators meet all three criteria used to justify investments in an SFA system:

1. Increased sales effectiveness
2. Improved sales efficiency
3. Higher customer satisfaction

We listed both the tangible and intangible ways in which inaccurate configurations can cost your company, and showed how a sales configurator can help your organization. This chapter covers the different approaches in solving the sales configuration problem, and describes how the products of one company, Calico Technology, provide the functionality you would need in a sales configurator.

CONFIGURING A SALES ORDER

The basic goal in configuring an order can be stated very simply: based on the prospect's requirements create a complete, accurate, and up-to-date list of offerings that fully meet the requirements. If only real life were that simple.

To configure an order, a salesperson must first map the requirements to items your company sells, then find each item in your product catalog, check that at least one of the options available for each item meets the requirements, verify that the items and options that are being considered work together, and then see if the items require additional items to be selected to work properly (for more detail read the discussions on sales configuration in Chapters 3 and 5). For example, if your company is a vendor of network equipment, and a prospect wants to purchase a global network solution from you, the salesperson must first identify all the requirements of the proposed solution, map these requirements into the routers, switches, cables, software, and other items your company sells; verify that the proposed configuration of hardware and software will work together as planned (order configuration); ensure that each item has the correct options selected (product configuration); and also confirm that the list of items selected is complete (i.e., there are no additional items required to make this order do what is planned).

If your product line is even moderately complex, configuring an order can be a tedious and time-consuming task fraught with potential for error. The two main areas in which problems can occur are:

1. Requirements Mapping: The salesperson may not be able to translate the prospect's requirements into products that your company sells.
2. Configuration Validation: The configuration that the salesperson has developed may not be valid.

Another problem area is in pricing, because in today's highly competitive world your company may frequently adjust its price list, run promotions, and offer discounts. It is important that a salesperson be able to apply the latest pricing to a sales configuration, and so offer the most competitive quote to the prospect. This discussion, however, will focus on sales configurations.

Requirements Mapping

Requirements mapping problems occur when the products, features, and options you offer are so extensive, or the product set so complex, that the salesperson cannot keep track of all the solutions, functions, and features that the company's products provide. Searching through product catalogs and marketing encyclopedias can eventually result in finding the right products, features, and options to configure an order; but that can be a very time-consuming process. Furthermore, if the information being used is out of date, or if there is no consistency in how the products and their features are described, the salesperson could still not be able to map the prospect's requirements to what your company sells. In the preceding network example the prospect may have stated it was a critical requirement that when configuring a network, the network downtime be kept to a minimum. This might suggest selection of particular network management software, which might then drive numerous other products and options.

The solution to problems in this area is to have accurate and up-to-date sales information available to all salespeople, and to use a consistent way to describe the features and benefits of each product. A salesperson could then use this information to select products, features, and options to configure an order. This can be implemented, for example, by having the current sales offerings catalog available to the sales force over an intranet as part of the Marketing Encyclopedia System. Style guides and rules can help ensure that the description of features and benefits is consistent across all products and solutions.

However, even with this information, in a complex sale the salesperson must be extremely knowledgeable of how all the products work, and, equally importantly, how they work together. Since this depth of knowledge is difficult to attain and maintain, a more cost-effective solution is to use a sales configurator system that allows you to capture the technical expertise of your best salespeople and technical gurus.

Configuration Validation

But will the products that the salesperson has configured work together, and is anything else required? Continuing with the preceding network example, the salesperson could have selected the K-Net Network Management System Software as part of the order, only to find that a particular router that had also been configured cannot work with that software. Clearly the salesperson must either change the selection of software, or the router. Changing either selection in the proposed sales configuration may have a ripple effect and cause other configuration incompatibilities. A way around this is to specify all the routers that work with the software in the description of the software, and conversely, specify all versions and types of software that can make use of the router. The rules that specify which items work with other items are called *constraints*. As you can imagine, without tools to maintain these rules, this becomes a huge maintenance problem in any but the most trivial product lines.

Moving on with our example, our salesperson resolves the product constraints by changing to another router that will work with the software selected earlier. But this router requires that a special software patch be applied to the software before it can be used. In other words, the router and software combination requires the patch to work together; sending an order to a customer without this patch will cause problems when the customer attempts to deploy the network. Again, the way around this would be to list this requirement, called a *dependency*, in the description of the router in the sales catalog.

Constraints and dependencies together make up a set of *rules* that must be met before a sales configuration can be considered valid. There can be a huge number of rules, both implicit and explicit, in a sales catalog; and it can be almost impossible to configure a complete and accurate order without some help from a sales configurator.

CALICO TECHNOLOGY'S CONCINITY

Calico Technology's Concinity family of products provides a sales configuration solution as part of their Interactive Selling System, as well as solutions for quoting and electronic commerce using the Internet. The sales configuration solution ensures that the configuration is valid, and enables sales representative or customers directly to interactively configure a solution. The system employs *user-guiding behavior* to enable the user to make selections in any order, revisit selections at any time, and to even select apparently unavailable options and see graphically why they can't be selected at that point. The user creates a configuration by making selections. As each selection is added to the configuration, the software checks rules (dependencies and constraints) specified in the system, and either validates the selection or displays the exact nature of conflicts in the configuration caused by the latest addition. If there is a conflict, the user can either select another product or remove or replace one that has been selected earlier.

The products also allow a user to save a draft configuration at any time and reopen it later and continue working from the stopping point. The application can also allow other users to work on the configuration in progress so that many members of a sales team can contribute to a configuration.

Using the earlier example of the global network solution, the way the Concinity product would handle the situation would be as follows: Using Concinity, the salesperson would see selections organized in logical categories, such as network management software, routers, cables, power supplies, and so on. The salesperson would then begin selecting required features in the order that made sense in that particular case. For example, one salesperson might start with the network management software, another with budget, and yet another with router features. With each selection the configuration software would evaluate all rules and constraints, and update the user interface to reflect what has been selected and what of the remaining selections are valid. Through this process the salesperson homes in on the configuration that meets the prospect's requirements, and is guaranteed that it can be delivered by the vendor. Concinity allows the salesperson to advance through this process nonprocedurally; in other words, to make selections in any order. Also, with Concinity's user-guiding behavior, salespeople can select grayed-out options and then see what earlier selections conflict with a desired choice.

Concinity Family Product Overview

The key components of the Concinity product family are the Concinity Workbench, the Concinity Configuration Engine, and the Concinity clients as shown in Figure 13.1. The functionality is implemented in a client/server application that can be used on a salesperson's laptop computer to support traditional selling, or over the Web to enable customers to buy without the direct assistance of a sales representative.

Concinity Workbench

The Concinity Workbench is used by marketing and line-of-business professionals to model the products or services that are

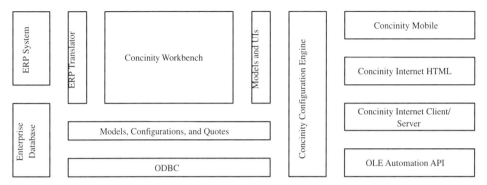

FIGURE 13.1   Calico Technology's Concinity family Concinity Workbench.

going to be sold. It allows the experts to identify the products that can be configured, available features and options, dependencies and constraints, and rules for actions that must occur during the selling process. Modeling is done using a high-level modeling language (similar to a spreadsheet language) and a point-and-click interface. All the business logic and data required to select and configure the product is specified in the model for each complex product or service.

Concinity Configuration Engine

This is where the logic and rules specified in the model are applied to selections made by a user during a configuration session. The engine runs the model in memory to ensure high performance, and provides interactive feedback to the user as each selection is made.

Concinity Deployments

Concinity can be deployed in three ways:

1. *Concinity Mobile.*   When deployed on a laptop, the user interface, engine, and model run on the same machine, enabling a salesperson to interactively configure a solution while disconnected from the network. This deployment allows a salesperson to provide on-the-spot configurations and quotes to a prospect, for even very complex configurations. Periodically, the sales representative connects to the network and synchronizes configuration models, marketing encyclopedia data, and order information (both new orders and order status information).

2. *Concinity Internet HTML.* When deployed with a Web server, the user interface is an HTML form that is created by Concinity, and displayed in any forms-capable browser. The Configuration Engine runs on a server connected to an HTTP server via a CGI. While this is the lowest common denominator for the Web, it lacks the interactivity of the laptop system. HTML is less interactive than a laptop or client/server installation, because HTML is a document-centric model. With HTML, the user is typically presented with a form that includes available options. Using that form the user makes selections and then has to submit the form to get feedback on selections and see what options exist moving ahead. This page-by-page approach does not provide the instantaneous feedback on each selection.

3. *Concinity Internet Client/Server.* Concinity can also be deployed as an Internet or intranet client/server application. Here the same user interface created for a mobile deployment is dynamically downloaded to the user's browser (using either ActiveX or Java) at the start of a configuration. This architecture makes it possible to support configuration over the public Internet or private intranets, and give click-by-click feedback as selections are made, as on a mobile deployment. If used with a wireless Internet connection, this deployment offers all the portability benefits of a mobile deployment.

Other Concinity Features

■ *Integration with ERP*. Most companies that manufacture or assemble products have an Enterprise Resource Planning (ERP) system that typically contains detailed product configuration information. This information can be taken from the ERP system, and fed into the Concinity system using Calico's ERP translation capability. Additional rules, pricing, and promotional information can be added to a Concinity system using the Concinity Workbench to develop a complete model that can be used in the configuration process. The ability to incorporate ERP data into Concinity means that product information is updated in only one place (the ERP system), which reduces the risk of introducing product configuration inconsistencies.

■ *ODBC Support*. An Open Database Connectivity (ODBC)-compliant database system can be used as an integration point between Concinity and other Sales Force Automation or customer information applications. Concinity uses ODBC to store configurations, and can read and import data from an ODBC database. For example, Concinity could get data on product availability from a manufacturing or warehousing application, and display to the user when a planned configuration would be available. This can give the user a lot of flexibility in making trade-offs between availability, pricing, and features.

■ *Integrated Pricing / Quoting.* Along with product configuration models and business rules, Concinity also stores detailed pricing schemes and promotional information. This means that the Concinity Engine not only shows an accurate price for any order, it also can detects configurations that qualify for special discounts or promotions. This is especially valuable for remote salespeople who may not be current on the latest promotions, because the configurator can guide them to finding the best, most accurate price to prepare a quote.

■ *Proposal Generation.* In addition to ODBC support, Concinity can also export a finalized quote to a spreadsheet, and then embed that quote grid into a complete proposal that includes marketing information, competitive points, standard terms and conditions, and so on. This ensures that the salesperson delivers a persuasive and accurate proposal for the prospect.

ADDITIONAL INFORMATION

Calico Technology has its corporate headquarters at 4 North Second Street, Suite 1350, San Jose, CA 95113; Fax: (408) 975-7410. Readers can find more information on Concinity products at Calico's Web site, www.calicotech.com; or can contact Calico at (408) 975-7400. Some additional information on Calico products is also included on the accompanying CD-ROM. Concinity is a trademark of Calico Technology, Inc.

The authors would like to acknowledge the assistance of Dave Rome of Calico Technology, in the preparation of this chapter.

14

Internet Reporting— Actuate Software

Information access has been a focal point of this book in enabling sales and marketing managers to view data in a flexible, timely manner so as to adjust their operations to the rapidly changing business climate. Whether your sales force is preparing quotes or processing orders, it is critical that they have easy access to the right information. In addition to easy access, online availability of this information is important whether a salesperson is in the corporate office, in a remote field office, or even on the road.

We have presented a multitude of reporting options that you can demand from your SFA system. Reporting via the Internet adds a new dimension to the traditional report writing solutions by providing point-and-click access to live data right from your browser tool. Also, by offloading report generation to reporting servers, you free up your network from runaway queries, and your desktop from processing huge result sets. Report servers provide server-side processing and report repository capabilities that directly address the needs of enterprise reporting.

SFA REPORTING

Much of the criticism of desktop reporting tools is that, while they have empowered the more technical user community to generate *ad hoc* queries and reports, they have left the novice users facing such challenges as:

- Complex data models
- Cryptic naming conventions
- SQL query syntax
- Report distribution to field offices

Sales and marketing have unique reporting requirements, in that the access to information in a timely manner can make or break a deal. These groups don't have the time to submit IT requests to generate reports, and wait weeks for a formatted report to be sent back to them. While this process may work for manufacturing and operations, the rapidly changing business climate faced by sales and marketing simply does not permit the traditional reporting structure.

The Internet has provided a medium to circumvent the traditional reporting hurdles. The SFA reporting requirements and capabilities of a report server can now be very specific to include:

- Point-and-click access to reports via the Web
- Flexible report distribution
- Meet the needs of mobile sales professionals
- Adaptable reporting components
- Integration with sales force automation applications
- Scalability

Point-and-Click Access to Reports via the Web

Ease of use is an important factor for the sales and marketing professionals, who shouldn't have to learn complex SQL syntax in order to access information easily and quickly. By providing a common Web browser interface, there is no user interface to have to learn how to navigate before you can get access to your vital SFA data.

Flexible Report Distribution

Reporting servers provide report repository capabilities that, similar to the marketing encyclopedia concept, centralize the report results in one place. By providing Web access to the report repository, physical report distribution is no longer necessary or needed in order to arm your field sales force with up-to-date sales figures.

Meet the Needs of Mobile Sales Professionals

A reporting server should allow users to access reports with any Web browser, which will enable the salesperson to view the status of an order directly from the customer's site. In addition, the report server should allow for offline viewing of report information directly on the mobile laptop.

Adaptable Reporting Components

Adaptable report components that can easily be reused and customized by end users shortens the report generation process. Users can generate *ad hoc* queries and reports from an existing report object or results set, without having to adversely impact the database server from which the original report was run.

Integration with Sales Force Automation Applications

The ability to support popular databases, such as Oracle, Sybase, Informix, and Microsoft SQL server, will provide access to most SFA applications on the market today. In addition, ODBC and desktop connectivity will allow integration with stand-alone contact managers or PC-based databases like Microsoft Access. A well-designed report server will be able to pull data from multiple data sources if needed to generate a single report.

Scalability

Any reporting packages should be able to run either from a PC or across a network, supporting 1 to 1000 users without any performance degradation. To support this scalability, network resources need to be conserved by allowing viewing of reports online without downloading large data results sets to the user's desktop. This type of reporting mechanism is limited with traditional HTML formatting. Implementing more robust functionality is accomplished by adding ActiveX controls, Java applets, or a browser plug-in.

BENEFITS OF INTERNET REPORTING

Adding to the benefits listed previously, Internet reporting allows more users access to much larger amounts of corporate data, within a familiar, point-and-click, Web-browser user interface. Corporations can distribute reports via Internet sites to broad user communities. Internet reporting enables anyone on the Internet to get the reports they need online at any time.

INTERNET REPORTING WITH ACTUATE SOFTWARE

The Actuate Reporting System provides distributed client/server reporting technology, which enables you to deliver Web-based reports to your Internet or intranet. Based on patent-pending Report Object technology, Actuate provides object-oriented reuse and a distributed architecture that balances tasks among three tiers—client, application, and server.

Actuate's products are used by Fortune 1000 customers, such as Chase Manhattan Bank, Fidelity Investments, Montgomery Securities, PacifiCare, and Kaiser Permanente.

The Actuate Reporting System product line includes Developer Workbench, End User Workbench, End User Desktop, Viewer, Administrator Desktop, Report Server, and ReportCast.

Developer Workbench

A visual, object-oriented development tool that provides a complete environment for designing, compiling, viewing, and debugging Live Report Document designs and components, Developer Workbench can be used either stand-alone on a single PC, or in conjunction with one or more Actuate Report Servers for team development. The Actuate Developer Workbench includes high-performance native database interfaces to Sybase, Oracle, Informix, and Microsoft SQL Server, as well as an ODBC driver for access to local PC databases and other data sources.

End User Workbench

End User Workbench enables users to adapt, customize, and assemble Live Report Object components built by developers, create new *ad hoc* queries and reports, and view and print Live Report Documents.

End User Desktop

Used for report scheduling, on-demand *ad hoc* reporting, and viewing and printing Live Report Documents.

Viewer

A royalty-free product for end users to view and print Live Report Documents.

Administrator Desktop

Used by system and network administrators to manage user accounts, set resource quotas and security, manage Report Servers, and schedule production activities.

Report Server

Used on UNIX and Windows NT server machines to generate, store, and distribute Live Report Documents using a unique Virtual Report Distribution architecture. Report Servers include the high-performance Actuate database interfaces to Sybase, Oracle, and Informix for UNIX platforms, as well as Sybase, Oracle, Informix, Microsoft SQL Server, and ODBC for Windows NT platforms.

ReportCast

Combines report notification (using push technology) and integrated Web reporting, producing dynamically generated HTML report pages using a browser plug-in, a Java applet, and ActiveX technologies. The user can be sent a report notification, rather than the entire report. When a report is requested by the user, Web report viewing has the same functionality as the client/server product, and graphics are transmitted to the browser as numerical data rather than large graphic files. This combination of technologies provides all of the elements that an Internet-based reporting server should contain.

Web Agent

Web Agent provides the critical secure link between the Internet and the Actuate Report Server feature available to the Internet via any standard browser.

Viewer Plug-In

Actuate Viewer Plug-in is a free product that provides browsers with active viewing capabilities necessary for navigation of complex and large reports. These capabilities include searching, table of contents, and hyperlinks between other reports or Web pages.

ADDITIONAL INFORMATION

Actuate Sofware's address is 999 Baker Way, Suite 330, San Mateo, CA 94404. They can be reached by phone at (415) 638-2000, or by fax at (415) 638-2020. Readers can find more information on Actuate products directly from their Web site: www.actuate.com.

The authors would like to acknowledge the assistance of Al Campa of Actuate Software and the Hurwitz Group in the preparation of this chapter.

Java-Enabled Sales Force Automation on the Web—Scopus Technology

As discussed in earlier chapters, there is no doubt that the automation of sales and marketing functions will explode through the use of Web-based technologies and the Internet. It is also important to note that even though the benefits of HTML and CGI technologies are very compelling the future of sales automation on the Web lies in the use of Java, which is quickly growing into the *de facto* standard for Internet- and intranet-based applications. In particular, Java provides the dynamic environment, efficient interactivity, scalability, portability, and security required by Web-based sales automation—from opportunity management to marketing encyclopedia to interactive unassisted selling. In addition the *write once, run anywhere* Java environment provides both the Information Technology and Sales Operations organizations with the ability to respond quicker to market pressures with sales application deployments, upgrades, and extensions, while lowering the overall cost of solution maintenance. At the same time a Java platform allows sales applications to reach out beyond functional barriers, leveraging existing system investments to embrace both the enterprise and the extended enterprise.

SALES AUTOMATION AND
THE CURRENT WEB PARADIGM

Sales automation on the Web today primarily falls into three categories:

1. *Electronic literature racks.* The number-one use of the Web today, where companies create Web sites that feature text-based product information for customers, prospective customers, and passers-by to browse.
2. *Lead generation forms.* Many Web sites provide an HTML form you can use to request more information, usually as a call-back or printed fulfillment; some forms even allow you to identify yourself as a bona fide prospect.
3. *A transport for disconnected users.* Many companies are creating internal Web pages with secured access, where traveling salespeople can pick up leads and other various information.

While these solutions based on the older HTML paradigm provide some value, they do not realize the full power and potential that is offered by new developments in Web technologies. At the same time there are several trends that impact the general information technology infrastructure, which are exacerbated by the demands of sales automation:

■ *Increasingly expensive desktops and bloated desktop (laptop) applications.* Putting Pentium 200 machines with 64MB on every desktop of a 500 seat call center can get expensive. Maintaining the applications on these desktops over time can make the initial hardware costs appear reasonable.
■ *Application deployment and maintenance in an increasingly distributed world.* At the same time rolling out a similar powered laptop machine to several hundred field sales representatives can also be very expensive. This does not include the costs to maintain the increasingly large monolithic applications remotely. Do the benefits of increased effectiveness outweigh the ongoing costs of sales automation?

- *A need to break down the functional barriers between applications.* Sales applications for the most part today reside as functional silos of processing and information. But that is not the nature of the sales process. As discussed in earlier chapters, the sales organization is highly dependent on other organizations, just as sales-automation systems are highly dependent on other corporate applications, such as accounting, inventory, and customer retention systems.
- *A need to leverage disparate platforms.* The differences in computing platforms, both within the enterprise and in the extended enterprise, is a major reason for high functional optimization in contrast to a highly interdependent enterprise systems. Some organizations in your company may use engineering workstations, others may use laptop computers with different operating systems, and your partners may be using yet another type of system.
- *Increased security demands in a distributed environment.* With mobile computing and the ability to move components among internetworked machines comes a heightened risk of security violation. For example, viruses on the net can destroy a mobile salesperson's forecast or order information, or unauthorized users can steal classified business data and directly affect revenue.

SALES AUTOMATION WITH JAVA

Java, as the implementation technology for Sales Force Automation over the Web, provides a unique opportunity to provide a dynamic, interactive sales environment for representatives, partners, and customers alike, and at the same time address some of your Information Technology organization's most vexing issues:

- *Full interactive selling systems.* Java allows for more than content consumption: It allows for manipulation and processing. Web sites can allow customers, partners, and sales representatives to find products and services that meet customer requirements, and play what-if games with configuration, pricing, and financing options. This is very difficult to do with HTML.

■ *Network-aware sales process automation.* Getting the names of leads is always a bona-fide first step, but by using Java you can implement a system that not only collects leads over the Web, but also is smart enough to know what systems on the network consume those leads, and what level of qualification each consuming application requires. Leads can get distributed to the appropriate system regardless of location, where additional workflow can be added to contact the lead through e-mail, direct mail, telephone, or direct contact. Java allows the building of applications that cooperate in a distributed manner across multiple platforms. For example, a Java-based system could evaluate a lead that comes in over the Web, and route it to the telesales application of a value-added reseller in another country. If the qualification criteria so dictate, another lead could be routed to the direct-sales application of the same reseller.

■ *Complete enterprise acquisition and retention process through Enterprise Beans.* Java Enterprise Beans will hide the complexity of cooperation with other business systems. A sales organization's opportunity management system can interact in real time with back-office inventory or order-entry applications even if they are run on a mainframe.

■ *Active publish and subscribe.* With Java application concepts, such as push-based marketing and sales information or publish and subscribe, marketing encyclopedias on the Web become a reality (for example, see the discussion on FirstFloor Software in Chapter 12). Java breaks down all barriers to integrating marketing encyclopedia servers (MES) to various network available resources, including news feeds, electronic commerce, educational sources, and so on. Java-based MES are not limited by content format. This allows businesses to provide access to non-Web-based content, including software in a cross-platform environment.

■ *Secure access through off-the-shelf browsers.* A Java-enabled Web browser can provide the rich application environment needed for sales automation. For example, you can perform channel forecasting or pipeline management without having to distribute and maintain an application at your channel partner's site. All this can be possible in a secure environment with Java's built-in security model that ensures *untrusted,* or malicious applications cannot gain access to system resources.

■ *Low-cost network computers.* A real benefit of Java will be found in the cost savings gained in the call center. Telemarketing and telesales desktops can now be outfitted with lower-cost NC machines, yet still provide robust operating environments that are server and Java based. Additionally, in a fast-paced world, where changes to call guides or whole applications are necessary to wage the latest campaigns, Java will provide for rapid, low-cost centralized development and deployment.

■ *The end of huge application clients.* The value and nature of sales automation components can change based on the sales engagement, salesperson's preferences, and product set. In today's market most applications are becoming increasingly large, where only a small segment of the functions is utilized. The highly object-oriented Java world will allow salespersons and channel partners to gain access to only those application components they need, when they need them. For example, if the current sales automation application has different client interfaces for different market segments, then in all likelihood the client that is installed on a salesperson's computer is very large, because the salesperson may be selling into any segment. In a Java-based system, the client will be small, because only the specific screens and functions that are going to be used to sell to a particular segment will be downloaded when needed, and discarded (actually removed from the salesperson's system) when the salesperson is done using the application.

SCOPUS SOLUTION

Scopus Technology is a vendor of customer information management applications, what Scopus calls *Customer Care.* One of its applications is SalesTEAM, which implements much of the sales automation functionality discussed in earlier chapters. At the time of writing, Scopus is in the process of rolling out complete technology-enabled selling functionality powered on the Web through Java. The rollout will occur in two distinct phases. The first phase capitalizes on Java as an aid in lowering the overall cost to implement technology-enabled selling in a call-center environment. The second phase focuses on using Java as an enabler to network-aware applications. The Scopus Java Architecture is shown in Figure 15.1.

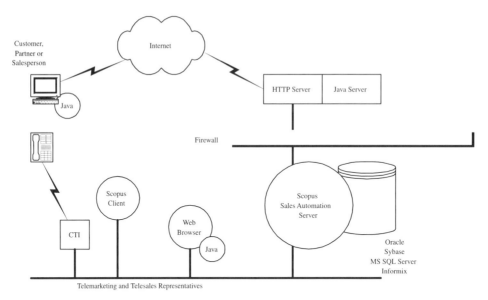

FIGURE 15.1 Scopus Java architecture.

Scopus Java Client

Today Scopus ships a complete Java sales automation system. The Scopus application set is a full metadata-driven architecture. That is to say, the look, feel, and even much of the application processing is stored in a relational database system. This repository-centric architecture has been in place since 1992. Until recently Scopus also delivered its own proprietary C++ browser to read and display the metadata application.

In 1996 Scopus set out to deliver a client built 100 percent in Java. This effort provides customers with true platform independence and lower cost of application maintenance. But the biggest benefit will be found in the call center, where telesales and telemarketing personnel can be outfitted with overall lower-cost desktop environments, including NC machines.

With the Scopus Java client, agents benefit from a fully functional application that includes marketing response, survey, lead generation/qualification, and order entry functionality in a common browser environment. Java clients coexist on the LAN or intranet with other traditional Scopus C++ clients.

Scopus SmartScript Java Bean

A major issue in any call center is the deployment, maintenance, and effectiveness of call guides or scripts. Scopus SmartScript call guide has been implemented as Java Beans, allowing call centers to deploy robust call-guide environments that move beyond simple information consumption to fully interactive environments that in the past were associated only with large desktop applications. Providing a call-guide environment in Java, implemented as Java Beans, allows for component reuse in script construction—providing standardized interfaces, unlimited customization, support for events, and persistence. In many call centers profitability hinges on the success of the call guide, the ability to get the script to the floor as soon as possible, and the ability to fine-tune the script to maximize potential. One of the biggest benefits of Java is quicker time to market, with call guides that are easily assembled and customized.

Scopus Java MES Server

The hallmark of a good marketing encyclopedia system is its ability to deal with heterogeneous information sources, and to fully pull those sources together in an integrated environment that can be accessed over the Internet as well as on intranet. Additionally, access to the MES must be independent of platform, and provide features for distributed and occasionally connected use. The Scopus MES server has been written totally in Java. Implementing an MES in Java allows remote sales personnel, channel partners, and customers—regardless of location and computing device—to access rich stores of product-based information that can be pulled from an abundance of content sources. In addition, occasionally connected users beat information overload through a publish-and-subscribe model. The subscriptions are also augmented by user profiles and behaviors that ensure latest information is not missed.

Scopus Java Channel Server

The Java Channel Server provides a complete extended enterprise solution for partners and value-added resellers. All a partner now needs to effectively interact are a browser and access to your company's application. The Channel Server distributes leads to partners based on profile and skill rules. Partners not only accept leads and the latest product and marketing information, but can also provide call-back reports and sales status. The Channel Server also works in concert with the Scopus MES to deliver content, including non-Web-based content, to channel partners. The two products working together let businesses control what partner gets what content, and when.

The Channel Server also protects business-sensitive information, since it is built using the Java security model components and protected domains. The security model enforces a *sandbox* that allows only trusted components to load, execute, and access system resources. In addition protected domains extend the protected area to the file system. This model is highly secure and flexible.

ADDITIONAL INFORMATION

Scopus Technology has its corporate headquarters at 1900 Powell Street, Emeryville, CA 94608; Fax: (510) 428-1027. Readers can find more information on Scopus products at the Scopus Web site www.scopus.com; or can contact Scopus at (510) 597-5800. Some additional information on Scopus products is also included on the accompanying CD-ROM. SalesTEAM is a trademark of Scopus Technology, Inc.

The authors would like to acknowledge the assistance of Mitch Bishop and Lyle Ekdahl, of Scopus Technology, in the preparation of this chapter.

Phased, Rapid, and Flexible Deployment— Borealis

Chapter 9 covered the steps necessary to deploy a Sales Force Automation solution in your organization. We described how you could set the goal for your system, develop your sales processes, develop the solution, deploy it, and provide ongoing maintenance. As pointed out, the overall cycle can take a long time, and you run the risk of having a solution that is out of date by the time it reaches the sales force. A better approach would be to develop and deploy your application in small pieces, and build on those pieces until you have the solution deployed to the entire sales force.

This chapter will describe a way in which you can do that, using the Arsenal suite of products from Borealis Technology Corporation.

RISKS WITH THE ALL-AT-ONCE APPROACH

Many Sales Force Automation implementations today adopt an *all-at-once* approach to development and deployment. In extreme cases of this approach, the entire functionality of the whole system is defined before development commences, then the people responsible for developing the system (usually the Information Technology organization of your company) go off and make the system, and when it is ready it is deployed to users all at once.

An enterprise SFA system is usually very large, so there are some risks with the all-at-once approach:

- Sales process changes
- Technology changes
- Technology assimilation

The first two risks stem from the time it takes to develop and deploy a large application. At best it will take a minimum of 9 to 12 months to deploy an enterprise solution for even a medium-size sales organization. Given the rapid changes in the business environment these days, the way your salespeople do business 12 months from now is almost guaranteed to be different from the way they do it now. Your organization may adopt another sales methodology, or enter new markets that require new selling techniques; or your sales strategy may change so that your organization now focuses more on channel sales. Whatever the case, there is a strong likelihood that by the time the sales automation solution is deployed, it will be out of date.

Much the same can be said of changes in the technological environment. The pace of technological change, especially in the computer industry in general and in Web technologies in particular, is simply amazing. Chapter 9 showed the gap that can open up if you get tied to a particular technology but cannot use it for some time.

The third risk is with technology assimilation: Can your salespeople be reasonably expected to learn and effectively use a large-scale application in a short period of time? Can you afford to let them take time out to do this, and let your sales suffer as they spend weeks, even months, figuring out the intricacies of the system? In all likelihood your salespeople will quickly decide that the solution doesn't work for them, and at best will use only isolated functions that are easy to understand and have clear value to them in their job: selling.

PHASED, RAPID, AND FLEXIBLE DEPLOYMENT

We believe that the best way to address the aforementioned risks is to adopt a phased, rapid, and flexible deployment strategy. In this approach, you would analyze your current sales processes and determine which processes would benefit the most from automation. As discussed in Chapter 9, you could then decide where the most value would be realized through automation, and implement only that automation first.

The advantage of this approach is that you can implement the SFA functionality in small pieces, or phases. As you implement each piece you can deploy it to the user community, and help them see the value in using the tools. If the functionality is limited, but of high value, salespeople will be motivated and able to use it. The IT organization can get feedback on the implementation, and can change the tool to incorporate the feedback and release that in the next phase. This allows users to get involved in developing the product, and gives them a sense of ownership, which in turn makes them want to use the tool even more.

As they get comfortable with the technology, you can deploy more functionality, perhaps to address the next big thing on your list of automation projects. Or you could find that your business environment has changed, and your tools need to be changed to work in the new environment. Because the functionality you have deployed is discrete you can easily modify it and redeploy within a very short time frame.

The key to implementing a phased, rapid, and flexible deployment strategy is an application development environment that allows you to quickly develop, test, prototype, deploy, and manage Sales Force Automation applications. One such application is Arsenal from Borealis Technology Corporation.

ARSENAL SOLUTION

Arsenal enables phased implementations, eliminating the risks and constraints of traditional sales automation systems. Arsenal's phased implementation approach takes the complexity out of the system, replacing it with a continuous improvement process. User feedback and adaptation to specific selling environments constantly update the implementation while delivering immediate and ongoing results.

Out-of-the-box applications let you quickly place applications into the hands of your salespeople, while the Arsenal Designer allows modifications or enhancements to be made within hours, not months.

As shown in Figure 16.1, Arsenal components include:

- Arsenal Applications
- Arsenal User
- Arsenal Designer
- Arsenal Server

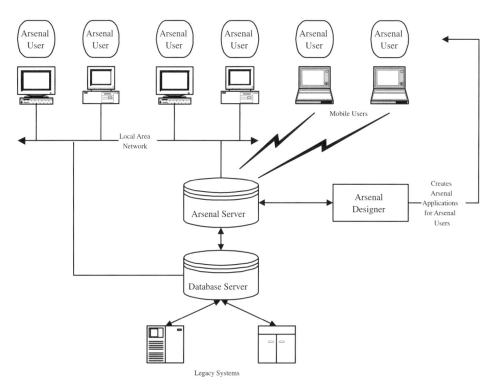

FIGURE 16.1   The Arsenal solution.

Arsenal Applications

Arsenal provides the capability to create end-user applications using the Arsenal Designer application or the Borealis-supplied library of applications. Applications are a selected combination of individual components, such as forms, database schema, menus, and scripts. Applications can be created from scratch, or can be updated versions of existing applications. Once the application is complete and checked in to the Arsenal Server, it can be scheduled for electronic distribution to Arsenal users.

The runtime application provides end users with the functionality and graphical interface they need to effectively do their job. This usually involves the ability to enter, view, and modify data about accounts, contacts, opportunities, and so on. This information is stored in either a database on the local computer (Arsenal Remote User) or in the corporate database located managed by the Arsenal Server (Arsenal LAN User). If a remote user, the data is sent electronically to the corporate database when the user synchronizes. If a LAN user, the changes are made directly on the corporate database.

Because Arsenal contains a complete development environment, it is beyond the scope of this document to attempt to identify what any given application can do. Arsenal applications could be as simple as a contact manager, or as elaborate as a complete opportunity management application with built-in literature fulfillment, Internet links, proposal generation, and pipeline forecasting. However, the key features of Arsenal applications include the ability to:

- Run an application created with the Arsenal Designer
- Transparently support Arsenal functional modules, such as the Calendar
- Execute scripts created with the script editor, which is part of the Arsenal Designer

Arsenal User

The Arsenal User is the runtime environment used to run Arsenal applications. The runtime environment is the *engine* that runs an application, communicates with the Arsenal Server, and performs local housekeeping. This includes running the Arsenal application that was created with the Arsenal Designer, the ability to send and receive data with the Arsenal Server, the ability to receive runtime application and/or database schema changes and Arsenal upgrades from the server, as well as integrate all changes. The Arsenal User also supports built-in functional modules, such as the Calendar, dynamic Searching, and Sorting.

There are several functional areas that the Arsenal User is responsible for and each is described in detail in Table 16.1.

TABLE 16.1 Functional Areas of Arsenal User

Functionality	Description
Arsenal Applications	Support for running the end-user application created with the Arsenal Designer. Allows Arsenal Users to view, create, and edit data, as well as perform other tasks, depending on the capabilities exposed in the application
Functionality Modules	Arsenal supports Borealis-supplied *canned* modules. Version 3.0 will support Calendar, Search, and Sort modules that can be included as part of the end-user application.
Roll Out	Ability to receive application updates and database schema changes from the Arsenal Server. Roll out also supports the ability for Arsenal Users to receive Arsenal upgrades.
Synchronization	Provides capability to communicate with the Arsenal Server for the purpose of sending data changes and receiving data, application, and database schema updates as well as Arsenal upgrades. Data on the client can be specified as private or public.
Integration	Ability to integrate changes (data, application, schema, and Arsenal upgrades) received from the Arsenal Server on the Arsenal User automatically and transparently to the user.

Configurations	Description
Arsenal LAN Users	Support for nonmobile, networked users that access the corporate database directly via the corporate network.
Arsenal Remote Users	Support for mobile, dial-in users that use a local database and occasionally synchronize with the corporate database.

Some of the Arsenal User's functionality involves the Arsenal Server and where applicable they are identified.

A typical configuration would have a combination of Arsenal LAN and Remote Users. Network-based Arsenal Users use the LAN configuration in which they are always connected directly to the corporate database via the local area network. The corporate database is the database that resides on the server in the runtime environment, and is managed by the Arsenal Server. Remote-based Arsenal Users are generally mobile users that connect occasionally to the corporate database via modems. Arsenal Remote Users have their own local database that they interface with, and when they connect to the Arsenal Server their local data is synchronized with the corporate database. The local database is typically a subset of the data located on the corporate database.

Arsenal Designer

The Arsenal Designer is the Arsenal development and project administration environment. The development environment is where all individual components (e.g., forms, scripts, menus) are worked on with the intention of including all or some of them in a runtime application. Components are created, deleted, or modified by using the supplied editors (e.g., Form Editor, Schema Editor, Menu Editor) embedded in the Arsenal Designer. Once created or modified, components are checked in to the Arsenal Server as part of a project, and the components can be used over and over again in different applications that belong to the same project.

The Arsenal Designer also provides the interface to the Arsenal Server, so objects (projects, applications, and components) can be checked out and in, and rollouts can be scheduled. Each component can be checked out individually, so multiple developers can work on a project simultaneously. Only one developer can work on an individual component at a time. The developer that checks out the component can modify it and check it back in. Other users can get copies of the component (for local testing of an application) but cannot make changes. Once the developer checks the component back in, it may be checked out by another

Arsenal developer. The Project Manager and Application Manager (contained in the Arsenal Designer) are used to manage the project and its applications. Once an application is ready to be implemented, the Rollout Manager (contained in the Arsenal Designer) is used to schedule a target user environment, and a date and time to integrate the changes and send the update to Arsenal Users (both LAN and Remote).

A typical configuration would have one or more nodes (either Windows or Macintosh) with the Arsenal Designer software installed. These nodes would be connected via LAN to the Arsenal Server. All development work is done on the local Arsenal Designer node after the project, application, or individual components have been checked out from the Arsenal Server. Checking out components actually copies those components to the Arsenal Designer while locking those files on the Arsenal Server to prevent others from modifying the same components. Once Arsenal Designer work is completed, the components are checked back into the Arsenal Server, where the version is updated and the components unlocked. The LAN connection is required only to check in and out files. Actual editing may be performed without a connection to the Server, thus allowing files to be edited locally from any physical location.

Arsenal Server

The Arsenal Server is a collection of processes and software tasks that reside on the server. The Arsenal Server must be accessible to Arsenal Designers, Arsenal Users, and other Arsenal Servers. Typically, Arsenal LAN Users will connect to the network through a LAN or WAN, while Arsenal Remote Users will connect to the network through a modem connection. Arsenal Designers may use either configuration.

Additional Arsenal Servers may reside on the same server or on separate servers. Separate servers must be networked in order to support application rollouts. Multiple Arsenal Servers are necessary, as each is responsible for managing its own environment. The two runtime environments, Test and Production, access their own Arsenal sales data located in separate corporate databases. The sales database is part of the environment and resides on the same server. The development environment, Designer, maintains all projects, application definitions, components, and scheduled rollouts that are stored in the corporate database assigned to that Arsenal Server environment.

ADDITIONAL INFORMATION

Borealis Technology Corporation has its corporate headquarters at 4070 Silver Sage Drive, Carson City, NV 89701; Fax: (702) 888-3215. Readers can find more information on Borealis products at the Borealis Web site, www.brls.com; or can contact Borealis at (702) 888-3200. Borealis and Arsenal are trademarks of Borealis Technology Corporation.

The authors would like to acknowledge the assistance of Colleen Kelly, of Borealis Technology Corporation, in the preparation of this chapter.

Customer Management via the Web— ONYX Software

17

CASE STUDY

Visio Corporation, headquartered in Seattle, Washington, develops and markets business graphics software. Award-winning Visio drag-and-drop products have emerged as the corporate standard for business drawing and diagramming. Visio employs more than 200 people around the globe.

Situation Analysis

After uniting its customer-focused team with ONYX Customer Center, Visio required a means to leverage its Web site and expand its contacts with customers and prospects between its Web site and customer database. A more active Web site would allow Visio to attract and better qualify more prospects, while customizing responses would give prospects and customers more of what they wanted to see. Visio investigated which options would provide the most cost-effective and timely ability to *activate* its Web site.

"What we were looking for was true, interactive-response marketing," said T. J. Evans, Worldwide Internet Manager for Visio. "A Web site should be about providing and personalizing.

We wanted to be able to capture information about who's coming on to our site, and give them what they're looking for. But we also needed to be able to do this quickly, with room for future growth, and with a budget in mind."

Visio's Goals

Visio required a system that quickly linked its Customer Center database to the Web so that it could:

- Better communicate with customers and prospects
- Rapidly capture qualified leads from its Web site
- Leverage its Web site for instant cross-sell and up-sell opportunities
- Position its Web site as its primary registration tool

Solution Description

ONYX Web Wizards for Sales enables a company to quickly extend its marketing and sales efforts to the Internet by instantly generating Web pages to interact directly with ONYX Customer Center. Using familiar *wizards* in a step-by-step process, companies easily create a Web enabled link to their Customer Center databases for lead generation, literature fulfillment, and prospect profiling. By extending the Total Customer Management abilities of Customer Center to the Internet, companies strengthen prospect and customer relationships by increasing responsiveness and knowledge.

Business Benefits

Visio attributes several benefits to the Web Wizards project:

- 67 percent savings on lead entry costs
- 30 percent increase in use of integrated fax system
- 10 percent product registration rate increase with attached customer profiles
- Inexpensive, instantaneous method to cross-sell and up-sell its products
- Reduced administration and internal Web development costs due to fast implementation

- Instant success: 220-seat license sale as a result of a *self-qualified* Web-generated lead
- Return on investment of three to four months

Flexible Solution

In order to change its Web site from a traditional reference area, where customers wandered the library of its site, Visio needed a *virtual librarian* to better serve customers by capturing profiles and directing them to areas most appropriate to them.

"We looked at building our own bridge to our database, and also looked at outsourcing the project to someone else," says Chris Bassett, Database Administrator for Visio. "But for cost effectiveness, implementation time, and data security, these other options didn't give us the flexibility we need down the road."

Based on the success of ONYX Customer Center, Visio implemented ONYX Web Wizards and has seen a rapid return on its investment.

Increased Opportunities

Increased user registration of the new Visio Professional release was a first goal of the Web Wizards implementation. From kickoff meeting to fruition of the project, Visio's project registration wizard took two weeks to implement, and Visio is now receiving over 300 Web registrations per week.

By embedding a hot link to its Web site in its new product, customers are now taken directly to the Visio Web site when they first open the application. Once there, Web Wizards registers and further profiles the customer through a survey form the customer is asked to complete. While only a few questions are enforced, most customers willingly answer the rest. With their prior fax-registration system, cross-sell and up-sell opportunities were not possible.

"Not only have we increased our registration rate, we now have the opportunity to sell upgrades and other services while cross-merchandising," says Bruno Gralpois, North American Direct Sales Manager. "Just because your customer is registered, doesn't mean the contact with them should stop. Incredible sales opportunities were potentially lost with our old registration system."

Within days of the implementation, Visio was receiving product registrations from both North American and European sales of its new release. Most initial registrants were existing customers in its database and by having them fill out the associated survey, Visio's customer profile has become more complete. Says Bassett, "Within days of the implementation, leads were being passed to sales for immediate follow-up based on survey responses. Web Wizards is helping us fulfill our worldwide registration strategy."

The increased opportunities of the Web Wizards implementation was immediately realized. Visio received a 220-seat license sale as a result of a self-qualified Web-generated lead.

Big Savings

The versatility of Web Wizards led Bassett to develop an interesting use of the product: lead capture from trade shows. Traditionally, Visio salespeople would return to their office with a flat file database of leads. They would then allocate space and resources for temporary employees to enter the data. With Web Wizards, Visio created forms that allow a remote temp agency to input trade-show leads remotely via the Web. With four people entering about 5000 leads, Visio saved $3600 at the first show. Visio attends 10 to 15 trade shows per year.

"ONYX Web Wizards has been a great time and money saver for Visio," says Neal Myrick, Information Systems Manager. "By extending our Customer Center database to the Web, we shaved 67 percent off our traditional lead entry costs. That's big savings when you're talking about thousands of leads."

Visio now has a rapid, two-day cycle for capturing a trade-show lead and establishing a second contact. "We're now more automated and responsive than our competitors," adds Myrick.

Looking back on the decision to implement the ONYX solution, Bassett says, "Web Wizards was a lifesaver. If we had cooked up our own system, it would have eliminated a lot of the functionality of this robust product, like multiple-option questions. It also would have taken much more time to implement. Looking at spending $15,000 on developing our own project versus the flexible solution we now have, I'd say Web Wizards was a great investment."

Says Myrick, "Not even counting the sale we made from a Web Wizards lead, the money we saved from product registrations and lead-entry costs has given us a three- to four-month return on our investment."

Quality Contacts

With its new ability to profile prospects and customers via the Internet, Visio has increased its knowledge as well as its ability to respond to customer needs. "Web Wizards is all about communicating with customers the way they want, on the level they want," says Evans. "It's about tailoring the customers' experience and giving them more choice."

"Web Wizards has not only helped us with our trade-show leads," adds Bassett, "it's a virtual trade show that just sits out there on our Web site and collects leads at minimal cost."

Web Wizards not only allows a company to learn more about its prospects and customers and leverage its Customer Center database quickly, but because it supports a sophisticated data model it also allows companies to reuse templates for future projects. For example, within days after its first project was completed, Visio created a new survey which profiles prospects before they download a demo version of a product from the Visio Web site.

"With Web Wizards, we are able to begin capturing the interactions of customers and prospects on our Web site," says Gary Gigot, Visio Vice President of Marketing. "Rather than measuring hits, we can now capture the quality of contacts and the nature of their businesses."

ONYX SOFTWARE

The ONYX Customer Center product shown in Figure 17.1 enables companies to provide marketing, sales, service, and support teams with a single tool to access all corporate customer information via the Internet, remotely, and from the desktop.

When combined as part of a holistic, customer-centric IT infrastructure, the Internet promises the progressive software company a rare opportunity to manage the entire customer life

FIGURE 17.1 ONYX Customer Center desktop.

cycle effectively and efficiently. It also enables a company to deliver greater value in the most critical customer interactions. For ONYX Software, the onslaught of the Internet brought change, and product development was focused on Internet-enabling products. In redefining the customer business processes to showcase how to leverage this new vehicle, ONYX analyzed the opportunities presented by the Internet and the Web:

- What are customers' expectations when they visit our Web site, be they a prospect, a recruit, or a current account?
- How can we use Internet technologies to consistently exceed customer expectations?
- At which steps in the customer life cycle can the Internet add value?

The customer life cycle is a holistic, integrated process. From this perspective, each department is a critical component of total customer management, with responsibility for the whole, recognized and shared by the corporation. Each step in the process fosters the seamless transition from marketing to sales to service and back again.

The marketing goals of the ONYX Internet strategy map directly to the corporate strategy of customer acquisition, retention, and expansion—acquire low-cost, highly qualified customers; achieve market-share objectives; retain profitable customers; and expand the business done with current customers.

To date over 30 percent of current ONYX customers first heard about ONYX through the Internet. For almost all others, the Internet was instrumental in supporting marketing, sales, and service efforts. In addition to being a major source of sales leads, Web leads are also the most cost effective. For example, at a big trade show ONYX will gather approximately 200 qualified leads at a cost of about $40,000, or $200 per qualified lead. By contrast, the ONYX Web site delivers at least 600 qualified leads per month, at a fully burdened cost of about $10,000 per month (less than $20 per qualified lead). Traditionally, people have looked at direct mail as inexpensive lead generation—it can't hold a candle to the economies of the Web. A $3 mailing to 20,000 targeted suspects may yield 300 leads at a cost of $200 per lead.

Customer Service/Support

Forty percent of all ONYX Customers use the Web for support issues. Every incident gets logged versus being left to individual determination. All incidents are automatically added to the knowledgebase—customers document problems in their words, versus ONYX reps interpreting problems over the phone. Customers can check any incident in the last thirty days, as well as query status of incidents. When a problem is solved, customers are automatically e-mailed the solution. They are also notified of status changes.

Marketing

In a recent, independent test of Web responsiveness, Matterhorn Consulting, a customer management consulting firm headquartered in San Francisco, visited over 3500 consumer and business-to-business Web sites, asking for information through the vehicle provided by the site. None of the requests were in the form of unsolicited mail. After requesting the information that was offered on the site, Matterhorn measured the speed, appropriateness, and completeness of the response. ONYX had the fastest response of the 3500 companies tested, responding to the inquiry in 90 seconds.

"The average company surveyed responded in 15 days," said Barry Goldberg, president of Matterhorn Consulting. "There were only four same-day responses, and only two of those within an hour of the request. *ONYX was on the phone before we were off their site.* This kind of instant response should be the standard for companies who see themselves as customer centered."

If prospects are truly interested in a product, they will provide this information in exchange for educational value. To this end, industry white papers, product demonstrations, and industry research are offered in exchange for prospects completing qualification surveys.

This survey asks a prospect to complete ten important identification questions that form the basis for prospect quality rating, including:

- Common demographic information (name, address, title, company name, phone, fax, e-mail, Web site URL)
- Company information (number of employees, annual revenues, industry classification)
- Which systems they currently use to manage customer information
- Whether they are actively searching
- Which departments need a system, and how many users in each department
- Where they first heard of ONYX

The prospect also is presented with a list of mailable, faxable, and e-mailable documents from which to choose. Once the person hits the Submit button on the survey page, the real fun begins:

- Information is immediately populated in their customer database. Requested faxes, e-mail, and literature are instantly processed.

- Using custom qualification rules, ONYX tailors specific, instant responses to the customer.

This shifts more of the sales process to marketing by automating the lead qualification step and delivering leads deeper into the sales funnel (and fewer inside salespeople are needed to qualify leads). Eight inside salespeople qualify and work a minimum of five leads per day. On average, 25 companies prequalify themselves via the Web each day. The inside sales team works these as well, but the need to *qualify* is complete.

In addition to being a source for over 30 percent of current ONYX customers, the Internet has also been instrumental in supporting and enhancing most of its traditional acquisition efforts. In general, for all programs such as alliances, advertising, public relations, and database marketing, the Internet provides an unparalleled call to action. Where the Internet has offered the most dramatic support is with seminars and trade shows.

Seminars

One problem with seminars is low response rates and high attrition rates. There is only so much you can do to attract attendees with a direct-mail piece. ONYX's solution is to Internet-enable this by:

- Supporting the direct marketing effort by making the call to action a visit to the Web site (and providing the visitors with far more information than can be given in a mailer)
- Quick registration
- Fax confirmation, directions, and so on, as soon as they click Confirm

Trade Shows

Scribbling of notes on business cards or forms. Weeks to follow up. Big data scrubbing and import needs. Sound familiar? ONYX has eliminated these headaches and long delays. All attendees at trade shows are given an electronically coded badge with name, title, phone/fax, company name, and full profile information. When these people stop by the booth, their badges are *swiped* and the encoded information is instantly pushed to their Web sites. While standing with prospects, ONYX can profile them, ask what type of literature they'd like to receive, and instantly report this information back to corporate headquarters.

Before prospects leave the ONYX booth:

- Their fax requests have been sent
- A personalized letter is printed and sent from headquarters
- An e-mail is waiting for them in their inbox
- Their profiles are pushed to the appropriate inside salesperson for follow-up. (At a recent DCI show in Chicago, inside sales called or responded back via phone to 609 people that saw the demo at DCI within 24 hours!)
- At the end of the day, when the announcer tells the attendees on the show floor, Thank you all for participating in this year's show, ONYX has already said Thank You! This type of lead follow-up should set the standard for other vendors in the industry.

Sales

The Internet has improved sales processes in two main areas. First, self-qualified Web leads shorten the sales cycle and improve ONYX's close rate. Second, selling efforts are more effective due to increased remote access capabilities via the Internet.

With the Web, some of the traditional lines between sales and marketing are being blurred. Marketing is focused on attracting the best, self-qualifying leads; and can fulfill the basic needs of these self-qualified prospects and then move them several stages through the sales process. Lead qualification is the first of five major steps in the sales process. Whereas traditional lead sources, such as bingo cards and telephone inquiries, require significant time on the part of telesales to qualify the prospect, Web leads are self-qualified—telesales can skip the qualification step and start assessing a prospect's needs immediately. As a result, Web leads produce higher close rates and shorter sales cycles. Incoming leads via the Web have shortened the sales cycle from six to four months.

In addition to serving as a primary interface with customers, the Internet is an integral interface for end users of customer information systems. The Internet allows considerable leeway in who uses the system and where they use it. For example, through a partnership with AT&T Wireless, ONYX Customer Center can be accessed via an Internet browser using a Pocket-Net Phone. This Internet access allows a field sales representative to review work notes en route to a client site; obtain a customer's name, title, and phone number while waiting for a plane; or e-mail a trip report to a team member back in the home office.

The Internet provides important capabilities at many points in the sales process:

Remote Demos

By using Microsoft's NetMeeting for remote live demos, you can eliminate the need to travel to the prospect site for initial demos, shortening the needs assessment and solution development steps of the sales process. In addition, allowing prospects to test-drive an application over the Internet provides increased convenience to the potential customer, and decreases the travel time and expense for the salesperson.

Partner Access

The customer information system can be integrated with financial/accounting systems, where you can share information on certain accounts with these system vendors. The Internet makes this possible. You can provide access to the relevant customer accounts via a Web browser, allowing partners to the system wherever they can get on the Internet.

Salesperson Access

The Internet allows a salesperson, armed with the appropriate password, to call up the information from the customer's PC via a Web browser, instead of taking the time to boot up a laptop. With the customer looking on, the salesperson can produce a quote and enter the order, closing the deal on the spot!

ADDITIONAL INFORMATION

ONYX Software's corporate address is 330 120th Avenue NE, Bellevue, WA 98005. They can be reached by phone at (425) 451-8060 or fax (425) 990-3343. You can find more information on ONYX products directly from their Web site: www.onyxsoftware .com.

The authors would like to acknowledge the assistance of Christina Schuetz, of ONYX Software, in the preparation of this chapter.

18

Delivering Web-Centric Solutions— NetDynamics

Companies looking to extend their enterprises to the Web must leverage their existing core applications in order to be successful. However, a significant amount of time and money have already been invested in these traditional client/server applications. To re-create them for the Web would be inefficient and expensive.

The technology architecture companies select will significantly impact the benefits they gain by using the Web as an application development and distribution infrastructure. Companies looking to establish a Web-centric business model, where the Web plays a critical role in the success and competitive advantage of the business, must adopt a Web-centric computing model. The Web-centric solution must first and foremost address the unique issues of the Web, everything from state management to server security. A successful Web-centric enterprise must look at leveraging its existing core applications while delivering new applications that are Web-native. Application scalability is very important. As the enterprise grows globally, the application must grow accordingly. A scalable application server is required. Furthermore, as the user community increases, so does the need for modifications to existing applications. Application extensibility must be easy and maintainable. A suitable language must be selected, ideally one that is open, extensible, and an industry-accepted standard.

NetDynamics provides the capabilities companies need to build their presence on the Web. NetDynamics provides Web-native technology, enterprise extensibility, scalability, and openness in one integrated package.

USING NETDYNAMICS TO WEB-ENABLE YOUR SFA APPLICATION

NetDynamics, Inc.'s flagship and namesake product, NetDynamics, is the solution for companies looking to build Web-centric enterprises. This integrated development environment and application server system is architected from the ground up for the Web. It takes the lessons learned from client/server implementations with regard to easy, rapid, but extensible development cycles. NetDynamics addresses the unique Web issues of scalability, state and session maintenance, security, and technology changes. The application server architecture delivers a Web-native, three-tier architecture that meets the scalability and performance demands of ever increasing numbers of users. To Web-enable existing core enterprise applications, NetDynamics includes the WebEXTEND product family. WebEXTEND technology allows developers working within a familiar visual development environment to build browser-based applications that access existing business logic on applications from PeopleSoft, SAP, and others.

NetDynamics Studio Development Environment

The NetDynamics Studio development tool provides an integrated, Java-based, point-and-click environment to develop Web/data applications rapidly.

Rapid Application Development

The NetDynamics Studio visual development environment automates the process of building Web/data applications through wizards that generate the application framework. These wizards generate everything from default HTML pages and tables to data-driven objects, such as text fields, list boxes, radio buttons, and so on. The wizards also perform automatic formatting and validation of data. Developers can set default formats or parse input entries based on regular expressions.

NetDynamics also automatically generates data objects that incorporate SQL statements for accessing databases. These data objects can perform all forms of SQL actions, from queries to updates to stored procedure access. The automatically generated SQL can be enhanced to include dynamic criteria that is appended to the SQL statement based on a user's individual responses.

Tight Language Integration with Java

NetDynamics is tightly integrated with Java, which is the underlying object-oriented development language of NetDynamics. In addition to generating Java code automatically during the wizards-based development process, NetDynamics also provides built-in Java classes. Over 250 classes and 2000 methods are available for developers who wish to create custom business logic for manipulating data access, interfacing with input and output data displays, managing user sessions and state, and controlling and authenticating user privileges. NetDynamics developers can also access existing application code by incorporating functionality within a Java-based NetDynamics application with external Java or C++ classes.

Open, Portable Integration

NetDynamics is based on an open architecture that allows developers to integrate any database, HTML editor, Web server, Web browser display (HTML, Java, JavaScript, ActiveX), and any Web browser across multiple platforms. For example, developers can edit NetDynamics-generated HTML pages within Microsoft Front-Page, then test the application on a Netscape Navigator browser. With built-in access to the Microsoft ActiveX Control Pad, developers can easily attach ActiveX controls to a NetDynamics page. The same can be achieved with Java applets. NetDynamics is designed to be used across a heterogeneous computing environment.

NetDynamics applications are completely portable. NetDynamics generates only portable Java bytecode, HTML templates, and ASCII-based parameter files. Moving an application from one operating system to another is a simple process of transferring the files (using Copy or FTP). No recompilation or code rewriting is required.

Security

NetDynamics leverages standard Web security mechanisms, such as Internet firewalls, Web servers, and database servers. Companies that have implemented environments with firewalls and secure transmission protocols, such as Secure Sockets Layer (SSL) or RSA-based encryption, will find that NetDynamics works seamlessly without modification. NetDynamics also provides built-in security on an application level, enforcing a security bridge between the Web server and database server. Developers can control the login process from Web server to application server to database server, even managing multiple users with single database logins. Table 18.1 describes some of the authentication and security options available with NetDynamics.

In addition to NetDynamics-based security mechanisms, NetDynamics also partners with a key security vendor to provide a single authenticated login that is propagated from Web browser all the way to the database server. The integration of NetDynamics with Gradient Technologies's WebCrusader security architecture allows developers to manage Access Control Lists (ACLs) that describe the access levels, priorities, and access times of individual users. NetDynamics uses the ACL to determine the proper level of accessibility within the NetDynamics application.

Session and State Management

In traditional client/server applications, a user's application session begins when the user logs on to the application (and consequently the associated database), and ends when the user logs off. The stateless nature of the Web server does not allow a similar handling of sessions. Each session on a Web server is limited to the length of time it takes to process a request for an HTML page. Once the HTML page is returned to the user's browser, that session is terminated. To maintain session information, developers have turned to browser-dependent *cookies,* for example. Others have written their own CGI-based mechanisms for maintaining state information.

TABLE 18.1 NetDynamics Security

Mechanism	Provider	Process
User authentication	Web server	The Web server authenticates the user and passes the Web ID to NetDynamics.
Navigation flow control	NetDynamics	Developers define navigation control within the NetDynamics application. They enforce application entrance points and prevent users from navigating through the application except through defined paths. For example, users will be unable to bookmark pages to bypass the initial login screen.
User authorization	NetDynamics	Developers define user privileges (query, insert, update, etc.) on a page-by-page basis. Users cannot execute procedures for which they are not authorized by developers.
Database access authorization	NetDynamics	Before sending the data request to the database, NetDynamics maps the Web ID to the database login. Multiple users with distinct Web IDs will be able to use a single database login ID. This approach minimizes the number of individual database logins required. The Web ID to database ID mapping takes place through a secure table lookup or through a developer-defined Java procedure.
Database security	Database Server	The database server provides standard database security. NetDynamics logs in to the database server using the proper method prescribed by the database vendor.

NetDynamics solves the problem by providing built-in, developer-definable session and state management. The Persistence Engine (PE), part of the NetDynamics application server, stores all relevant information about a user. Everything from the Web ID to the exact table row the user is currently viewing can be maintained in the PE. A user session is automatically initiated for each browser upon the user accessing the first page of the application. The session terminates on a developer-defined timeout, or on a specific application termination event, such as a button that reads "Exit application." When the session is terminated, the server stops holding the session information for that user.

NetDynamics maintains state information on both the server and on the client page. Application state information is maintained by the application server, and local state information is maintained on the page. NetDynamics provides manipulatable state objects for both server and page state information.

On an application level, NetDynamics automatically maintains the user's database login, password, and page privileges. Developers can define server-based application objects that maintain their state even as users browse through many pages of an application. An example of such an application object is an object that maintains state information on the content of a user's shopping cart.

On a page level, NetDynamics automatically generates a session ID for each page. The ID, which is generated for each application session, is encrypted and changes from page to page. The session ID enforces secure access to data by preventing users from moving to pages for which they are not authorized. The ID also contains information about database cursor position in order to accurately handle future data record retrievals.

Take, for example, a user who is browsing through an application that displays five rows of data at a time. The user is currently looking at the page that displays items 1 through 5. Because NetDynamics maintains database cursor position, the user can click on the Next button and retrieve the next page to display rows 6 through 10. This is true regardless of whether the user arrived at the first page through initial entry into the application, or whether the user proceeded further into the application and then clicked on Back in the Web browser to return to the page displaying items 1 through 5. This handling of browser and application server interaction through the use of the intelligent Persistence Engine is all automatic with NetDynamics.

Transaction Management

NetDynamics manages transactions through the Data Server interface, part of the NetDynamics application server. NetDynamics provides built-in support for autocommit and rollback on SQL actions. NetDynamics also supports developer-controlled transaction blocks that include:

- Start transaction before executing SQL
- Rollback upon failures
- Commit upon success

NetDynamics Application Server

The NetDynamics application server delivers the high processing speed and scalability required by commercial applications. The server is based on a distributed architecture that provides automatic load balancing. As usage of an enterprise-scale NetDynamics application grows, the system administrator simply adds more CPUs (or individual machines) to the NetDynamics application server system. The application server manager can then funnel the increased incoming requests to the new CPUs. No custom coding whatsoever is required.

Architecture Overview

Figure 18.1 is a schematic of the NetDynamics application server.

In Figure 18.1, application requests flow through the NetDynamics application server in the following manner:

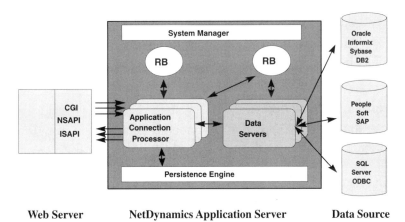

FIGURE 18.1 NetDynamics Application Server architechture.

- The Web server passes a browser's HTTP request to the NetDynamics server through a lightweight CGI *stub* (approximately 16Kb), a Netscape Server API (NSAPI)-based dynamic link library (DLL), or a Microsoft ISAPI DLL.
- The application server request broker (RB) receives the request. The request broker oversees one or more connection processors (CP) within the application server system. It finds an available connection processor and sends it the request for processing. Each CP incorporates a Java Virtual Machine (JVM) and can execute the necessary Java code.
- When a data source request is made, the request is sent to the data server request broker. The data server request broker manages one or more data servers.
- The data server request broker looks for an available data server that is already connected to the requested database with the same user ID and password. When a free data server with the matching connection is found, the request broker sends the request to the data server. If no matching one is found, the data server will initiate a new connection to the data source.
- After the connection is made, the data server sends the request to the data source. When it receives the response, typically in the form of a data set, the data server sends the results back to the CP that invoked it.
- The CP completes processing of the request and generates the dynamic HTML page that will be sent back to the Web server.
- The Web server then serves the page to the Web browser for display.

Optimized Data Access

As discussed earlier, CGI-based executables are inefficient means of providing data access. With CGI executables, each time a user requests a page with data, the Web server starts a new CGI process, connects to the data source, receives data, closes the connection, and shuts down the CGI executable. The larger the CGI executable (and they can range from several Kb to several Mb), the greater the overhead and the slower the performance.

Likewise, performance overhead is also incurred in the opening and closing of the data source connection.

NetDynamics's optimized interface with the Web server and database server eliminates this overhead. The application server, which is always resident in memory, caches applications. Users requesting the application do not incur the cost of starting and stopping the application. NetDynamics also eliminates the overhead involved in opening and closing the database. Each data server maintains one or more cached connections to the data source or sources. Consequently, requests for data can be made to the data source without incurring the overhead of opening and closing the connection.

Scalability and Automatic Load Balancing

The NetDynamics application server is based on a distributed architecture that allows it to be easily scaled across multiple hardware systems. System administrators can increase processing by adding more CPUs to a multiprocessor machine, or networking individual machines together. Within each machine, the system administrator can also allocate the number of running CPs and DSs for optimal performance. This distributed architecture enables the system administrator to partition the application by placing each set of processes on different systems. The NetDynamics application server system's request brokers continue to balance request loads across this networked, multi-CPU environment.

Availability

The NetDynamics server integrates built-in system monitors to provide availability. The monitors check running CPs and DSs, and will automatically shut down and restart abruptly terminated processes. NetDynamics delivers the reliability and self-running capabilities required for an enterprise-scale application.

WebEXTEND

Recognizing the need to extend existing core applications to the Web, and the costs involved, NetDynamics introduces WebEX-TEND, application interfacing technology that leverages existing business logic. WebEXTEND allows NetDynamics application developers to access PeopleSoft, SAP, or CICS applications from within the NetDynamics Studio development environment. Developers create Web-based displays that access existing application logic. The developer does not rewrite the application but instead creates a new interface—a Web-centric one—to a familiar application. The WebEXTEND technology interfaces the application through native APIs (e.g., Message Agent with PeopleSoft, and BAPI for SAP R/3). Developers work with the business logic in these applications, and can extend them by adding their own custom logic within the NetDynamics development system. As a result, users now have the benefit of accessing these applications from any Web browser, on any platform, anywhere in the world. Furthermore, the capabilities of the application are extended with the addition of new NetDynamics business logic. With WebEXTEND, current technology investments are leveraged for a new medium—the Web.

ADDITIONAL INFORMATION

The NetDynamics corporate address is 185 Constitution Drive, Menlo Park, CA 94025. They can be reached by phone at (415) 462-7600; or fax, (415) 617-5920. Readers can find more information on NetDynamics products directly from their Web site: www.netdynamics.com.

The authors would like to acknowledge the assistance of Sherrick Murdoff, of NetDynamics, in the preparation of this chapter.

Supporting the Extended Sales Enterprise—NetGain

19

Many medium-size to large companies have already implemented Customer Management Automation (CMA) in some form. Solutions range from implementing something as simplistic as e-mail to multimillion-dollar, highly customized client/server-based Sales Force Automation and customer support projects. While companies have clearly experienced some measurable benefits from their CMA projects, solutions today do not support corporations as they really exist: an extended enterprise consisting of the corporation and the business partners that enable the delivery of its products and services. Current solutions do help companies communicate and collaborate better, know more about customers to address their needs in a timely manner, and gain insight into aspects of the Customer Management equation within the corporate boundary. But these solutions do little to support organizations whose sales efforts include a heavy emphasis on resources beyond the corporation. Our experience with companies points to a need for supporting communication and collaboration beyond the internal organization—to fully support the Extended Sales Enterprise.

By extending CMA beyond the traditional boundaries of the enterprise to business partners, companies can yield substantially higher returns, especially if the enterprise depends greatly on other organizations such as sales, service, and distribution channels. This white paper attempts to define the Extended Enterprise, and discusses the issues surrounding the type of technology solutions needed and available today to help address the unique requirements of the Extended Enterprise. As this paper will support, these solutions will need to be based on the emerging standards for Web-based application architectures that will address CMA problems more effectively than traditional client/server applications.

WHAT IS THE EXTENDED ENTERPRISE?

Today's corporations extend far beyond their traditional boundaries. The real organization is a *virtual corporation* that includes a complex web of relationships between the company's internal workgroups and its customers, suppliers, resellers, dealers, vendors, systems integrators, and prospects. There is a need to provide and share information throughout the extended enterprise about products, customers, and projects—quickly, accurately, and securely. Traditionally, providing technological support for these extensions to the enterprise required high-end, highly customized, and often proprietary technologies (such as EDI or in-house developed systems). These solutions were expensive to build and often impossible to integrate with each partner's own unique information systems. So, the virtual corporation continued to communicate and share information in a cumbersome, paper-intensive fashion.

In spite of the complexities, the extended enterprise is here to stay. To successfully compete in this global marketplace, many companies are shifting from direct selling to selling with and through business partners via *indirect channels*. The benefits of an indirect channel strategy are multifold:

- Greater market reach or pull with wider company/product representation
- Reduced time to market for new products or services
- Reduced cost of sales and distribution to price sensitive markets
- Ability for customers to have a wider choice of suppliers and support

Additionally, organizations are increasing efforts to integrate their entire supply chain. Often, the lines between various suppliers, manufacturers, and distributors are transparent to the end customer. With the requirement to effectively and securely bring together customer and vendor, manufacturer and supplier, the role of technology is expanding dramatically. The recent rapid and pervasive rise of the Internet and the World Wide Web has created a paradigm shift in the business world by changing the fundamental way in which business interaction will occur. The incredible opportunities that the emergence of the Internet has created by essentially changing how business is conducted will trigger a new era of customer management.

In this new era, companies will utilize the Internet and Web platforms to communicate, collaborate, and drive commerce like never before, using best-of-breed tools and applications that are optimized for this environment. The Gartner Group states:

> The Web will evolve from a passive publishing medium to an interactive computing environment that subsumes client/ server and expands into transaction processing, electronic commerce, and network dynamic functionality. The technology architecture for the sales system in 2000 will be radically different from the ones used today.

Forrester Research forecasts that by the year 2002, companies will spend 45 percent of their IS budgets on extended enterprise applications. These applications will need to integrate disparate organizations or individuals in the same IT-enabled processes, independently of formal boundaries. Companies need to be looking at technology solutions that allow them to consider and integrate whole value chains, regardless of geographical or organizational boundaries.

In Figure 19.1 the intranet, which is the corporate network, consists of information that a firm's employees can access. This access is secured by directly connected dedicated cables within a building or buildings. The information is typically proprietary company, product, and customer information. The extranet consists of a firm's customers, vendors, and partners. This is also sensitive information, so the network is secured through data encryption and password-protected access. The Internet is used to transport the in-

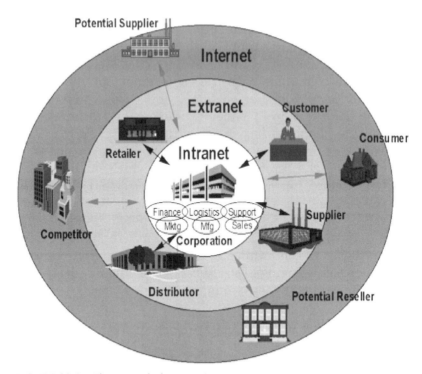

FIGURE 19.1 The extended enterprise.

formation, but it is only available on a need-to-know basis. Finally, the Internet consists of prospective customers, suppliers, business partners, and others that have access to certain *generally available* company, product, and customer information. This information is not sensitive, so security is not required.

ISSUES IN SUPPORTING THE EXTENDED ENTERPRISE

The Internet provides the intraenterprise (intranet) and the extended enterprise (extranet) connectivity and application hosting on a scale unimaginable just a few years ago. The Internet is not the solution in and of itself, but it provides the platform needed to build the types of systems necessary for the next generation of Customer Management Automation systems. Many of today's solutions only utilize the Internet in a passive fashion for activities like lead capture and information gathering. This clearly provides some positive benefits, but fails to address some of the major issues relative to supporting the requirements of the extended enterprise. The market drivers pushing the world toward support for the extended enterprise are as follows.

Customer Expectations

Customers have an expectation that they can acquire information from suppliers that is accurate, timely, and easily accessible. They expect that when the information they need requires collaboration and confirmation among multiple companies in the supply chain, that the complexities of assimilating that information will be transparent to them. We are a self-serving nation brought about by the evolution of technology-enabled conveniences such as ATMs, self-service gasoline, cellular phones, pagers, and now the Internet. The *how* behind such conveniences is not relevant to customers who rely on technology to work.

Work Anytime/Anywhere

Whether it is called telecommuting, the mobile sales force, disconnected or remote users—the solution needs to allow the remote worker to execute his or her job where it matters most, close to the customer. Technology needs to allow a remote worker the same access to company systems that an office worker has, wherever he or she happens to be working.

Information Sharing and Access

There is a need for the ability to collect, analyze, and share information beyond the enterprise that includes not only data, but multimedia, graphics, documents, video, sound, and dynamic pricing. These requirements mandate information-processing tools that provide quick search and retrieval, and the capacity to index the massive amounts of available information.

Elimination of the Middleman

Companies are increasingly concerned about the lack of communication between the original supplier and the ultimate consumer. While this does not mean eliminating the middleman (i.e., wholesale distributor), it does call for organizations to remove some of the barriers that directly prohibit them from understanding end-user issues and concerns. There is a need for the extended enterprise to share information and communicate openly—but with security and controls.

CURRENT SOLUTION—CLIENT/SERVER-BASED SALES FORCE AUTOMATION OR CUSTOMER MANAGEMENT

The industry continues to struggle with a phrase that captures all of the elements associated with acquiring and keeping customers. Customer management is a current term that is defined as the set of activities businesses perform to find customers that are best suited for the company's products and services. By managing ongoing customer relationships better, both companies and customers can realize long-term value. Customer management is primarily used to define those processes where direct interaction with the customer occurs—sales, marketing, and customer support. Providing good customer management is increasingly challenging. The very attributes that on one hand make companies competitive in today's economy—size, multiple distribution channels, global presence, and so on—add more complexity to the organization, making it harder to deliver satisfactory customer management.

Automating aspects of customer management can greatly increase both the levels of customer management quality that a company and its business partners can deliver, and the breadth of the delivery. Mark Anastas and Douglas Root write in their article, "Islands of Automation vs. a Company-Wide Customer Information System":

> A company-wide customer information system empowers individuals and groups to achieve company goals by automating the contact management processes of all departments. Because it is designed as a workgroup software application that all departments can use, individual workers are connected to each other, and departments are connected to other departments.

Automation can help companies communicate and collaborate better, know more about customers, address their needs in a more timely manner, and increase their insight into all aspects of the customer management equation. There are a variety of solutions available today for customer management. They are primarily client/server-based applications. Most of these solutions offer robust functionality for opportunity management, account management, marketing encyclopedia systems, customer management, sales administration, marketing campaign management, and telemarketing. Other products that are often classified as customer management include sales configurator and proposal generation systems. Although current customer management solutions have been implemented successfully and with measurable results in numerous companies, they are associated with a failure rate as high as 65 percent. They are also insufficient for providing technology-enabled selling for the extended enterprise for the following reasons:

■ *Sales professionals don't use the product.* As Gartner Group has noted for several years, mid- and high-tier customer management applications have been designed for management control, typically at the expense of the end user. Sales professionals in particular frequently find these applications on the market today to be more of an administrative burden than a productivity tool, and eventually stop using the applications. Once universal participation is lost, the shared information becomes useless.

■ *Complexity of customer management.* Sales professionals are typically mobile users, operating in a *frequently disconnected mode.* Users require applications that allow them to generally use their application offline, while occasionally connecting to a network to synchronize their local data store with a central database. CMA applications, by definition, must automate processes across multiple user types and functional areas. These issues add a significant degree of complexity to the engineering problem for designing CMA application, as well as implementation and ongoing maintenance processes.

CMA vendors today are just now bringing to market first-generation solutions that functionally address the issues of variations in customer requirements, mobile computing, and cross-functional process integration. However, vendors have not yet been successful in protecting end users and application administrators from the complex underlying engineering problem. These applications result in big-bang implementations typically associated with high up-front costs and labor-intensive ongoing application maintenance afforded only by the largest organizations.

■ *No solution for the extended-enterprise.* In order for current CMA solutions to offer connectivity and extend data access to myriad partners and suppliers with a collection of disparate systems, the partner must implement the same system as the enterprise—compatible network platforms, or try to develop integrated links. This approach is not only cumbersome and expensive but it is also unrealistic with a large extended enterprise.

■ *Internet-enabled, not Internet-based applications.* None of the current customer management solutions are true Web applications. They are merely Internet-enabled versions of their enterprise-centric client/server products. In most cases they are utilizing the Web only to provide very basic features, such as reference library lookup or elemental lead capture. This approach reduces much of the real benefits that could be gained if the Web was leveraged to its fullest potential. Internet-enabled CMA solutions are nothing more than monolithic client/servers with an Internet interface bolted on. They do not support full browser-based usage, so it cannot be deployed as true Web application, or run as a highly functional client/server solution in its entirety over the Internet.

THE NEXT GENERATION—INTERNET/INTRANET CUSTOMER MANAGEMENT

The recent rapid and pervasive rise of the Internet has fundamentally changed the way business interactions will occur. The opportunities that the emergence of the Internet has created have triggered a new era of customer management. In this new era, companies will utilize the Internet and Web platforms to communicate, collaborate, and drive commerce using best-of-breed tools and applications that are optimized for this environment. The new era of Web-based customer management applications will exploit the Internet and the Web's powers and economies by effectively and securely bringing together customer and vendor, manufacturer and supplier, into an increasingly internetworked economy.

GartnerGroup, in a 1996 conference, stated:

> The Internet is changing the nature of computing and communications as we know it. It promises universal connectivity, linking everyone with everyone else, and interconnecting all computing devices, providing unprecedented and unparalleled access to information of every conceivable type.... Predictions of the Internet's future range from a solver of the majority of the world's problems to a disastrous implosion in the making. We expect that the Internet will result in neither Utopia nor disaster. Rather, the Internet and its technologies will be used increasingly for both intraenterprise (intranets) and interenterprise communications over the next several years as enterprises attempt to provide a common information and communication environment to all employees, as well as to key customers, suppliers, and business partners.

The NetGain Virtua Enterprise suite of applications is a packaged Internet solution for the extended enterprise that has been designed and developed from the ground up as a Web-based application. NetGain provides companies with the ability to deploy Virtua Enterprise applications to any user anywhere in the world with a Web browser, thus supporting customer management for the entire extended enterprise.

NetGain is leveraging broader Web-inspired concepts to create an entirely new category of customer management solutions defined not only by wide deployability, but also by a unique way of presenting information to the end user. Internet content delivery vendors such as PointCast have opened a Pandora's Box of available information made useful by combining push-model Web-content delivery mechanisms, along with intelligent filtering and a dynamic user interface that continuously presents users with updated information. Windows open and close, ticker symbols scroll by, and news pages turn to bring the most important information to the user in a more engaging and easy-to-use format.

Using the current push model for a basis, NetGain created its own version of push to be what it calls the Virtua Workplace.

NetGain's Virtua Workplace takes customer management to the next generation by aggregating Web content, structured SQL data, and e-mail with a variety of personalized end-user application services. Unique features of Virtua Workplace include:

- *End user personalization* through a subscription-based desktop.
- *Built-in links* between transactional data and Web content with the ability to pull the content from the Web, associate it with transactional data, update the corporate database, and push it out to other users who need it.
- *Workflow* that presents high-priority tasks directly to the user, along with a constant stream of new information agents that alert the user to important changes to customer data, such as new leads or service calls for an existing account.

NetGain presents all of these powerful features and personal application services to the user in one dynamic, Web-inspired user interface that supports continuous scrolling and animated graphics. The interface is presented in Figure 19.2.

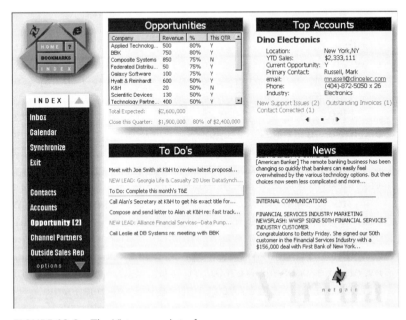

FIGURE 19.2 The Virtua user interface.

The Virtua suite of products incorporates a tightly integrated workflow engine to define the order and routing of tasks. As a component of Virtua Workplace, workflow enables Virtua Enterprise applications to present users with dynamic lists of tasks associated with active workflows in which those users participate. Virtua Workplace isn't merely active, it is interactive. Not only can users adjust routing rules on the fly and add additional documents and voice annotations, but they can also use it with Microsoft's NetMeeting, contact other members of the workflow team, and collaborate on a work item in real time. The workflow engine is also capable of collaborating with and learning from the end user. Another key workflow feature is the ability to include anyone in the extended enterprise in the workflow—all they need is a browser and an e-mail address. The Virtua Enterprise suite of products include:

- Virtua Sales
- Virtua Marketing
- Virtua Customer
- Virtua Executive—EIS Module

WHAT MAKES NETGAIN UNIQUE FOR THE EXTENDED ENTERPRISE?

- NetGain applications are true Internet/Web-based applications versus Internet-enabled client/server applications. This means that NetGain's applications are completely browser based and can be deployed with a browser to anyone, anywhere with an Internet connection. All of NetGain's Virtua Enterprise applications are fully Web deployable and operational over corporate intranets and beyond to indirect channel partners over an extranet.
- In contrast to the passive windows style user interface of current vendors' products, NetGain's Virtua Workplace raises the bar in end-user effectiveness. NetGain combines a unique Web user interface (WUI) and push model to create a highly interactive, user-friendly desktop of integrated Web content, subscription news services, SQL transactional data, workflow, and *new information* alert agents.

- Configurable business objects in NetGain's Virtua Enterprise suite of Web-based applications offer multiple levels of customization facilities, from end user to administrator to programmer. End users have the freedom to customize their desktops by subscribing to different business objects, including different views, depending on their personality and individual style, while remaining consistent with emerging Internet browser standards. NetGain's configurable business objects support a high degree of variability in industry and customer requirements with a data-driven configuration model.

- NetGain's Virtua Enterprise applications are assembled out of many small components rather than existing as a single, large executable program such as today's traditional client/server solutions. Specific business objects, like a marketing encyclopedia or lead tracking, can be deployed incrementally and in multiple combinations. This design model provides unique implementation flexibility in addition to its ideal Web-based architecture for Web deployment. It allows a high degree of variability in industry- and customer-specific object data and relationships on a single code base.

BENEFITS OF AN INTERNET/INTRANET APPLICATION FOR THE EXTENDED ENTERPRISE

We have explored the value of leveraging technology and taking advantage of the Internet to provide customer management solutions for the extended enterprise. The following are some of the more tangible benefits for this type of approach:

- *Ubiquity of a browser.* The ability to widely deploy Virtua Enterprise applications to any user anywhere in the world with a Web browser is a reality with NetGain. This approach enables organizations to extend Customer Management Automation beyond the enterprise and achieve an integrated selling environment across multiple sales channels. With only a Web browser, partners come together as a virtual selling team to share and collaborate on information, and then pass this benefit on to customers in the form of consistent, timely, and accurate information critical to buying decisions and service issues.

■ *Interactive, Web user interface.* An additional benefit of being browser based is the ability to present both intra- and inter-enterprise end users, regardless of computing platform, with an easy-to-use interactive Web user interface similar to the push model deployed by such vendors as Pointcast. This is an important key to extending the enterprise, because it provides channel partners with an affordable solution acquisition to effectively participate as a member of a virtual selling/service team. NetGain provides all enterprise users and its extended users with an easy-to-use, consistent application interface to control and manage opportunities without the traditional limitations. NetGain's application interface provides a single, alert-driven, interactive desktop, aggregating daily transactional data from enterprise database servers, with relative subscription-based Web content to deliver the most up-to-date account information required by an individual end user to be personally effective. This also enables a virtual selling/service team to collaboratively manage and service shared customers accounts.

■ *Component-based architecture.* NetGain's Virtua Enterprise solution is designed according to object-oriented concepts that encapsulate logic and data inside small business objects, addressing the bandwidth and latency issues faced by other CMA vendors trying to enable their large, monolithic client/server applications for the Internet. NetGain's unique component-based architecture reduces enterprise-class implementation nightmares and failures by allowing customers to implement a Virtua application incrementally, one business object at time, such as lead tracking, forecasting, marketing encyclopedia, and so on. Implementing a component-based application as a series of frequent and quick installations is much easier to manage than the big-bang, all-or-nothing alternative of monolithic client/server solutions. A component based implementation approach is most beneficial for companies that need to show a faster return on investment by getting end-user support and confidence early on.

SUMMARY

When it comes to choosing a CMA solution today, many businesses specifically in the midtier market find themselves torn between selecting a practical, user-friendly, low-end solution that meets the contact management requirements of a sales rep or choosing an expensive, high-end, client/server solution that meets the distributed computing needs of an entire enterprise. Until now, enterprise-class applications for the middle market have been risky, with high implementation failure rates and low-end alternatives unable to support a distributed computing infrastructure. Neither of these solutions addresses the requirements of the extended enterprise.

Extending CMA beyond the traditional boundaries of the enterprise to customers, suppliers, and business partners with a solution that is easily implemented over the Web will allow substantially higher revenue returns never before possible with traditional client/server CMA solutions. Next Generation CMA solutions will address the fundamental limitations associated with traditional client/server: implementation, usability, inter-enterprise connectivity, and collaboration.

As more companies look for ways to drive up revenue by developing closer ties with their customers, suppliers, and partners, the appeal of the Internet will grow. Customer Management Automation will evolve into a new generation of Web applications that make corporate data ubiquitous, allow freedom from specific platforms, and make universal connectivity and collaboration a reality.

ADDITIONAL INFORMATION

NetGain's corporate address is 430 10th Street, NW S-005A, Atlanta, GA 30318. They can be reached by phone at (404) 872-5050. Readers can find more information on NetGain products directly from their Web site: www.netgaincorp.com.

A 100 Percent Web-Based Sales Automation Solution— UpShot Corporation

We have seen throughout this book many examples of how you can put your existing SFA system to work using Web technologies and many of the tools outlined in previous chapters. Your sales organization, however, may not already have a fully integrated SFA system to build upon. What if you have a small sales organization using stand-alone contact managers on each salesperson's laptop? How are you integrating these systems together today? Are you able to view all sales activity or run forecast reports across the entire sales organizations data? Consider the following problems:

PROBLEM

- Leads come back to a company in the wake of a successful trade show. Telesales follows up with calls and eventually sets up an appointment for the Chicago sales rep to call on a decision maker at one of the companies that responded. Two weeks later the sales rep enters the prospect's conference room not knowing who the decision maker is, what he knows, or what material he has been given.

    A small company sends out 20,000 direct-mail pieces announcing its newest product promotion. Six-hundred business reply cards are returned. The cards are sent to the regional sales reps and local distributors. Three months later the CEO asks the Marketing VP how many of those leads have resulted in sales. What was the cost of each sale obtained through the mailing? The VP smiles wanly and promises to get answers soon.

■ The company has been trying to get its foot in the door of XYZ Corporation for years. The salesperson drops by and discovers that the company had been sold to one of his best customers. "Oh, I wish I'd known sooner," he moaned, head in hand. "I could have made my numbers last quarter."

■ The company comes up with a new scaled-down, less expensive version of its mainstay software program. The Marketing VP wants to send a special offer notice to everyone that telemarketing had spoken to in the last year, who had said that the current product was too expensive. Uh oh!

■ A salesperson is calling on the CEO of her key customer who accounts for some 10 percent of the total sales in her territory. She wants a complete record of every contact that her company has had with the customer in the past six months—technical support calls, telesales calls, the results of the design review done by her sales engineer. She also needs to know every product she has sold to the customer, and what the customer is doing with them.

■ Telesales calls a hot prospect. He finally reaches the prospect. "Why are you calling me?" the prospect asks. "I just met with Elsie, your local sales rep, yesterday."

Anyone in sales or marketing has faced problems like these. Well-run, large companies may have the means to handle them today. They may have an integrated and powerful database from Oracle, Sybase, or Informix—customized by an expensive consultant so that the company can view every contact with the customer, and measure the success of various programs. With the database, they could be purchasing one of the enterprise Sales Force Automation products. Unfortunately, this kind of solution costs $2500 to $7500 per user for the software alone, and has an entry price of $50K to $100K or more;

this price floor puts the solution beyond the reach of small to medium-size companies.

Instead of making a six-figure investment, a company of under 200 employees improvises. Smaller companies often have a haphazard *ad hoc* system. As Jack Gold of the Meta Group jokes, "The biggest vendor [in this space] is 3M with their Post-It notes." Some companies might use a product originally designed to be an individual contact manager; users find they are ill suited to manage the flow of a customer through a pipeline (in addition to being hard to use and administer). There is no follow-through to determine which of the initial responses turn into sales. That means the success of a marketing program is not really being measured. It can mean that solid leads are not being followed up, while weaker ones are. It means that the best customers for a new release are not even contacted.

SOLUTION

The dream then is to bring the power of the high-end Sales Force Automation systems to small and medium-size companies. This dream product would be affordable—of course. As long as we're dreaming, why don't we ask for the power of a high-end enterprise system for roughly the same price as a contact manager? But that wouldn't be enough. We'd also want to have a product that's intuitive, that's so easy to use that it requires virtually no training. (Good salespeople should be selling, not trying to figure out how to use a system.) As long as we're dreaming, let's make the product scalable. We could use the same product in a small team of three people, and it could spread throughout the company; then when we grow it can grow with us. All this with the same product. And while we're on a roll, let's close our eyes and imagine a product that is easy to administer, one that a small workgroup could administer itself without any IT or MIS staff. Sounds great doesn't it?

As Frank Sinatra used to sing, "Fairy tales can come true, they can happen to you." It's the mission of UpShot to deliver Sales Force Automation solutions for small and medium-size companies with unrivaled ease of use, scalability, and low cost of ownership. And we can do this today thanks to Web technology. What UpShot has brought to the market is not a Web form that can be used to access information, not a Web front-end running on top of a complex client/server system, not a system with a big piece of client software on every desktop, but a product designed for the Web from the get-go with a thin client. As Bill Gurley of Deutsche Morgan Grenfell writes, "New Internet application companies . . . are able to build their applications from the ground up, with the absence of restraints put in place by a legacy code base." It's that leapfrog over existing systems that brings users in small or medium-size companies a whole raft of advantages:

Ease of Use

The UpShot product uses the Netscape or Microsoft browser as the user interface. All of us are growing accustomed to using a browser as our primary information viewer. It's the interface we use to ask for information, to search for it, to view it. And because we already know how to use it, because we know its idioms, language, and assumptions, we almost know how to use the UpShot product before we ever see it. As one user of UpShot said, "Anyone who can use a browser can use this!"

Ease of Administration

Because the UpShot application sits on a server and because all a user has on his or her machine is a browser, the product is simple indeed to administer. Upgrade the server and users are upgraded when they log on. Again according to Bill Gurley, "The lightweight nature of Internet applications will make them faster and easier to deploy."

Team Orientation

The days of Willy Loman—a bag-carrying salesperson working on his own—are past. Now the sales function involves a team whose work must be coordinated throughout the sales cycle—

from lead generation to literature distribution to telesales, and finally to face-to-face calls. Coordination among salespeople, between sales and marketing, between field sales and telesales is not a wish: It's a requirement. The architecture of a Web-based solution is ideally suited for this environment. Customer information, changes, requests, and to-dos are all instantly accessible by any authorized team member as soon as he or she opens the browser and logs on to UpShot.

Architecture

UpShot is an intranet application. That means it uses Web technology for an application within one business. As seen in the following, it is software that resides on a server. For users on the intranet, there is no client-side software other than a browser and the Java applets automatically downloaded to it. (Be careful of claims that a Sales Force Automation product is Web-enabled or Web-ready. Just ask if there is client software besides a browser. Client software means more administrative work and consequent higher costs.) UpShot comes packaged with a Web server and database for a small workgroup, as seen in Figure 20.1. For larger teams, it can work with a Microsoft or Netscape Web server and SQL Server or Oracle databases. Communication between the server and clients is via any standard TCP/IP net-

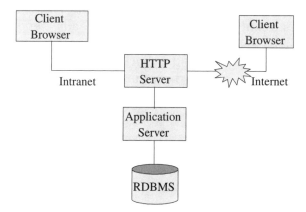

FIGURE 20.1 UpShot architecture.

work. Remote users can use the Internet itself to communicate with the application.

Scalability

Enterprise Sales Force Automation systems just aren't practical for small and medium-size companies. Leaving aside other problems, there's an entry price for the product that includes server software, database software, customization, installation, and so on. (There's usually a big hardware component as well.) But a Web-based solution like UpShot is inherently scalable. A small workgroup can try out the product for a couple of thousand dollars. Deployment throughout the organization can proceed incrementally. There's no need to commit tens or hundreds of thousands of dollars before ever using the system. Instead of starting with a low-end system and having to transition to a high-end one, UpShot scales as users are added and as the business grows.

Accessibility and Synchronization

Anywhere there is a Web browser, there's access to UpShot. It's that simple. Just log on to the Internet, type in the URL of your Web server, and you're in. You can obtain access from customers' offices, from hotel rooms, from airports, wherever you can log on to the Net. Remote users can work from their laptops. They can enter comments about prospects, enter new leads, send e-mail and letters to their laptops. The next time the laptop user logs in to the main server to get hot leads, check for new appointments, or have literature sent, all this new data is sent down to his or her machine, and the new data entered on the laptop is sent back to the main server.

Features

UpShot brings the features of the high-end Sales Force Automation system to small and medium-size companies. It's more than the corporate phone file that contact managers provide. UpShot offers features traditionally found in the enterprise products, such as:

- Opportunity management
- Automated forecasting
- Sales pipeline stages
- Accounts and contacts
- Tracking and management of lead-generation programs
- Sales territories
- Workflow—action items and delegation
- Group calendaring
- Marketing program effectiveness

At the same time, we have simplified and streamlined these features so that their use is straightforward and intuitive.

Customization

A lawyer's office, high-tech company, and medical supply company work differently. They have different processes and different terminology. UpShot then can be customized through a series of easy-to-understand, flexible forms to suit the needs of virtually any business.

Platform Independence

Microsoft or Netscape server? And whose browser? UpShot works with browsers or servers from either company. Moreover, because the UpShot client is simply a browser, it can run on Windows machines and Macs; in fact it will run on any machine that has a Netscape or Microsoft browser, including the much-heralded network computers (NCs).

Tracking Prospect and Competitor Activity

UpShot contains agent software that, with an Internet connection, can keep watch on the Web sites of customers and competitors. Salespeople will use this feature to stay informed about prospects and competitors. Major customer announcements can

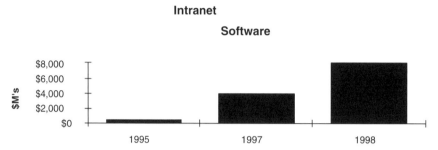

FIGURE 20.2 Zona Research: intranet software market. (Source: Zona Research)

also provide what salespeople are so often looking for—a reason to call a prospect.

WEB-BASED PRODUCT

Does it make sense to use a Web-based intranet solution for sales force automation? Between now and the end of the century, explosive growth will come in intranet applications. Zona Research estimates that the size of the intranet software market *alone* will be $4B in 1997 and $8B in 1998, as seen in Figure 20.2.

That's impressive growth indeed. And why? Because with the Web, old applications will be done new ways. It's the Web that enables UpShot to bring simplicity and affordability to Sales Force Automation. It's not the platform of the future. It's the right way to do sales force automation today.

ADDITIONAL INFORMATION

UpShot Corporation's address is 400 Convention Way, P.O. Box 5267, Redwood City, CA 94063. The fax number is (415) 482-3737. Readers can find more information on UpShot's products at UpShot's Web site www.upshot.com; or can contact UpShot at (415) 482-3730. UpShot is a trademark of UpShot Corporation.

What's on the CD-ROM

The accompanying CD-ROM consists of documents and source code referenced throughout this book. The following file types can be found on the CD-ROM:

- HTML Files: *.htm
- Microsoft Word Files: *.doc
- Visio Files: *.vsd
- Vendor Supplied Files

HARDWARE REQUIREMENTS

The software on this CD-ROM has the following system requirements:

- 486 PC (or higher) processor, CD-ROM drive
- Microsoft Windows operating system, version 3.1 or later; Windows 95, or Windows NT
- At least 8MB of RAM
- At least 8MB of available disk space
- 256-color palette and small font setting
- Web browser

INSTALLING THE SOFTWARE

The software on the accompanying CD-ROM can be accessed from the Web pages provided. Simply start at the homepage and go from there:

1. Start Windows on your computer.
2. Place the CD-ROM into your CD-ROM drive.
3. Start your Web browser.
4. Load the file, homepage.htm, from the root directory of the CD-ROM. You should see the page shown in Figure A.1.

From here you will be able to navigate through the hierarchy of Web pages provided.

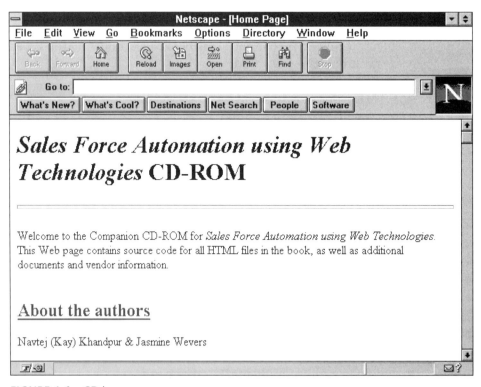

FIGURE A.1   CD homepage.

USER ASSISTANCE AND INFORMATION

The software accompanying this book is being provided as is, without warranty or support of any kind. Should you require basic installation assistance, or if your media is defective, please call our product support staff at (212) 850-6194, weekdays between 9 A.M. and 4 P.M. Eastern Standard Time. Or, we can be reached via e-mail at: wprtusw@wiley.com. You may also contact Jasmine Wevers via e-mail at: jwevers@mjmtech.com.

Resource List

The following is a partial list of vendors of Sales Force Automation products and services, and some other resources for additional information. This is by no means a complete list of all vendors; rather it is a list of some vendors whose names we came across while researching material for this book, and whose Web sites we browsed.

For each vendor we have included a brief excerpt from the Web site, with no editorial comment. The *copyright* to the excerpted material is owned by the owner of that Web site. All trade names mentioned are *trademarks* and/or *registered trademarks* of their respective owners.

Actuate (www.actuate.com) Founded in 1993 and headquartered in San Mateo, California, Actuate Software Corporation is the developer of the industry's first reporting system designed specifically to meet the needs of the enterprise. Actuate's solution facilitates a new level of intelligent searching and navigation through business reports, and efficiently manages data access in an enterprise client/server environment.

Antalys, Inc. (www.antalys.com) Classys is an enterprise-wide software solution that automates the configuration and pricing of products and services. Classys works effectively across industries, and provides implementation tools that allow customization to your business and technical environment. Classys integrates data from all parts of the organization to quickly provide accurate information to employees and customers.

Aurum Software, Inc. (www.aurum.com) The Aurum Customer Enterprise is the leading customer-relationship management solution that empowers global companies to evaluate and improve processes, resulting in transformed sales and service to their customers. It is the most advanced and integrated suite of applications that automates, adapts, and transforms enterprisewide field sales, telesales, telemarketing, and customer service functions of your business.

Baystone Software, Inc. (www.baystone.com) BayStone's integrated suite of Customer Interaction Software (CIS) applications are focused on automating the sales, marketing, customer support, and quality assurance functions within an enterprise. They address the entire spectrum of business processes that directly affect customer satisfaction and loyalty, including lead generation and qualification, account management, proposal/ quote generation, product design, development and quality, and customer service and support.

Bermac Communications (www.bermac.com) SalesWare's modular design lets your company pick just the right application for your sales process, system capabilities, and corporate image. You can plug in additional modules, such as a configurator and proposal generator. To make implementation even easier, SalesWare products can integrate intelligently with many of the popular Sales Force Automation applications you may already be using.

Borealis Technology Corporation (www.brls.com) Borealis is dedicated to delivering the highest customer success rate in Sales Force Automation by providing solutions that help customers quickly identify their specific needs, and rapidly deploy customizable applications that are optimized for high user adoption. Arsenal is the only fully customizable opportunity management system that can be deployed in weeks instead of months.

Brock International, Inc. (www.broc.com) Brock International, headquartered in Atlanta, Georgia, developed the Integrated Sales Performance solutions market, in 1984, to answer the demanding needs of sales and marketing professionals. Integrated Sales Performance solutions encompass sales, marketing and customer service software, industry best practices, consulting, and advanced, open technology to provide customers with a process for developing quality customer relationships from initial contact through ongoing support.

BT Squared Technologies, Inc. (www.btsquared.com) BT Squared develops Interactive Selling Systems that put the expertise of your entire organization in the hands of your salespeople. The BT Squared Interactive Selling System can help you shorten your sales cycles, ensure accurate and timely orders, and maximize sales volumes by using leading-edge technology to streamline communication and business processes throughout your enterprise.

C3i, Inc. (www.c3i-inc.com) C3i, Inc. provides comprehensive support services designed to make field-based users of sales automation more productive. Our services are designed to achieve one objective: help sales organizations realize the potential of their sales automation initiatives.

Calico Technology (www.calicotech.com) Calico Technology is a leading provider of electronic business solutions that enables interactive buying and selling of complex products and services. Calico develops and markets Concinity, software that is designed to allow sales organizations, customers, and end users to analyze requirements, access marketing data, configure solutions, develop quotations, generate proposals, and place orders using the Internet, intranets, laptop computers, and CD-ROMS. Concinity allows Calico's customers to achieve increased sales rep efficiency, expand channels of distribution, reduce costs, and increase customer satisfaction.

Clarify, Inc. (www.clarify.com) Clarify is the leading provider of customer-centric solutions for the front office, including sales and marketing, customer service, field service and logistics, quality assurance, and Help desk applications.

Clear With Computers (www.cwcinc.com) CWC's mission is to enhance the professionalism, productivity, and profitability of its clients' sales process through the development and implementation of technology-based products and services.

Concentra Corporation (www.concentra.com) Concentra Corporation is the leading provider of object-oriented sales and engineering software solutions. Using Concentra's software, market-leading companies worldwide in the aerospace, automotive, industrial equipment, and construction industries are creating customer-driven product designs, product configurations, and sales proposals in minutes, not months.

Configuration Systems & Consulting (www.configsc.com) Develops and delivers to *mass customization* industries superior quality and leading-edge product configuration application software solutions, consulting and support services, and operational technologies that provide significant competitive advantages and eliminate *nonvalue-added* activities and costs.

Contact Management Systems (www.contact-mgt.com) Founded in 1989 as a specialized Information Technologies consulting firm, Contact Management Systems has established a successful track record by providing clients with a full array of efficient and cost-effective Sales Force Automation-related services.

Data Code, Incorporated (www.datacode.com) Data Code is committed to providing the leading solutions in corporate sales and marketing automation. From account management and marketing analysis to decision support and database marketing, Data Code empowers the end user.

Data Systems Support (www.dssny.com) Sales Information Response System (SIRS) is an advanced client/server customer asset management suite designed to manage enterprisewide sales, marketing, and customer support activities. With an Internet marketing module, an opportunity management system, Sales Force Automation, and much more, no other solution offers more features to maximize your competitive advantage.

Davox Corporation (www.davox.com) Davox Corporation is a leading provider of unified call-center management systems that are currently meeting the collections, telemarketing, tele-sales, customer service, fundraising, and other critical customer contact needs of call centers worldwide.

Endpoint! Marketing Information Systems, Inc. (www.epleads.com) LEADS! is a powerful and complete company-wide sales automation system designed to *fill the gap* between contact managers and complex enterprise systems. The program gives reps a set of tools for managing contacts, accounts, and sales opportunities, while also providing a flexible and scalable architecture for automatic data synchronization between local and remote locations with support for team selling.

Enact, Incorporated (www.enactinc.com) Selector is de-signed for companies that want to implement buyer-enabled sales to meet increasingly specific customer needs without the traditional cost and market reach sacrifices. Selector allows you to be interactive with your customer during the buying decision. Selector allows you to deliver graphically rich, interactive buying applications via CD-ROM and over the Internet, opening new markets for your company's products and services. Selector is used for deployment to dedicated sales forces, distributors, retail POS, and customer-direct channels.

FirstFloor Software (www.firstfloor.com) FirstFloor Soft-ware is the premier supplier of Web-based document-delivery products and technologies for application developers. The First-Floor Smart Delivery product line enables the delivery of up-to-date documents and Web pages so that users have only the information they need, when they need it, and includes innova-tive technologies, such as agents, targeted notification, and off-line viewing.

Interactive Edge (www.interactiveedge.com) Interactive Edge, an acknowledged leader in the development of automated sales tools, has a unique approach to business software develop-ment—they let your requirements drive the final product. Inter-active Edge combines business and marketing expertise with cutting-edge graphic design and the best, most innovative programming and technology available today.

Interwoven, Inc. (www.interwoven.com) Interwoven, based in Silicon Valley, develops and markets solutions for industrial-strength Web-site production control. Interwoven's solutions are designed for large, complex Internet and intranet Web operations maintained by multiple development teams, and potentially thousands of content contributors distributed throughout the enterprise.

K&V Information Systems, Inc. (www.k-v.com) K&V rapidly delivers state-of-the-art, open, scalable sales and marketing solutions that are completely configurable to precisely meet the needs of corporate clients. Through cutting-edge technology of the highest quality and demonstrated industry competence, K&V assists clients in creating and sustaining value-added sales advantages.

Knowit Software, Inc. (www.knowitinc.com) KNOWIT/SFA is sales software for your entire sales force. The standard KNOWIT/SFA system provides a turnkey solution for expediting the information flow to your sales force. It is a lot easier than you think to go from mailing reports that become quickly out of date, to using KNOWIT/SFA and electronic mailboxes.

Market Power, Inc. (www.mpinet.com) MarketPower's suite of software provides the only fully integrated solution for technology-enabled selling. From opportunity management to proposal generation to in-depth sales analysis, everything you need is available at the click of a mouse—no matter what your company sells or where your sales force travels.

MarketWare Software, Inc. (www.mktware.com) Market-Ware is an industrial strength system for businesses where contact management software alone is insufficient. MarketWare software is an ideal system to upgrade to when your account management and sales information needs have outgrown the capabilities of shrink-wrap contact management software packages, such as ACT and Goldmine.

Maximizer Technologies, Inc. (www.maximizer.com) Maximizer Enterprise is an enterprisewide, comprehensive Sales Opportunity Manager introduced in summer, 1995, that was developed specifically for business-to-business marketers. This collaborative workgroup system helps shorten the sales cycle, close more sales, reduce selling costs, and decrease wasted effort. Using Maximizer Enterprise, sales teams and their managers—working on long, complex sales cycles—are able to track the progress of a sale through a series of predetermined steps based on strategic selling principles.

MFJ International (www.mfj.com) MFJ International is the world's leading provider of Lotus Notes-based sales automation solutions, with OverQuota as its flagship product. Lotus Notes is one of the most significant technological advancements of the decade, creating a whole new framework for sharing information, and helping people work together in ways never before possible.

NetDynamics (www.netdynamics.com) NetDynamics sets the standard for Java-based enterprise Web application development and delivery. The NetDynamics product set is built around a high-performance Java application server; a powerful visual RAD environment that generates Java, HTML, and SQL; and WebEXTEND, which enables integration with core business applications and corporate databases.

Newtonian Software, Inc. (www.newtonian.com) Newtonian has developed Sales Mechanix, the world's most flexible and productive configuration, pricing, and proposal generation framework. Sales Mechanix is fast becoming the *de facto* standard for configuration tools in Sales Force Automation.

OAC Software (www.oacsoftware.com) OAC designs, configures, and installs PC-based software programs that can convert your mainframe data for PC use; give your sales, marketing, and customer support team the most powerful sales and information management tool on the market; and let your company display select interactive information on the Internet for your customers or independent reps/agents.

On!Contact Software Corporation (www.oncontact.com)
On!Contact develops easy-to-use Sales Force Automation software packages for an entire organization. On!Contact Client Management Software is a 100 percent customizable sales, marketing, telemarketing, and customer service package designed for companies that need more than an out-of-the-box software package.

ONYX Software Corporation (www.onyxsoftware.com)
ONYX Customer Center enables companies to exceed their customers' expectations by providing sales, marketing, service, and support teams with a single tool to access all corporate customer information via the Internet, remotely, and from the desktop. By using Customer Center, a company is better able to acquire, retain, and expand customer relationships.

OpenPlus International (www.openplus.com) OpenPlus International provides enterprisewide applications that integrate the entire selling chain—from marketing and sales to order management, distribution, warehouse management, financials, and analysis and planning. Unlike manufacturing-oriented ERP vendors, OpenPlus focuses on integration of the front end of the enterprise back to the supply chain to create a customer-centric enterprise, providing a whole view of the customer from any point across the enterprise.

Optima Technologies, Inc. (www.optima-tech.com) ExSellence is a client/server solution providing the tools needed to increase productivity and effectiveness. The bottom line—Sales reps are more organized and better equipped to handle the challenges of complex territories, while management increases its ability to drive results and improve business decisions.

ParaVision Technologies, Inc. (www.paravision.ca) Developers and vendors of ParaGrafix automated sales configuration and quotation solutions for engineered and assemble-to-order products and services. These interactive solutions revolutionize the way customer-driven companies design and deliver their products.

PC Works (www.pcworks.com) Focus is on providing corporate clients with top-notch solutions for sales automation and reporting.

Pivotal Software, Inc. (www.pivotal.com) Pivotal develops and markets adaptable, enterprisewide software applications that harness leading computing and communications technologies to give businesses the competitive advantage in interacting with customers. Pivotal Relationship is enterprisewide customer interaction software that helps companies find, win, understand, and retain customers. Relationship consolidates all customer information in one system, allowing sales, marketing, customer service, and operations staff to target prospects, close sales, fulfill orders, and solve customer problems.

PowerCerv (www.powercerv.com) ADAPTlication for Sales Force Automation reflects the needs of today's complex selling environment, providing for team selling, team buying, agents, consumers, and traditional business-to-business selling. And ADAPTlication for Sales Force Automation accommodates individual styles within a sales methodology; for example, some sales staff work best from a personal calendar, others prefer to organize their activities in worklists. ADAPTlication for Sales Force Automation supports both!

Sage Solutions, Inc. (www.sagesoln.com) Specific services include strategic planning, project management, technology selection, and software development for mission-critical Web systems. Domain of expertise includes financial services, high-tech manufacturing and quality assurance, healthcare, government, legal, human resources, Sales Force Automation, customer care solutions, and Internet-based electronic commerce solutions.

Sales Automation Association (www.saaintl.org) The Sales Automation Association is the only professional association dedicated to supporting the needs of organizations working to improve their entire sales process through enhanced methods and high technology. Their purpose is to promote and advance improvements in the field of sales and related areas involving automation, information management, process improvement, and the philosophy of sales and customer service. The SAA helps its user members to be more successful in their automation efforts, thus promoting the profession as a whole, including suppliers.

SalesDesk Automation, Inc. (www.salesdesk.com) Sales-Desk Automation has developed distributed, scalable, enterprisewide quotation and pricebook management applications. Unlike current quotation systems, SalesDesk's applications focus not only on sales representative productivity and efficiency, but also on the effective use of frontline forecasting and product movement information for the corporate data warehouse.

Sales Productivity Systems, Inc. (www.spsinc.on.ca) SPS was founded in 1990 to develop and market Sales Force Automation solutions. SPS provides sales consulting, software integration and development, system implementation, training, and support for a complete cost-effective SFA solution. Clients include many Fortune 1000 companies in a broad range of industries, including telecommunications, advertising, banking and financial services, manufacturing and high tech. SPS leads organizations through the reengineering of the sales process and the implementation of state-of-the-art technology.

Sales Technics, Inc. (www.salestechnics.com) Sales Technics is the single source that you can turn to for Sales Force Automation planning, design, software, training, and implementation. They offer both strategic and tactical implementation services.

Sales Vision (www.salesvision.com) Sales Vision offers progressive companies a fundamentally new model for sales and marketing automation. Sales Object Framework for Power-Builder is an innovative, object-based hybrid between packaged and custom software, comprised of customizable business-object templates bundled around a powerful application framework technology. Sales Vision's holistic, business-object approach empowers organizations to create, evolve, and apply reusable intellectual assets to sales automation initiatives.

SalesKit Software (www.saleskit.com) SalesKit Software is the industry leader in open-architecture Sales Force Automation solutions. SalesKit is dedicated to leveraging its extensive industry experience and open integration model to allow customers the greatest speed and flexibility in deploying sales systems for distributed enterprises.

SalesLogix Corporation (www.saleslogix.com) SalesLogix is developing solutions for the largely ignored yet vast middle market—companies that have outgrown the functionality delivered by contact managers, but don't want the implementation burdens and high prices that are trademarks of traditional high-end sales automation software.

Saratoga Systems, Inc. (www.saratogasystems.com) Saratoga Systems is the leading developer and supplier of Sales Force Automation software, helping enterprises manage information about the customer/prospect relationship. Their Sales Force Automation and productivity system is called SPS. Their software is currently being used by over 500 customers worldwide, with over 40,000 users of their Windows application. The product is comprised of a number of productivity tools for sales-people in field sales, telesales, and telemarketing. It is easy to use, and transparently accesses popular database systems to store information.

Scopus Technology, Inc. (www.scopus.com) Scopus is the industry's leading provider of extended enterprise customer-care solutions. Scopus's client/server software applications enable you to efficiently capture, manage, and share customer information throughout the enterprise and the extended enterprise; include applications that automate external customer support and internal Help desk support, the product design change process, and sales and marketing activities; can be used individually to improve critical business operations, or integrated with one another and with third-party applications to provide comprehensive, enterprisewide customer interaction management solutions.

Siebel Systems (www.siebel.com) Siebel Systems is the world's leading provider of sales and marketing information systems. Siebel's flagship product, Siebel Sales Enterprise, is a comprehensive information solution for multichannel sales forces in even the largest global corporations. The Siebel Sales Enterprise is a robust family of Internet-enabled, object-oriented, client/server products. These products empower sales and marketing professionals with comprehensive up-to-date information about customers, products, and competitors.

SIMiN Business Systems, Inc. (www.simin.com) SIMiN Business Systems provides leading-edge contact management, Sales Force Automation, opportunity management, customer service, and customer asset management software.

Sirius Systems (www.siriusg2.com) Sirius Systems competes in the high-growth Sales Force Automation and customer information management marketplaces. Sirius's mission is to provide software tools that help sales and marketing professionals become more successful. This is accomplished by helping individuals and sales organizations more effectively control, communicate, forecast, and win sales.

Smartsales, Inc. (www.smartsales.com) SmartSales supplies industry-leading sales automation software to companies throughout North America and around the world. Aimed at the sales forces of small and large companies alike, SmartSales helps you be more competitive by making you a better salesperson, and your business a more effective sales organization. More than an opportunity manager, SmartSales is an innovative coaching tool that distills the essence of successful sales into your personal sales cycle, and then guides you through the entire process.

SoftAd Group (www.softadgroup.com) SoftAd is a provider of enterprise selling systems that support cross-department productivity and effectiveness. SalesExcelerator, SoftAd's client/server product suite, is a flexible, easy-to-use system that enables salespeople to involve customers through a process of qualification, consulting, configuration, and proposal generation. It includes everything from accessing updated customer information to creating proposals and presentations.

TeleMagic, Inc. (www.telemagic.com) TeleMagic is the leading provider of fully customizable software for contact-centric solutions for support and general business automation. The company was established in 1985 by a sales and computer programming entrepreneur who believed that a software program could be created as a productivity tool for salespeople. His vision of automating sales tasks, such as managing appointments, scheduled calls, mailings, and meetings, resulted in the development of award-winning TeleMagic software. Since its launch, TeleMagic, Inc. has provided businesses worldwide with innovative, feature-rich products and services to enhance business automation, productivity, and communication.

Touchstone Software International, Inc. (www.wintouch.com) The Wintouch Bundle provides a powerful, integrated solution to all your organization's office automation needs, be it Sales Force Automation, sales management, marketing, customer service, administration, or any other function of a similar nature.

TPS Call Sciences (www.callsciences.com) TPS Call Sciences is an international corporation that develops and markets integrated communications services for delivery over global intelligent networks. With a unique emphasis on human factors and standards, we give control back to the end user, and make it easy for service providers to deliver enhanced personal communications services.

Trilogy (www.trilogy.com) Founded in 1989, this company is the leading architect and provider of enterprise software for sales and marketing. The Selling Chain is a revolutionary suite of applications that enable the dynamic exchange of mission-critical information between the enterprise, sales, and customers. Selling Chain's open architecture facilitates integration with other business systems, and its platform portability and client/server architecture enable its delivery in virtually any computing environment. Trilogy's patented technology enables corporations to streamline and/or completely transform the sales and ordering function, delivering unprecedented results in increased profitability, customer satisfaction, and competitive advantage.

Unitrac Software Corporation (www.unitrac.com) Welcome to Unitrac Software Corporation, the supplier of UNITRAC, a worldwide, industry-leading information management software package for Sales Force Automation, inbound and outbound telemarketing, account management, customer service, mass mail management, client and prospect tracking, membership management, and Help desk management.

Vantive Corporation (www.vantive.com) Vantive Enterprise is an integrated software suite that automates marketing, sales, customer support, quality tracking, field service, internal Help desks, and Web interaction. Vantive software enables companies to achieve a competitive advantage and treat customers as valuable assets. Vantive Enterprise is differentiated by its rich functionality, enterprise performance, scalable multitiered architecture, powerful flexibility, robust security, and rapid implementation.

Versatility, Inc. (www.versatility.com) Versatility is one of three companies that founded the computer-telephony integration (CTI) industry in the early 1980s. Today, Versatility is the fastest-growing call-center application company in the world. The company's flagship product, Versatility Series, is a family of state-of-the-art telesales, telemarketing, teleservice, account management, and order servicing applications. These products are based on an object-oriented, client/server architecture that makes them highly flexible, scalable, and affordable.

Web Ingenuity, Inc. (www.webingenuity.com) Web Ingenuity is a provider of sophisticated Internet and World Wide Web-based Sales Force Automation, quotation, and product configuration solutions. They use a combination of leading-edge tools from leading software publishers to produce polished Web-based applications for delivery to the Intranet, extranet, or internet.

XcelleNet, Inc. (www.xcellenet.com) XcelleNet is a leading developer of remote access software utility products. Marketed under the RemoteWare brand, these products provide advanced system management capabilities, including administration and control of corporate intranets. RemoteWare allows remote and mobile users to easily access corporate information systems while reducing operating and support costs associated with remote access computing.

Glossary

This glossary defines some of the terms used in the book. There are few industry-standard definitions in either of the Sales Force Automation or Web technology areas, so many of these definitions are in our own words, and in the context in which they are used in the book.

Account A customer or a part of a customer organization that is for all intents and purposes a separate entity

Account Management The activities that go into managing the account after the sale. This includes periodic contact with the account, as well as normal postsales support.

Account Team The key people in your organization responsible for account management.

ActiveX An application environment for interactive Web-based applications.

Application The combination of computer programs and databases that automate elements of business processes.

Application Programming Interface (API) A way for an application to use data from another application.

Automation Application of technologies to business processes.

Back-Office Applications Those applications that support corporate functions not normally visible to customers, such as manufacturing and accounting.

Business Case The combination of strategic and financial reasons to follow a particular course of action.

Business Rules Conditions, which when met, should result in certain actions and notifications taking place.

Buy versus Build A decision to either purchase a commercially available application, or build an application customized to meet your particular needs.

Buying Influences Anyone in the purchasing organization who can influence the outcome of a sale.

CGI Common Gateway Interface A way of transferring data between HTML forms and back-end databases.

Client/Server Model A kind of application systems architecture.

Close The action of completing a sale.

Complex Sale A sale in which there are many buying influences, and usually more than one person from the selling organization involved in the sale.

Constraints In sales configurations, constraints are the rules that specify the selections that are not available with the current selection.

Contact Manager A tool that allows a salesperson to manage activities around *contacts* at a prospective customer.

Customer Loyalty The inclination of a customer to continue to maintain a purchasing relationship with your company.

Customer Satisfaction The degree to which a customer is pleased with the relationship with your company.

Customer Service The nontechnical postsales services delivered to a customer.

Customer Support The technical postsales services delivered to a customer.

Data Mining The act of analyzing databases for *nuggets* of information, such as trends and purchasing habits.

Data Synchronization Bringing two different databases into alignment so that they both have the (same) latest information in them. This is especially useful for salespeople in the field, who may be working off a local copy of a database that is resident on a laptop computer.

Demonstration Showing a customer how a product works.

Dependencies In sales configurations, dependencies are the rules that specify the selections that must be made with the current selection(s) to have a properly configured system.

Deployment Plan The plan that you will use to roll out your Sales Force Automation solution to all users.

Development Plan The plan that you will use to develop your Sales Force Automation solution.

Economic Model An analysis of the business and financial implications of a sale, often used to make a business case for the sale.

Enterprise Approach An approach in which all the major applications in a company are viewed in the context of the whole enterprise, rather than just the organization that is the primary user.

Enterprise Resource Planning (ERP) An application used to plan resources in the manufacture and distribution of products.

Extranet A private network that uses Internet technologies, but is available only to the company and trusted partners.

Field Service The technical postsales services delivered to a customer, at the customer's location. Usually applied to the maintenance of hardware.

Firewall A security feature that protects intranets from the general public.

Forecast An estimate of the potential revenues in a sales organization.

Forecasting System A methodology, usually implemented in a computer application, that enables forecasts.

Front-Office Applications Those applications that support corporate functions visible to customers, such as customer support and customer service.

Functional Requirements The specific functionality that is required of a Sales Force Automation application.

HTML (HyperText Markup Language) A programming language that specifies the layout and look of Web pages.

Information Technology Organization The organization or function within a company that is responsible for selecting, implementing, and deploying computer-based applications.

Installation Doing what it takes to get your products up and running at a customer's site.

Interactive Selling Systems Web-based applications that guide a prospect through the sales cycle, with minimal involvement from a salesperson.

Internal Support The organization or function within a company that is responsible for supporting the users of business applications (usually a part of the Information Technology organization).

Internet A *network of networks* originally established for research, but now a worldwide system of computer networks available to the general public.

Intranet A private network that uses Internet technologies but is available only to users within a company.

Java An application environment for interactive Web-based applications.

Lead Distribution The act of passing on a lead from the marketing organization to the sales organization or person responsible for making the sale.

Lead Generation The act of finding and acquiring leads.

Lead Qualification The act of finding out if what your company offers can meet the requirements of the lead, and if the lead has the wherewithal and intention of purchasing.

Leads An individual that has contacted your company and expressed a purchase interest in your products.

Marketing Encyclopedia A collection of marketing and sales-related information that is used by a salesperson in all phases of the sales cycle.

Opportunity A qualified lead that represents a real revenue possibility.

Opportunity Management The actions taken to manage all the activities and tasks that go on during the sales cycle.

Opportunity Management System A sales automation tool used to enable opportunity management.

Order Fulfillment The shipment of a sales configuration, as specified in a sales order.

Order Processing The act of collecting information from a quote or proposal, verifying it, and scheduling products for manufacture or shipment.

Partners Third-party organizations that have formed a selling relationship with your company.

Personal Productivity Tools Applications, such as presentation programs and word processors, that enhance the productivity of a salesperson.

Post-Sales Service All the activities that go into managing the customer relationship after a sale.

Postmortem An analysis of the circumstances that led to a particular outcome.

Presentation Showing a customer information about a product.

Problem Tracking Identifying a customer-related issue, and then being able to follow it and the actions associated with it as it moves through the organization.

Project Manager The individual with the primary responsibility for the Sales Force Automation project.

Project Team The other individuals that work with the project manager on the project.

Proposal A formal offer to a prospect to sell products and services.

Proposal Generator A sales automation tool used to create proposals.

Prospect An opportunity that is moving closer to being a sale.

Push Technology A way on the Web to selectively send information to users, rather than wait for a user to *pull* it.

Quotation System A sales automation tool used to create quotes.

Quote A part of a proposal that associates pricing information with a sales configuration.

Rapid Application Development A development methodology used to create and deploy applications in short time frames. Often uses prebuilt *objects* that can be used repeatedly.

Remote Connectivity The ability of someone not physically proximate to a *server* or *host* system to connect to that system, over a network or by dialing in to the system using a modem.

Request for Proposal (RFP) An articulation of the issues a purchasing organization is facing, and a specification of the desired solution to those issues.

Requirements The specific needs that a customer has of any solution that is purchased.

Sales Activity Any task related to the ongoing work on a sales opportunity.

Sales Configuration A list of products and services offered by your company that are meant to address the requirements of a prospect.

Sales Configurator A sales automation tool used to create sales configurations.

Sales Cycle The sequence of steps and tasks taken to convert a lead into a customer.

Sales Effectiveness How good your organization is at meeting its primary goal of generating revenues.

Sales Efficiency How much time and cost is associated with generating revenues.

Sales Force Automation The tools and technologies that enable the sales force to improve its effectiveness and efficiency.

Sales Methodology The particular selling system or technique used by salespeople in your organization.

Sales Model The means by which your products are sold to the users of your products.

Sales Operations The functions performed to support a salesperson in making and following through on a sale.

Sales Processes The consistent and repeatable steps and activities taken during the sales cycle.

Sales Team The key people in your organization responsible for making a sale.

Salesperson The single individual that is responsible for the sale; usually runs the sales team.

Site Visits The visits a prospect takes to either your company, or to some of your customers who are willing to demonstrate their use of your products.

Team Selling When more than one individual is needed to make a sale, because of the specific expertise required, or because of the complexity of the sale. Team selling requires tight coordination.

Technical Support See *Customer Support.*

Telemarketing The organization responsible for lead generation and qualification. Works on the telephones, hence *tele*marketing.

Telesales That part of the sales organization responsible for selling products and services by telephone. Often used in sales to an installed base.

Web Page One instance of a collection of images and words (and perhaps more) that are shown over the World Wide Web.

Wireless Connectivity The ability to achieve *remote connectivity* without using any physical connection to a telephone.

Workflow The ability to specify tasks, activities (work), and their routing (flow) in the execution of a sales cycle.

Workflow Engine That part of an Opportunity Management System that makes workflow possible.

Index